Criminal Lives

CLARENDON STUDIES IN CRIMINOLOGY

Published under the auspices of the Institute of Criminology,
University of Cambridge, the Mannheim Centre, London School of
Economics; and the Centre for Criminological Research,
University of Oxford.

GENERAL EDITOR: ALISON LIEBLING
(*University of Cambridge*)

EDITORS: MANUEL EISNER AND PER-OLOF WIKSTRÖM
(*University of Cambridge*)

PAUL ROCK, JILL PEAY, AND TIM NEWBURN
(*London School of Economics*)

LUCIA ZEDNER, JULIAN ROBERTS, AND IAN LOADER
(*University of Oxford*)

Recent titles in this series:

Criminal Lives

Family Life, Employment, and
Offending

**Barry S. Godfrey, David J. Cox, and Stephen
D. Farrall**

OXFORD
UNIVERSITY PRESS

OXFORD

UNIVERSITY PRESS

Great Clarendon Street, Oxford OX2 6DP

Oxford University Press is a department of the University of Oxford.
It furthers the University's objective of excellence in research, scholarship,
and education by publishing worldwide in

Oxford New York

Auckland Cape Town Dar es Salaam Hong Kong Karachi
Kuala Lumpur Madrid Melbourne Mexico City Nairobi
New Delhi Shanghai Taipei Toronto

With offices in

Argentina Austria Brazil Chile Czech Republic France Greece
Guatemala Hungary Italy Japan Poland Portugal Singapore
South Korea Switzerland Thailand Turkey Ukraine Vietnam

Oxford is a registered trade mark of Oxford University Press
in the UK and in certain other countries

Published in the United States
by Oxford University Press Inc., New York

British Library Cataloguing in Publication Data
Data available

Library of Congress Cataloging in Publication Data
Data available

Typeset by Newgen Imaging Systems (P) Ltd., Chennai, India
Printed in Great Britain
on acid-free paper by
Biddles Ltd., King's Lynn

ISBN 978-0-19-921720-5

1 3 5 7 9 10 8 6 4 2

Dedicated to the memory of
Sidney Frederick Arthur Godfrey, 1928–2005

My father grew up in the East End of London in the 1930s, moving out to Buckinghamshire as a young man and working as a skilled welder until he retired and moved again, this time to Nantwich in Cheshire. Like many of the people in this book he married and raised children, worked with metal, and enjoyed a full life. He experienced many of the structural forces that our sample of offenders did. This book is, in part, an attempt to discover why some people from his generation drifted into and stayed in crime, whilst others left crime behind, or, like my father, did not ever trouble the police or the courts.

BG

General Editor's Introduction

Clarendon Studies in Criminology aims to provide a forum for outstanding empirical and theoretical work in all aspects of criminology, criminal justice, penology and the wider field of deviant behaviour. The Editors welcome excellent PhD work, as well as submissions from established scholars. The *Series* was inaugurated in 1994, with Roger Hood as its first General Editor, following energetic discussions between Oxford University Press and three Criminology Centres. It is edited under the auspices of these three Criminological Centres: the Cambridge Institute of Criminology, the Mannheim Centre for Criminology at the London School of Economics, and the Oxford Centre for Criminology. Each supplies members of the Editorial Board.

This highly original book, *Criminal Lives: Family Life, Employment, and Offending*, by Barry Godfrey, David Cox, and Stephen Farrall, continues a longstanding tradition of key studies of criminal lives, applying modern concepts of desistance, criminal families, and the links between victims and offenders, and 'visiting them upon the late nineteenth and early twentieth centuries'. The authors document a preoccupation with habitual crime, respectability and contagion, drawing on the life stories of 101 individual offenders living from the 1870s through to the 1940s. These life stories evolve in a rapidly growing, single industry town in the northwest of England. They allow the authors to test contemporary theories of crime against what is known about those involved. They discover, for example, that marriage may not have had the same braking effect in the late nineteenth century as it seems to have in the contemporary period, raising questions about the changing nature of marriage and its increased significance in contemporary offending careers. Poverty and disadvantage played a large role in the lives of persistent offenders, but paradoxically, it was easier for those who wished to change their identities to find gainful employment, reasonable housing and a sense of community. The book constitutes a highly readable, theoretically informed account of the onset and ending of many criminal careers, exploring the relevance of their family lives, their work and education experiences, and criminal justice response to their offending. It has considerable relevance to contemporary debates about crime and its persistence as well as constituting a fascinating study of the life histories of these serious offenders.

The editors welcome this important addition to the *Series*.

Alison Liebling
Cambridge, February 2007

Preface and Acknowledgements

The Preface is a curious creature. It is always—in our experience—written last; always placed at the start of a book; and runs the risk of never being read at all. This confusion of temporal ordering is reflected in some aspects of the nature of our subject matter. Our core chapters take issues (desistance, intergenerational transmission, the victim-offender overlap, the geographical dispersion of crimes) which many criminologists of the modern era would find familiar and visit them upon the late-nineteenth and early-twentieth centuries. This criminological time travelling inevitably reveals certain continuities and discontinuities. Whilst debates about 'persistent offenders', 'hoodies', 'petty offenders' and terms such as 'the underclass' appear all the rage at present, similar debates resonated in the Victorian era. Whilst some may claim (à la Garland) that a concern with crime is now a feature of middle-class life, this would also appear not to be an altogether new preoccupation.

Prefaces are also one of the most satisfying elements of any book to write. By the point one has reached the stage at which the Preface needs to be written, one has battled one's way through coming up with a new research idea; drafted and redrafted the research application; secured the funding and commenced upon the research itself. Debates about methods, anxieties about fieldwork, worries about coding have long receded by the time one reaches one's Preface, as has the work of analysing and writing about the data, of course. In this respect, the humble Preface provides the authors with a chance to reflect upon the work they have completed and thank all those who have helped them along the way.

Naturally, we have incurred very many debts of gratitude over the course of our research. We would particularly like to thank the following people and institutions for their help and assistance. First, we must acknowledge the support of The Leverhulme Trust, whose generous funding allowed us to pursue our interests (as award no. F/00130/H). We are immensely grateful for the assistance of staff and archivists at the Cheshire Records Office; Chester Records and Heritage Centre; Crewe Central Library; The National

Archives; and Bombardier Transportation UK Ltd (especially Phil Bateman). All of these staff made us feel welcome amongst their records and afforded us the time and space to work uninterrupted. We drew much insight from the advice and comments of colleagues at Keele University, notably Susanne Karstedt, Tim Hope, and Julius Sim. We have also been fortunate enough to benefit from the accumulated wisdom of colleagues at other institutions, and as such we thank Jonathan Jackson (LSE), Keith Soothill (Lancaster), Di Drummond (Trinity and All Saints College, Leeds), Graeme Dunstall (Canterbury, NZ), Martin Wiener (Rice), and Clive Emsley (Open University). We also enjoyed discussions following presentations at Lancaster University's Applied Social Studies Department, Keele University's Criminology and History Departments, Hull Criminology Department, the ANZSOC 2006 conference in Hobart, the British Society of Criminology Conferences in 2003 and 2006, and the International Association of Crime and Criminal Justice Historians at Paris, Budapest and Geneva. A special word of thanks must be extended to Dr John Locker, who assisted with the pilot fieldwork, data analysis and grant application before departing for distant shores.

Tracing individual life and offending careers through historical sources is never easy, and although we have been as rigorous as possible, it is conceivable that some mistakes have crept in. In order to avoid unnecessary embarrassment, we have anonymized all of the cases we refer to directly in the text. We apologise for any mistakes we have inadvertently made, and hope that they are few and far between.

BG, DC and SF
September 2006

Contents

List of Tables

List of Figures

1

Introduction

'A hard core of prolific offenders—just 5,000 people—commit around one million crimes each year, nearly 10% of all crime. That's only fifteen or twenty people for each of our Crime and Disorder Reduction Partnerships. Yet they are wreaking havoc. The financial loss is estimated to be at least £2 billion a year [. . .]. We are determined to tackle this small group of offenders who do so much harm.'

> (Tony Blair, 30 March 2004, speech to a joint Local Government Association and Home Office conference on crime in London)

In an article entitled 'Crime, Persistent Offenders and the Justice Gap' Richard Garside launches a severely critical attack on the use of such statistics and the claims made about them.[1] He remarks that 'the idea that a significant proportion of all crime is committed by a relatively small number of persistent offenders is not new, but the current government has placed it at the centre of its criminal justice policy. Examination of the government's own evidence casts serious doubt on the legitimacy of this approach.'[2] He then proceeds, in a withering critique, to demonstrate how such statistics can be manipulated and misquoted by both the Home Office and politicians. Regardless what one makes of Garside's claims vis-à-vis the use made of statistics about offenders, he is certainly correct to remind us that interest in and use of such statistics is not new.

An extraordinary amount of public imagination throughout the last four hundred years has been given over to the idea of the hard-core persistent or habitual criminal. As early as 1566 Thomas Harman had written of a criminal 'subculture'. In a pamphlet entitled

---

[1] Richard Garside, *Crime and Society Foundation Discussion Paper Number 1* [2004].
[2] ibid 5.

A Caveat for Common Cursitors he described several types of what he regarded as habitual criminals.[3] Similarly, in his examination of the literary representation of crime in the eighteenth century, Ian A. Bell states that 'the notion of a widespread criminal class stealthily at work throughout the land [. . .] was a very potent idea in the eighteenth-century popular imagination' (Bell, 1991: 15). Naturally enough, in the nineteenth century the debate as to the nature and existence of habitual or persistent criminals was still raging. In 1815 Patrick Colquhoun could confidently announce that around 1,300,000 of Britain's total population of c.10,500,000 (approximately 10%) were indigent or criminal (and contemporaries did not often differentiate between the two).[4] In the early 1860s, an editorial in *The Times*, printed as a result of the 'Garrotting Panic' of 1862, remarked that 'we have an entire class, though perhaps not a very numerous one, whose freedom is fraught with peril to the rest of the community'.[5] Since then historians and criminologists have debated the numbers and characteristics of prolific offenders (see for example, McGowan, 1990; Soothill, 2003 and 2005) as well as penal and legislative approaches to this perceived problem (Pratt, 1997).

It is clear that interest in the hard core of offenders said to be lurking within British society was by no means peculiar to the late-nineteenth century; indeed notions of criminal families, incorrigible offenders, predatory sex offenders, and rampant juvenile offenders can be found in abundance in modern media discourse. However, many of the reasons behind this perception were products of their own time, and the validity and the extent to which views of persistent criminality were modified throughout the latter half of the nineteenth century and the early decades of the twentieth century are amongst the subjects discussed in this chapter.

[3] Harman, Thomas, 'A Caveat for Common Cursitors Vulgarly Called Vagabonds' (1566): reprinted in Arthur F. Kinney (ed.), *Rogues, Vagabonds and Sturdy Beggars: A New Gallery of Tudor and Early Stuart Rogue Literature* (Amherst: University of Massachusetts Press, 1990) 109–53.

[4] Colquhoun, Patrick, *Treatise on the Wealth of the British Empire* (London: Joseph Mawman, 1815) 111–12.

[5] Quoted by Jennifer Davis, 'The London Garrotting Panic of 1862: A Moral Panic and the Creation of a Criminal Class in mid-Victorian England' in Gatrell, V.A.C., *et al*, (eds), *Crime and the Law: a social history of crime in Western Europe since 1500* (London: Europa, 1980) 192. The 'Garrotting Panic' was the result of a media-driven campaign against the 'ticket of leave' system, whereby prisoners could be released from gaol under a licensing system. Such men were thought to be behind a 'wave' of garrotting attacks in London during 1862.

The nineteenth century was a period of unparalleled change in many aspects of British society. The country developed from a relatively low level of industrialization to an increasingly complex and sophisticated level of technological know-how. It is easy, from the position of the early twenty-first century, to forget that humankind went from the horse and cart to reusable spaceships within the length of a single human lifespan. The twentieth century saw both the rise and 'rolling back' of the welfare state, involving the creation of large arms of the regulatory-state, the development of widely accepted and supported forms of state intervention and the establishment of this as the 'consensus' before being rejected in the last quarter of the century (Garland, 2001; Farrall, 2006). People in the UK went from living in tithe cottages or lodgings given to them as part of their employment as farm hands, to terraced housing in what were becoming amongst the first of the UK's large industrial towns and cities. Many individuals left the countryside to take up or find work in the cities, creating the wholesale displacement of people; people who had previously travelled little and never far from their place of birth. Perceptions of crime and criminality were inevitably bound to be modified as a result of such socio-economic, demographic and political upheaval. Throughout the period, as a result of various changes including the reform of criminal codes and the growth in availability of, and refinement to, statistical information, these perceptions were altered and occasionally deliberately manipulated by both an increasingly sophisticated socio-political system and an emergent media.

These demographic and socio-economic changes, including the increasing percentage of the population that moved to urban settlements such as Crewe in Cheshire (the focus of our study), together with the related rapid growth in industrialization, led to a perceived threat in the minds of many of the constituents of the middle and upper classes with regard to political stability. This fear of losing political control undoubtedly contributed to the promulgation in the minds of many middle- and upper-class individuals of the creation of a hardcore of itinerant, idle and often drunken working-class men—what Sir Archibald Alison, the Tory Sheriff of Lanarkshire referred to in 1844 as 'the dangerous classes' (Philips, 1977: 13).

For our purposes, we are particularly interested in discussions around the habitual offender that surfaced around the last quarter of the nineteenth-century, as these helped create and modify views on how to treat criminals and the construction of the legal framework by which they were dealt with, both aspects that are reflected in the crime statistics of Crewe. When fears of social and political revolution had subsided from the turbulent early decades of the century, and the 'war on crime' was well underway, there still appeared to be a small, predominantly urban group of persistent offenders who bucked the trend; who seemed unaffected by increased surveillance, harsher penal policies, and the general rise in standards of living. Debates in medical and criminological tracts of the period posited the idea of a generally respectable working class, subsumed within wider democratic and social processes, but within which lay a smaller 'residuum'—those who, by virtue of their inability to adapt to the realities of mature industrial capitalism were confined to poor housing, poor education, the workhouse and ultimately the prison (for examples of such tracts see Maudsley, 1873; Rylands, 1889).

This putative group was not creating a rising tide of crime that could engulf respectable society or challenge the authority of the state, but was considered by some commentators to be a persistent nuisance and drain on national resources; debilitating in their own way on the progress of the nation, and also socially contagious, capable of infecting those who could not resist temptation and 'the easy life'. The perceived demise of the dangerous criminal class, and its decline into what Stedman Jones has described as a 'small and hopeless remnant' of habitual drunks, petty thieves, vagrants and wandering lunatics was almost complete by the early decades of the twentieth century, and was commensurate both with the professionalization of welfare services and an increasing belief in the efficacy of medical treatment and social rehabilitation (Stedman Jones, 2002: 320).

However, although there was considerable debate on the subject of criminal persistence, there was by no means universal agreement on either its causes or its cure. The main thrust of the argument for a residuum of habitual and persistent offenders had, by the last quarter of the nineteenth century, become largely anthropometric in nature, with Henry Maudsley, Cesare Lombroso and Francis Galton all promoting ideas based on the theory that there was a genetic and hereditary disposition to criminality and that certain types of physiognomy were related to this genetic factor and could therefore be used to identify those predisposed to a criminal nature.[6] Such

---

[6] Maudsley, *Body and Mind*; Lombroso, Cesare, *L'Uomo Delinquente*, 1876); Galton, Francis, 'Hereditary Character and Talent' (published in two parts in *MacMillan's Magazine*, vol. 11, November 1864 and April 1865, 157–66, 318–27). The parallel with the growth of the theory of eugenics is disturbingly apparent.

beliefs, described in detail in Horn (2003), Kelves (1985), Kerr and Shakespeare (2002), Pick (1989), and Rafter (1997) have long since been discredited, however they re-emerge from time to time. In Nazi-occupied Germany in the 1930s we see the emergence of a discourse which drew heavily upon physiognomy. In the late 1980s Norris suggested that more attention ought to be given to the genetic make-up of serial killers (Norris, 1998).[7] Later still, in the late 1990s and early 2000s we saw some suggest that scientists might be able to find the gene responsible for crime. Closer to our own interests, some of the research on the intergenerational transmission of criminality also looks towards genetic and hereditary factors for explanatory models (this literature is reviewed in Chapter Five).

The increased literacy of the latter half of the nineteenth century and the concomitant growth in the number and circulation of newspapers and other journals (for example the *News of the World* (launched 1843) and *Household Words* (1850–1859) fuelled debates in the nineteenth century. Admittedly these publications were aimed squarely at the emergent literate middle class, but then this was the class whose perceptions and thoughts have predominantly been preserved. The *Saturday Review* in 1862 talked opprobriously of 'our moral sewage' when referring to ticket-of-leave men (convicts granted early release to start a useful life), and such talk helped to embed 'the idea of a separate, irredeemable criminal class [. . .] in popular consciousness' (Davis, 1980: 192, 212). However, it has been argued with regard to the still largely semi-literate working class of the mid-nineteenth century that 'it seems doubtful that any clear division existed either in reality or in the minds of the working class between the poor but honest and the merely poor' (Davis, 213).[8] The boundaries between criminality were perhaps not as clear-cut as the editor and readers of the *Saturday Review* would have liked to have believed.

---

[7] In his chapter on episodic aggressive behaviour, Norris argues for a fundamentally anthropometric approach to the study of serial killers' behaviour.

[8] ibid 213. Literacy rates are notoriously difficult to ascertain, but current general consensus suggests that around two-thirds of the English population was literate to varying degrees by the 1840s. This accords with a table of convicts' literacy printed in the *Manchester Guardian* of 25 April 1838:

Convicts	unable to read or write	−35.85%.
	read and write imperfectly	−52.08%.
	read and write well	−9.46%.
	received superior instruction	−0.43%.
	unknown standard	−2.18%.

After the publication of Darwin's *On The Origin of Species* in 1859, scientific thought was increasingly devoted to the study of the human animal; 'sciences' such as phrenology and physiognomy enjoyed something of a resurgence after their original flourishes in the late eighteenth century. This in turn led to several scientists promulgating the idea that not only was there a distinct 'criminal class', but that this class could be recognized by attributes such as facial features and lack of intellect. Maudsley's *Responsibility in Mental Disease* of 1874 went so far as to state that 'individuals are born with such a flaw of warp or nature that all the care in the world will not prevent them from being vicious or criminal' (Gregory, 1987: 373). There was, therefore, a move from attempts to create social reform in order to dissuade the perceived criminal element from becoming recidivists to a media-generated bugbear of a race of biologically-determined criminal savages, intent upon wrecking the very fabric of society. This fear has never quite left society's psyche—one only has to look at the banner headlines in today's more lurid tabloid publications to sense that this fear of the unknown or the different (especially if foreign and 'other') is still very much with us.

Although at the time these theories proved to be a popular and persuasive argument, chiming with the growth in anthropology fuelled by (an often-misunderstood) Darwinian theory, ever-increasing medical expertise and the wish to understand why people behave as they do, they did not meet with universal acceptance. In a recent essay on late-nineteenth and early-twentieth views of Lombroso's theories, Rebecca B. Fleming has brought to light much contemporary debate on the criminal classes, especially from the medical profession, including Dr David Nicholson, Medical Officer of Broadmoor, and Dr H. B. Donovan, medical adviser to the Prisons Commission, who both severely criticized such views after carrying out their own empirical studies (Fleming, 2000: 195–217). Chassaigne's work on the persistent violent offender has similarly clearly shown that contemporaries were far from being of one mind even on the existence of such a class; he argues that subsequent historians, sociologists and criminologists may have been swept along by the rhetoric of the late Victorian commentators rather than examining the evidence (Chassaigne, 2003; see also Norman and Erdos, 2005: 29–30).[9]

[9] Chassaigne, Philippe, 'A new look at the Victorian Criminal Classes: a view from the archives', paper given at Social Deviance in England and France c.1830–1900

Chassaigne's research suggests that whilst the 1860s and 1870s saw a real increase in the criminalization of violence and other activities, the verdicts of the courts showed very little evidence for a widespread belief in a large criminal class. Others such as Jennifer Davis have argued that such theories fed on moral panics engendered by events such as the 'Garotting Panic' of 1862 and the activities of Jack the Ripper in the late 1880s, and were often overblown reactions and commentaries by the concerned middle-classes on very rare events rather than a rational examination of the facts.[10] The confident and exact statement of the 1908 *Criminal Statistics Report* that 'the police in England and Wales estimate that on the first Tuesday in April 1908 there were 4,255 habitual criminals at large in England and Wales'—0.0125% of the population—suggest that at least some contemporaries did not think that habitual criminality was a major problem.[11]

The creation of a separate and therefore feared class has nevertheless had powerful repercussions throughout the nineteenth and twentieth centuries. Dee Cook remarks in her 1997 critique of New Labour's attitude toward poverty that 'although the language and the categorising of the 'dangerous' and the 'dishonest poor' may at first appear dated, these historical concepts still shape the ways in which we think and speak about today's 'undeserving' poor' (Cook, 1997). The underlying assumptions about the lives of the 'unrespectable poor' and their links with habitual criminality certainly appear to be enduring ones, and are still found under various guises in popular and academic works such as Charles Murray's 1995 thesis on the

Conference, Maison Française d'Oxford, Oxford Brookes, 4–5 July 2003. A recent publication by Civitas (Dennis, Norman, and George Erdos, *Cultures, Crime and Policing in Four Nations* [London: Civitas, 2005]) has deviated from the consensus of historical opinion and argues that the statistical evidence of the late nineteenth and early twentieth century should be viewed as more credible than generally thought, and that England should be seen as 'a country that enjoyed a very low crime rate in the second half of the nineteenth century and the first half of the twentieth'. 29–30.

[10] Davis, Jennifer, 'The London Garrotting Panic of 1862' 191–212. 'Jack the Ripper' has perhaps generated more discussion (much of it facile) than any other individual persistent offender; for a detailed and generally less salacious account of his crimes and the failure of the police in his detection, see Sugden, Philip, *The Complete History of Jack the Ripper* (London: Constable and Robinson, 2002).

[11] Quoted in Dennis, Norman, and George Erdos, *Cultures, Crime and Policing in Four Nations* 25–6.

'underclass' (Murray, 1995: 23–53; see also Alcock, 1995; David, 1995; Slipman, 1995).[12]

It was against this backdrop that we embarked upon our studies of persistent criminality in the late-nineteenth and early-twentieth centuries. Our period, which runs from the late 1870s through to the first few months of the Second World War covers a huge period of social, economic and cultural (not to mention criminal justice) change. The period encompasses the very end of the long nineteenth century, the consolidation of engineering works and the growth of a panoply of social organizations which people of all ages and most social classes would have to become used to—at least until the 1970s and 1980s. We 'pass' along the way, the rise of the regulatory state, the heyday of the British Empire, the build-up to, commencement, and conclusion of the tragedy that was to become the First World War, and the austere period between that and the late 1930s.

As we detail in Chapter Two, Crewe came into existence following the decision of the Grand Junction Railway to relocate its main Works from Edgehill to a new site. Before the railway moved to Monks Coppenhall (as the parish was then known), Crewe did not exist. We chose to base our study in Crewe for a number of reasons. Firstly, because Crewe grew virtually out of nothing, it represented a relatively small town (initially) and so it had a known 'starting point', thus making the complex influence and exploration of too many earlier phases of the town's existence unnecessary. The town, by virtue of the Works, also had a relatively stable population, making at least one of our goals easier to achieve. Again due to the Works, we were able to trace specific individuals and their employment over time. In addition to this, Crewe had a virtually complete run of petty sessions (magistrates' courts) records from 1880–1940 and a complete run of at least one of the local newspapers, namely the *Crewe Chronicle*. Chapter Two outlines in far greater detail our chosen site and some of its salient characteristics.

Chapter Three outlines the nature of crime in Crewe during the period which we explore, and introduces the reader to some of the people whom we shall encounter during the remaining chapters.[13]

---

[12] Murray has since referred to habitual criminals as 'outlaws' in several articles for the *Sunday Times*.

[13] All the names of offenders and victims mentioned in this book have been changed to avoid causing any offence or distress to surviving relatives or acquaintances.

We outline the broad contours of our sample of persistent offenders, what they did, who they did it to and how well they knew one another. Chapter Four explores the role of the Works in the lives of offenders (and some non-offenders). To what extent did engagement at the Works encourage our persistent offenders to stop offending? Did the culture of the Works encourage offending amongst some men but not others? Why might this have been? Another factor commonly cited as important in the termination of the criminal career is marriage. Did this social institution have the same effect in the period we are interested in? If not, why might that be? What can this tell us about the role of social institutions in processes of desistance? As will become apparent, many of our persistent offenders had sons and daughters of their own, and Chapter Five explores the persistence of criminality through from our persistent offenders' parents to their grandchildren (four generations in all). From our sample of 101 persistent offenders, sixty-four had children, and in all there were 318 children born from unions involving these sixty-four individuals. What explained the transmission of criminality? Was it genetic, as some claimed, or were social and cultural processes also at play? Chapter Six explores the extent to which our 101 persistent offenders were also victims of crime.

We know of no studies which have followed persistent offenders through the whole of their lives and have also explored their victimization. Herein we recount the tales often left untold. Chapter Seven—our conclusion—makes sense of key findings and locates our findings within (in particular) the wider literature on desistance and the intergenerational transmission of criminality. It is our contention that to fully appreciate the processes by which people stop offending or their children also become involved in crime, one needs to understand the social institutions and organizations within which their lives are embedded, and also the ways in which these same institutions change over medium to long periods of time. In short, similar social processes may produce differing outcomes from one another at two time-points because of wider historical changes which alter the symbolic meanings they hold for individuals and communities. At the end of Chapter Seven, we come full circle back to where we started—the continuing development of criminal justice policy towards persistent offenders.

2

The Social History of Crewe[1]

They were pioneers, willing to take up their place in a new venture, in an embryonic town, that was compared with the Wild West of America for the roughness of its life and provisions.

(Drummond, 1995: 213)

Inspector Robinson, of the National Society for the Prevention of Cruelty to Children, stated that he visited the house and found the defendant's wife and four children. Two of the children were rather poorly nourished, but the other two were fairly well nourished, but were badly clothed and shed. The house was absolutely destitute of furniture with the exception of a child's stool and a butter tub. In the front room there was a piece of sacking filled with straw. There was nothing in the second bedroom. In the kitchen there was a frying pan, an old corned-beef tin, two cups, a saucer, and a basin. The only food on the premises was a mouthful of cheese and sufficient butter for one slice of bread.

Details of a case of parental neglect reported in the *Crewe Chronicle*, 19 April 1913

Celebrating the remarkable history of its town in 1887, the *Crewe Guardian* placed the birth of Crewe in the year 1837. At 8.35 a.m. on 4 July 1837 the first train passed through Crewe Station headed for Birmingham on the Grand Junction line and this marked the beginning of the history of Crewe. A few years later in 1843, the opening of the Grand Junction Railway's Works at Crewe signalled the beginning of the town's rapid growth. From this date onwards the expansion of the town was extraordinary. Within a generation of its opening the Crewe Railway Works emerged as 'the most advanced railway and locomotive workshops in the world' (Drummond, 1995: 1) as well as 'the most steadily productive of all the railway companies' works' (Simmons, 126). According to one nineteenth-century contemporary, Crewe quickly became 'the most

[1] This chapter builds upon Godfrey, Farrall and Locker 2005.

important station on the London and North Western Railway' (Head, 1849: 100). What is more, the town's population increased at a phenomenal rate within a few years, and continued to do so for much of the second half of the century. This chapter charts the population growth and development of a social infrastructure in Crewe for roughly a century (1843–1940), before outlining the scale and character of crime that existed in the town over that period.

The 'Railway Town' *Par Excellence*

Crewe was the railway town *par excellence*, launched into existence and almost a century of spectacular industrial growth by the decision of the directors of the Grand Junction Railway (GJR) to base its engine sheds and repair workshops in south Cheshire. Before then, Monks Coppenhall (which would later become known as Crewe) was little more than a small hamlet comprising a few dispersed labourers' cottages and farms. The 1831 census recorded Monks Coppenhall as having twenty-seven dwellings, housing the same number of families with a total population of 148 individuals (eighty-one males and sixty-seven females). Ten years later the situation had changed little (see Fig. 2.1). However, by the early 1840s the population of Monks Coppenhall had reached approximately 1,000, boosted by 800 men and their families who were moved to the newly formed London & North-Western Railway Company (L&NWR) works from Edgehill (near Liverpool). These migrants joined labour drawn in from local areas to give Crewe the character of a rapidly growing but single industry town with few civic amenities. Thereafter railway employment and population growth increased steadily as a result of both step-migration (where unskilled and low-skilled workers moved from village to nearby town to regional industrial centre) and chain migration (where skilled men moved a long distance and were later joined by their families, or if unmarried, formed relationships in the new area).

Whilst a national economic depression during the late 1840s affected the Railway Works, and therefore the development of the town, by the early 1850s an upturn in the economy encouraged further growth and expansion. Thus, by 1851 (eight years after the development of the Works), its population had grown by 2000% to roughly 4,500. As a result of expansion at the Works, the period

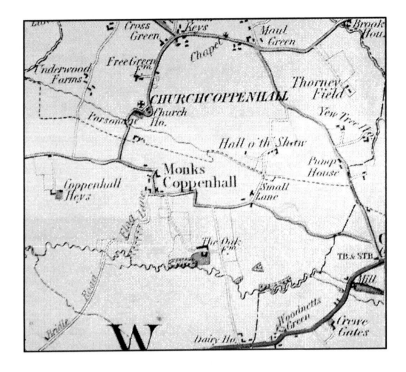

Fig. 2.1 Extract from Byrant's 1831 Map of Cheshire.

1851–1861 saw the population increase by 76%, the figure reaching 8,801 in 1861. The importance of the Works to the fortunes of the town can be further seen by the fact that in 1861 the L&NWR Company employed over half (59%) of all heads of households at Crewe (Drummond, 1995: 11–12). The Works expanded yet further during the next decade. Five years later, in 1876, the year in which the town celebrated the construction of its 2,000th engine, the *Crewe Guardian* put the figure at 5,951 men with a further 6,762 men employed at the out-stations, making a total of 12,713. The recruitment of more men and their families from outside of south Cheshire led to an even sharper increase in the population of the town during this decade. Between 1861 and 1871 the company opened a steel works (1864), and also decided to centre all L&NWR locomotive construction and repair at its Crewe site. In consequence the number of men employed at Crewe Works increased to 3,665 (Drummond 1995: 226) and the general population also increased. In 1871 the population of Crewe reached 19,904 (an increase of 126% from 1861), with Crewe Works having developed into a huge production facility located at three sites in the town, employing men in a variety of different industrial processes. By 1887 the Works took up 116 acres of space, with over thirty-seven acres of roofed workshops. Population growth rates continued to remain high throughout the century expanding to 24,385 in 1881, and to 32,926 by 1891 (Drummond, 1995: 13).

In this period the railway company provided the little institutional structure there was. The company originally built and owned a large number of houses for their workers. These redbrick plain workers' houses built by the L&NWR for the first generations of workers were generally of good quality, designed to attract and keep skilled and semi-skilled labour. By the 1890s the needed labour was unskilled and plentiful, and the houses built for them were 'thrown up'. This was the golden age of the Crewe 'jerry-builders' (Chaloner, 1950), however Crewe inhabitants still enjoyed relatively good housing stock, especially foremen and managers whose grander houses were set back from the grimy noisy centre of town.[2] Mains gas became widely available after the railway took over provision of gas cooking and heating apparatus in 1900 (it had only been available to one in five houses in 1888). Electric street lighting was introduced in 1900, many years after it had been pioneered in London.

As well as residential buildings to house the workforce, the company also endowed the town with civic and public establishments: a Mechanics' Institute; all of the Anglican churches built in the town between 1845 and 1920 (some with furniture painted in the company colours); and schools, gas and a water pumping station. Queen's Park (named in honour of Victoria's Jubilee) was also given to the town by the railway company in 1888. Hospitals were built in 1894 (Victoria Cottage Hospital) and 1897 (Isolation Hospital); and numerous additional buildings were appended until the First World War (a mortuary in 1898; staff accommodation 1900; children's ward 1901; enlarged general premises in 1909). Health care

---

[2] 'Jerry' was a Victorian term for circus clowns and acrobats. In 1854 the L&NWR built a row of houses in Victoria Street specifically for foremen of Crewe Works, following representations from eight such foremen for the provision of suitable housing. These houses became known as 'Gaffers' Row'.

was also improved by sporadic attempts to improve sanitation. In 1895 dustbins were collected fortnightly, and weekly from 1900.

The Borough of Crewe

In 1877 a town council was formed as a result of the incorporation of Crewe. From then on, the influence of the railway company was tempered and combined with the growing importance and activity of the local borough councillors. In order to impose some measure of control over the large number of people flowing into Crewe, the main police station was built in 1877, but there was little sign of other kinds of official or county bureaucracy. Crewe remained under the control of a Superintendent of Police who resided in Nantwich and who reported to the Chief Constable of Cheshire, and indeed Crewe never appointed a Chief Constable for their Borough Force. However, the growth in population was given as a reason to build another police station in 1909, and Crewe division was eventually made responsible for policing their long-established market-town neighbour of Nantwich in 1922. Partly to facilitate efficient bureaucracy and partly in recognition of Crewe's increasing claim to be a civic centre (see Fig. 2.2 which shows the town in 1911), a full Commission of the Peace had been granted to Crewe in 1881, and regular petty sessions were then held in the town (previously they had been held three miles away in Nantwich, and occasionally in Willaston, a nearby village). In contrast to other single industry towns, the predominating company was not over-represented amongst the judiciary as Table 2.1 below illustrates.

By 1901 Crewe housed more than 42,000 residents, 7,471 of whom were employed in the Works. Whilst the rate of population growth slowed down into the twentieth century some growth was, nevertheless, noticeable. Between 1901–1911 the population of Crewe rose to just under 45,000. According to Drummond, the decline in the growth rate of the town was a result of the failing health of Crewe Works, and was a reflection of the town's reliance upon its railway industry. She states that from the late 1880s onwards the Works was overstaffed, and large numbers of dismissals were made at various times. In 1911, for example, 500 men were dismissed from the Works (Drummond, 1995: 13). Nevertheless, as Reed noted, 'the great Crewe Works and town, grew and grew until through many years of the twentieth century the Works employed 7,000 to 8,000

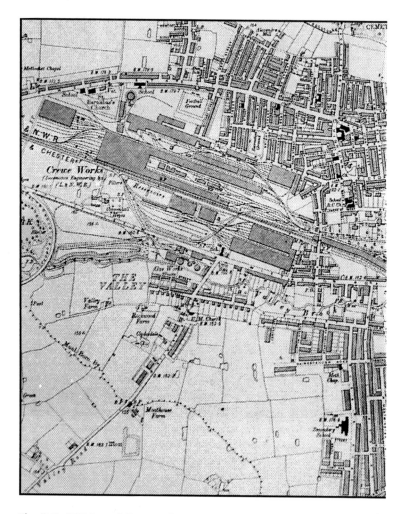

Fig. 2.2 OS Map of Crewe, 1911.

men and boys and the town housed over 45,000 persons, who until around 1940 were nearly all dependent on the railway for their subsistence' (Reed, 1982: 8–9). Certainly, well into the twentieth century the Works employed a significant proportion of the town's population. Chaloner, for instance, notes that by 1920 the works employed slightly more than 10,000 men and boys (Chaloner, 1950).

Both the World Wars and imperial growth meant that Crewe avoided the worst of the downturns in the 1920s and 1930s.

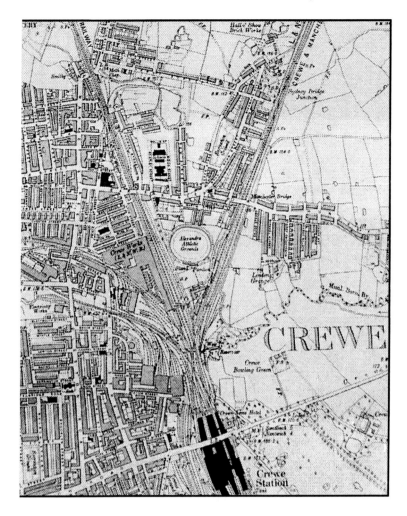

Nevertheless, significant job cuts were made—to take one example, a hundred employees were made redundant when materials ran short in 1938. The growth of Rolls-Royce, which established a plant in Crewe in 1936, and its subsequent war-work sustained Crewe into and beyond the Second World War. The broadening of the economic base and the development of the town into a regional retail centre meant that Crewe continued to grow at a steady but unremarkable rate well into the final quarter of the twentieth century.

Table 2.1   The railway interest on the bench, 1892 and 1902.

Year	Name	Address	Occupation	L&NWR connection
1892	William Adamson	Wellington Square	Mechanical engineer	Yes
	John Ainsworth	Heathfield, High Town	Inland Revenue Officer	No
	James Atkinson	Mirion House	surgeon	Yes
	Thomas Castley Bailey	Havelock House	Crewe Borough Medical Officer of Health	No
	James Briggs	Linden Grange	Stockbroker	No
1902	James Atkinson	Mirion House, 57 Earle Street	Surgeon (Mayor)	?
	Thomas Bailey	Havelock House, 6 Havelock Street	Surgeon	?
	Benjamin Silvester Bostock	Sandfield Road, Haslington	Provision dealer	No
	James Briggs	Linden Grange	Pawnbroker (Mayor)	No
	Douglas Henry Earl	Deva House, Wellington Square	Manager of Crewe Works	Yes
	Wilmot Eardley	4 Chester Bridge, Crewe	Printer	No
	Arthur Griffiths Hill	136 Nantwich Road	Solicitor, practising in Market Street	?
	William McNeill	8 Herdman Street	Taylor and draper	No
	Kenneth McRae	Wellington Villas	Locomotive accountant	Yes
	Thomas Glover	West View, West Street	Grocer with three shops	No
	William Hodgson	Hightown	Surgeon	?
	John Knott	Gatefield Street/ Victoria Street	Butcher (Mayor)	No
	Wallace Lumb	Gatefield House, Crewe	Wine and Spirit Merchant, 23–25 High Street	No
	Richard Pedley	Winterley	Cheese Factor	No
	James Robertson	Hungerford Road	Not known	?
	Peter Swinton	38 High Street	Ladies' Outfitter	No
	John Thomas	Nantwich Road	Cheese Factor	No
	Henry Wallwork	Chester Bridge, Crewe	Jeweller (Mayor)	No
	George Whale	Wellington Square	Mechanical engineer (Mayor)	Yes
	J. W. Wilding	Linden Grange, Hungerford Avenue	Shopkeeper and grocer with many premises	No

Crime in Crewe

Rates of crime can be charted across time by reference to the judicial and criminal statistics published annually (since 1857). Broad changes in the rates of violent, property, and public order offences have been interpreted and summarised by historians such as Emsley (2005: 21–56), Godfrey and Lawrence (2005: 90–5), and Taylor (1998: 7–48). Broadly Crewe did follow the same trends, and experienced the same types of crime that people experienced across the country. Readers of local newspapers in Crewe also took the same high interest in serious offences committed in and outside the area. Crewe newspapers published details of the trials of serious offences and weighty offenders—for example, Jeremy Johnson, a sixty-year-old sometime labourer who found himself in Crewe magistrates' court in 1895 on a charge of obtaining money by false pretences. Since that was an indictable offence, his case was committed by the local magistrates to Cheshire quarter sessions at Chester, where he was subsequently convicted and sentenced to imprisonment. This must have been a familiar scenario to Jeremy, since this was his thirteenth custodial sentence in a fourteen-year period.

His record of offending, which has been pieced together from petty and quarter sessions' records, shows a man who moved around the northern industrial towns committing fairly serious offences, for which he was regularly imprisoned. As a prolific and apparently incorrigible offender, without regular legal employment, and committing serious offences of dishonesty, the Victorian elite would have quickly recognized him as a member of the 'criminal classes'.[3] This putative criminal grouping supposedly existing in the heart of the purlieus and rookeries of the working-class districts has cast a large shadow over criminological research for the last hundred years or so (Emsley, 1996: 168–78). Although this book is not an inquiry into the existence and extent of the criminal classes in Crewe, it was possible for us to identify a few of the serious offenders that were said to make up the criminal classes. For example, we assiduously traced one such offender in the newspapers and court records:[4] Joshua Tinker

[3] In the working-class districts, peoples' belief in a 'criminal class' may not have not been so strong, but their views were less documented, see Godfrey (2006).

[4] We found only one other serious persistent offender who started their career between 1880 and 1890. In 1887 Walter Bennett, a fitter at the Works, left his wife-to-be at the altar whilst he burgled his own wedding guests (presumably because he knew their houses would be empty at the time). Not content with this betrayal, he

(a.k.a. James, and Chalky) was born in Crewe in 1863 and began his offending career by the age of eight, when he was sent to Bradwall Reformatory School for an unspecified offence. His father was charged in 1871 with being in arrears of his maintenance, and Joshua remained at the school until 1873/4. In 1874, the thirteen-year-old was sent to reform school for a further four years after stealing a jacket in Crewe High Street. In 1879, Joshua left reform school and began at the Works as an apprentice on 4s. per week.[4a] The following year he was sacked for losing time and also charged with a felony against Timothy Weston. The offence was the first of a series of crimes of a sexual nature and resulted in Tinker spending the next few years in Pentonville Prison. By 1887 he had been released and returned to Crewe, where he was described as a 'loafer' and convicted of the larceny of calf-skins from Crewe Market. The following year he was convicted of a misdemeanour, and in 1889 he was convicted of housebreaking. In the 1891 census he was recorded as being an inmate of Knutsford Prison following convictions for burglary and larceny at Crewe Market. In 1896 he assaulted Joseph Longton (probably a young boy) and in the following year committed his most serious offence; that of the rape of Nellie Court, the eleven year-old daughter of Peter Court. He was sentenced to a further term in prison and spent the next seven years in Dartmoor Prison. In 1903 he returned to Crewe (his parents having both died in 1899) and was convicted of vagrancy, two charges of obscene language, and failure to report to the police as a convict on licence.

The *Crewe Chronicle* carried a detailed report on Tinker with regard to his obscene language in front of a funeral procession, where 'there were about a 100 boys collected around the prisoner. There have been numerous complaints about Tinker [. . . who] had a terrible record'.[5] Similarly, with regard to his failure to report, the newspaper reported that 'in 1897 he had been sentenced to seven years' penal servitude for an assault on a child. At the beginning of the present year he had been liberated from Dartmoor and had reported regularly to the police until recently, when he disappeared.

later demanded the wedding presents back from his wife at knife-point. Her father, not surprisingly, said he would try and run the reluctant groom out of town. This resulted in Walter Bennett burgling the father's house and threatening to shoot him with a loaded revolver.

[4a] Prior to decimalization in 1971, British currency was made up of pennies (d.), twelve of which made a shilling (s.), twenty of which made a pound (£).

[5] *Crewe Chronicle*, 15 August 1903.

He was traced to Sandbach where he was living with a girl under the age of sixteen, an imbecile. The prisoner said he meant to marry her, and that the banns were being arranged for. The girl's mother had given information to the police'.[6]

Tinker's abuse of children continued for the rest of his life; in 1904 he was convicted of an indecent assault on an eight-year-old boy; in 1907 of a similar assault on a seven-year-old girl; in 1910 he was convicted of the unlawful carnal knowledge of a thirteen-year-old girl and a twelve-year-old boy, receiving a ten-year prison sentence and a further two-year sentence for another offence carried out with the young girl; and in 1918 he received two months in gaol for assault and gross indecency against a young boy (we explore the impact of Tinker's offending on some of these victims in Chapter Six). He died in 1920 a thoroughly disreputable and disturbed character. He was not, however, typical of the type of offenders in Crewe courts, as few dangerous offenders were resident in the town. Most serious property offenders, like Jeremy Johnson, were just passing through, and even the statistics of serious sexual or violent offences (where local people tended to be the defendants) were very low. Between 1880 and 1940 for example, there were thirty-seven cases of wounding/GBH; eight cases of manslaughter; six rapes or attempted rapes; and thirteen murders or attempted murders—ranging from William Peters, a boiler riveter at Crewe Works who shot his wife and seven children with a revolver in 1892 before attempting suicide, to a case of infanticide in 1936 (one of the very few infanticide cases prosecuted in the twentieth century).

The common trade of the courts were the minor offenders who traipsed through the courts for a variety of petty offences. A breakdown of the approximately 49,000 prosecutions between 1880 and 1940 is revealed below (Table 2.2).

Serious crime then was a relative rarity in Crewe, and the largest categories of minor crime involved public order or regulatory offences. These offences had their own rhythms that rose and fell over time as can be seen in the following section.

Crime Rates Over Time

Both property and violent offences in Crewe maintained at a low level throughout the period. The violence statistics for Crewe,

Table 2.2 Categories and sub-categories of crime in Crewe, 1880–1940.

Offence category	% of total	Largest sub-categories	% of total
Public Order	39	Vagrancy/indecency	8
		Driving behaviour	
		(speeding, drunken-driving, etc)	7
		Annoyances	7
		Gambling	3
		Public order violence	2
Regulatory Offences	32	Vehicular regulations (faulty brakes/lights; licence offences, etc)	10
		Animals (moving animals without licences; over-working animals, etc)	5
		Health and cleanliness (public health and sanitation acts)	3
		Education Act offences	3
		Retail (open after hours; employing children, etc)	3
		Wartime (blackout/ rationing offences)	2
Court Orders	15	Taxation	14
Property	10	Larceny (minor thefts; shoplifting)	7
		Major (burglary; breaking and entering; receiving)	1
Violence	3	Minor (assaults)	2.5
		Sexual/Major	0.5
TOTAL	99		78

although lower than the national rates and much lower than the county town of Cheshire, do follow the same downward trend (see Fig. 2.3). In 1881 there were twelve assaults per 10,000 people in this small but growing industrial town. The rates had fallen again by the turn of the century (mirroring national trends) but fell even lower to less than two assaults per 10,000 of population by 1940. It was a similar story when it came to assaults against the police, which most commentators concerned with violence (both contemporary and modern) tend to consider offences of violence. The decline was less sharp here, but was still notable. In 1871 there were sixty assaults on police officers per 10,000 of population. By 1901 there had been a fall to forty per 10,000, and thereafter the rate fell more steeply, to less than ten assaults per 10,000 people in 1931.

Property offences never rose above forty offences per 10,000 people in Crewe, a figure which was higher than national rates, but

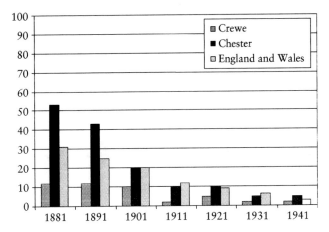

Fig. 2.3 Prosecutions for violence per 10,000 people, Crewe, Chester, and England & Wales, 1881–1941.

which can still be regarded as 'low'. Trends in property crime did not appear to coincide with economic cycles, and the depression of the 1930s does not appear to have increased prosecutions for acquisitive crime (at least in Crewe, see Fig. 2.4).

Turning to the two largest categories of crime in Crewe, public order and regulatory offences, it is clear that Crewe police division were kept busy in controlling the streets. The bulk of public order offences related to drunkenness. Prosecutions against drunkenness (simple drunkenness; aggravated drunkenness; and drunkenness & disorderliness) peaked in 1881 in England and Wales. There were approximately seventy-five offences per 10,000 people in that year, and the rate stayed fairly high until 1901. They declined only after wartime legislation (reducing opening hours and introducing stricter licensing controls) more than halved the rate to approximately thirty prosecutions per 10,000 people in 1921, and halving again to fifteen prosecutions per 10,000 people by 1931. In Crewe, as elsewhere, drunkenness 'drove' the public order figures, however, the sharp rise in the figures after 1900 reflects not just a rise in prosecutions for drunkenness, but also for street gambling, as new legislation came into force. Nevertheless, Crewe rates of public disorder broadly followed national trends with prosecutions declining throughout the early twentieth century (see Fig. 2.5).

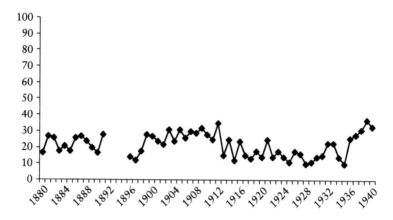

Fig. 2.4   Property offences per 10,000 people, Crewe 1880–1940.

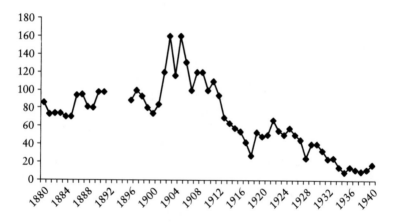

Fig. 2.5   Public order offences per 10,000 people, Crewe 1880–1940.

Moving against the general downward trends in property, violence and public order offending, there was a considerable rise in prosecutions for regulatory offences. As can be seen from Fig. 2.6 below, there was an uneven but gradual rise in prosecutions from 1880 to 1940. Britain's economic success in the late Victorian and Edwardian period relied on *laissez faire* economic policies and liberalizing markets, but the market struggled to solve social problems. Governments turned to directive legislation and social regulation delivered through local agencies to alleviate poverty and deprivation (see Davis, 1999: 4,

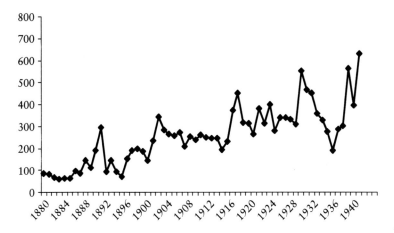

Fig. 2.6   Regulatory offences per 10,000 people, Crewe 1880–1940.

also Emsley, 1993: 366). As the nineteenth century ended a number of private or local authority agencies sought to regulate economic and social activity to an unprecedented degree, and central government also accelerated this process during periods of crisis and uncertainty. For example, the Defence of the Realm Act (DORA) passed in 1914 gathered to an 'otherwise liberal, anti-interventionist government' extensive powers of social control (DeGroot, 1996: 141). The capillary growth of regulation through areas of retail, health, welfare, and leisure activity; the activities of public and private enforcement and prosecution agencies; and the people upon whom the regulatory gaze fell, is relatively unresearched, yet statistically, regulatory offences were growing exponentially during this period as Fig. 2.6 shows.

In Crewe between 1880 and 1940 there was a large number of prosecutions under the 'regulatory umbrella'—health, sanitation and safety (3,034 cases), family regulation (1,733 cases), traffic offences (8,673 cases), the regulation of economic transactions (3,179 cases), and wartime regulations (1,488 cases). Together these offences constituted 53.4% of all criminal cases dealt with at Crewe petty sessions (1880–1940). The Crewe figures are not anomalous. As Emsley stated, 'In the second half of the century penal punishments were imposed to back up legislation on education, registration and vaccination; legislators saw failure to comply with the requirements of the state as the products of a defective conscience'(Emsley, 1993: 360). Contemporaries estimated that half-a-million parents were

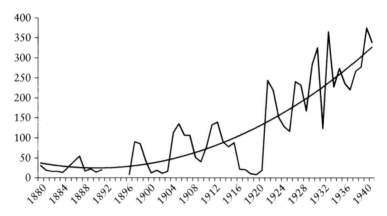

Fig. 2.7 Prosecutions for non-payment of borough rates, Crewe, 1880–1940 (with added trend line).

prosecuted in the twenty years following the passage of the 1870 Education Act for failure to send their children to school. Between 1880–1940 there were over 800 cases in Crewe alone.

If one adds together the people prosecuted for not sending children to school or to be vaccinated; having a chimney fire or unsanitary drains; riding a bicycle without lights or a bell; selling unsound meat or margarine disguised as butter; buying scrap metal without proper documents; leaving curtains open during an air-raid; or not paying local authority rates, the numbers are considerable (over 18,000 prosecutions just in Crewe). Those charged with regulatory offences might not be considered to be ' "criminals" in the accepted sense' (Emsley, 1993: 360) but they did find themselves in court, paying fines, and occasionally being sent to prison. Christopher Morley, for example, was imprisoned for six months for neglecting the welfare of his eleven-year-old child.

As with other categories of offending described above, particular offences tended to direct the general trend. In the case of regulatory offences, it was the numbers of rate defaulters in the 1920s and 1930s (possibly due to the national economic downturn) that helped to inflate regulatory offences figures (see Fig. 2.7 above).[7]

---

[7] Between 1880 and 1940 in Crewe there were 6,864 prosecutions for non-payment of borough rates or income tax (over a thousand of which were prosecuted by Joseph Harding).

Conviction Rates

This chapter would be incomplete without an examination of the conviction rates and penalties imposed in this period since they are widely accepted as a reliable indication of sentencers' attitudes (see Critchley, 1970; Gurr *et al*, 1977; King, 1996; Gurr, 1981; Monkkonen, 2001; Stevenson, 1994; Indermaur, 2000).

Turning first to rates of conviction, the following figures (Figs. 2.8–2.11) demonstrate there was a certain amount of 'sentencer volatility', with rates fluctuating across the years. Nevertheless, by the addition of trend lines, it is possible to identify sea-changes and major trends in rates of conviction. In a period when the evidence for public order came mainly from police sources (in cases of drunkenness; criminal damage; street gambling; street football etc) and when the magistrates were more trusting of police evidence, it is unsurprising that the conviction rates for public order offences were high. Fig. 2.8 shows the rate falling from approximately eight out of ten defendants being convicted, to around six out of ten. The fall may have been due to the police bringing more speculative prosecutions to court. Police campaigns against drunkenness and gambling, and the pre-selection of strong cases to take before the magistrates, may have led to almost certain

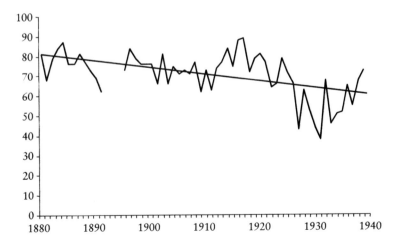

Fig. 2.8 Conviction rates for public order offences, Crewe, 1880–1940 (with added trend line).

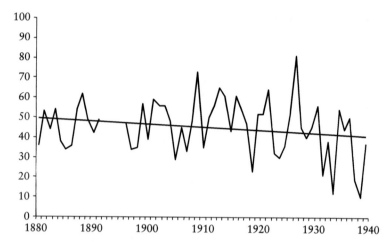

Fig. 2.9 Conviction rates for violence, Crewe, 1880–1940 (with added trend line).

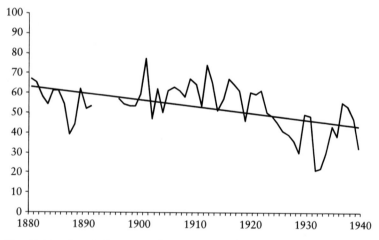

Fig. 2.10 Conviction rates for property offences, Crewe, 1880–1940 (with added trend line).

conviction in the nineteenth century, but possibly the magistrates had more sympathy for offenders in the 1930s and gave more defendants the benefit of the doubt.

Conviction rates were most volatile (and also lower) when it came to offences of violence. Magistrates had to judge the stories of competing private individuals in cases of assault, and also made

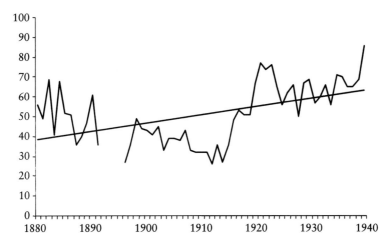

Fig. 2.11 Conviction rates for regulatory offences, Crewe, 1880–1940 (with added trend line).

decisions whether minor cases of violence, neighbourhood rows, and drunken brawling were worth taking the time in court to sort out (see Godfrey, Farrall and Karstedt, 2005). In many cases the newspapers make it clear that the magistrates did not think the cases were worth their efforts, and simply dismissed both parties as being as bad as each other. Therefore the conviction rates in Fig. 2.9 vary between high rates (70–80%) in some years, to low rates (10–20%) in others. Nevertheless, the general trend was a very slight decline in rates between 1880 and 1940.

Conviction rates in property offences also declined (see Fig. 2.10). This is perhaps more surprising since developments in forensics—fingerprints, plaster of Paris for footprints, and so on—should, one would have thought, have increased the chance of conviction. It may be that the increase in juvenile shoplifting from shops with open self-serve counters, which were first introduced into Crewe in the 1920s, both increased the number of shop thefts, and also made it harder to prove offences in court.

The trend line is slightly misleading in Fig. 2.11. In reality, rates of conviction were broadly decreasing until the First World War after which they rose steadily. By 1940 almost nine out of ten defendants were convicted of regulatory offences, a good many of which were blackout offences (riding bicycles or driving cars with lights undimmed; not having blackout curtains in place; shops still using

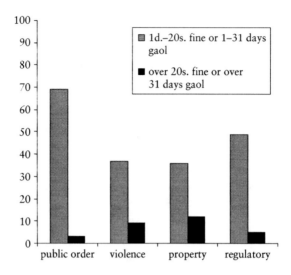

Fig. 2.12   Penalties imposed (%), Crewe, 1880–1940.

lights in their front windows, and so on). It is hardly surprising that during wartime the magistrates tended to convict for these type of offences—not least because Crewe rail yards and the Rolls-Royce factory were bombed during the Second World War. Whether or not a conviction is made in court is primarily decided by the strength of evidence. With the exception of assault cases perhaps, magistrates may have found it relatively easy to decide guilt or innocence. For those reasons, it is likely that the penalties imposed on offenders are a more reliable guide to sentencers' attitudes.

Sentences Imposed

In Crewe, between 1880 and 1940, convicted property offenders and violent offenders were more likely to receive a longer gaol sentence than other offenders (approximately 10% of violent/property offenders received fines above 20s. or a period of gaol of over one month). It is clear that sentencers and the general public considered these offences, and offenders, as more serious than the general run-of-the-mill public order and regulatory offences (see Fig. 2.12).

Thus far we have sought to document rather than explain the crime figures for Crewe. However, because (as is explained in the following chapter) the offences for which persistent offenders

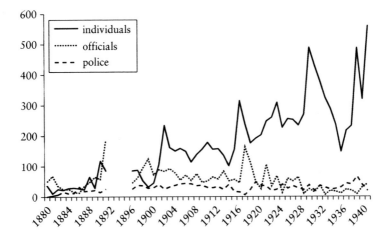

Fig. 2.13 Agencies involved in prosecutions for all offences in Crewe, 1880–1940.

were prosecuted, to some extent, were affected by policing and prosecution practices, we ask the following questions. First, how did the route to prosecution change between 1880 and 1940? Second, how did this alter the statistical landscape over this period?

The Prosecution Process, 1880–1940

After police forces were established across the country under legislation passed in 1856, prosecutions were overwhelmingly brought to court either through police action, or through private individuals taking out summonses and prosecuting the offences themselves. This situation continued until the 1880s after which other agencies increasingly became involved in the prosecution process (for example, the National Society for the Prevention of Cruelty to Children; Royal Society for the Prevention of Cruelty to Animals; Borough Market Inspectors, Nuisance Inspectors, Rates Collectors, Truancy and School Inspectors etc, see Fig. 2.13).[8]

---

[8] Samuel Stockton and William Urqhuart, the borough's nuisance inspectors, prosecuted 323 cases; the two market inspectors proceeded against 475 people; the RSPCA advanced seventy-three cases to Crewe courts, and the NSPCC another forty-five.

The involvement of private individuals and semi-official agencies remained fairly constant, whilst the activity of the police increased dramatically. Regulatory offences formed the bulk of the work of Crewe magistrates' courts, and within that category of offence, the police were the most active prosecution agency. This was mainly due to the increased number of traffic offences, and the willingness of the police to prosecute them (the police prosecuted 99.6% of the 3,402 vehicular offences in Crewe between 1880 and 1940). There was, as can be seen below, a very notable shift in policing and prosecution focus around the First World War, when public order offences (ie drunkenness) decline steeply, and are overtaken by vehicular (predominantly motoring) offences (see Fig. 2.14 below). It was not just the increase in car and motorcycle ownership, but a substantial shift in police attention after 1918 from offences of public order to vehicular offences of all kinds (including bicycles and horse-drawn vehicles) that caused this situation to occur.

Conclusion

We have identified two major changes in the prosecution process between 1880 and 1940. First, the growth of private and semi-official

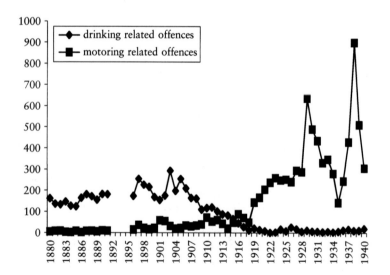

Fig. 2.14 Prosecutions for drunkenness and motoring related offences, Crewe, 1880–1940.

prosecution agencies, which together with the growth of by-laws designed to bring about higher rates of urban civility, engendered a huge growth in regulatory offences dealt with in the courts. Second, the attempt to govern public spaces and mobility in the period after the First World War focused police attention away from public order offending in the entertainment areas of town, towards the control of traffic on the major public highways. This caused traffic offences to rise exponentially during the early twentieth century. These changes affected the number and type of offences brought before the Crewe courts generally (habitual drunks; speeding drivers, and so on). They, therefore, also affected the number, type, and offending careers of persistent offenders that were brought before the courts. The following chapter describes 101 prolific offenders in Crewe between 1880 and 1940, all of whom were brought into the courts partly because of their own behaviour, but also because of the changing focus of the police and the prosecution process in this period.

3
Persistent Criminality in Crewe 1880–1940

The Chief Constable of Cheshire has given the record of John Oldcastle, recently dead, who made 130 appearances before the city justices: 86 being for drunkenness and 44 for assaults. Oldcastle's father appeared before the bench 35 times, a sister 67 times, and another sister 29 times. The father, son and two sisters were charged 347 times; it has been estimated that in the expenses of prosecution, prisons, and poor-law maintenance, the Oldcastle family has cost the city £2,000.

'The Cost of a Criminal Family', *Crewe Chronicle*, 28 Sept 1895

Cohort A: Characteristics

In this chapter we focus on those individuals that we have identified as being persistent offenders in Crewe between 1880 and 1940. Briefly, 101 individuals were identified as having committed five or more offences during their offending career since their first crime in the 1880–1890 period. We refer to these 101 as 'Cohort A' persistents.

To what extent are contemporary late-Victorian views of the criminal classes confirmed by our sample of 101 prolific offenders in Crewe? Would they have fitted into a kind of 'residuum'; were they unrepentant and irredeemable habitual criminals, drawn from the dregs of the 'dangerous classes', habitual drunks and petty thieves? Did they begin their prolific offending careers from adolescence, being virtually 'born into crime'? We first looked at the aggregated characteristics of these offenders to see what they could tell us about the nature of persistent criminals in Crewe, and then we illustrated some of the issues raised in a series of case studies drawn from the offending careers of our persistent offenders.

Gender

Our offenders were predominantly male (82%), and therefore our sample conformed to the generally accepted pattern of male/female

Table 3.1   Offences committed by Cohort A offenders, by gender (%).

Offences	Males (%)	Females (%)
Drunkenness	30	45
Education Acts	19	0
Work-related offending	8	17
Larceny	6	0
Vagrancy (including prostitution)	5	5
Rates arrears	4	0
Unlicensed dogs/dog collar offences	2	0
Deserting family	2	0
Public Health Acts	1	0
Fraud	1	0
Bastardy	1	0
Indecent/obscene language	0	17
Unclassified	15	5

offending—only 18% of the group were female. The female persistents committed a smaller range of crimes, perhaps reflecting their reduced opportunities to engage in as wide a range of activities as males—some crimes such as bastardy and desertion being exclusively male (see Table 3.1 above). However, our aggregated female persistents exhibit some further differences when compared to our male offenders. The females are over a third as likely again to be habitual drunkards than males (45% of females compared to 30% of males), and are also more likely to be physically abusive (11% of females compared to 6% of males).[1] They are also more likely to be convicted for persistent work-related offences (17% of females compared to 8% of males), but this figure is undoubtedly skewed by the fact that the majority of the working male population of the town was employed by the railway company. As a result, the majority of work-related offences such as pilfering or

---

[1] This categorization of violence includes assault and sexual offences (excluding prostitution). This finding resonates with the findings from the *Home Office Research Study no. 275* (Budd, Tracey, Clare Sharp, and Pat Mayhew, *Offending in England and Wales: first results from the 2003 Crime and Justice Survey* (London: Home Office, 2005), which found that 'female offenders aged over twenty-five were more likely to have committed a serious offence than their male counterparts. This is entirely due to them being more likely to commit an assault with injury; 31% of female offenders aged twenty-six and over had done so, compared with only 21% of male offenders of the same age' (p. 32.). These figures refer to habitual offenders who re-offended in the subsequent twelve months.

breaches of regulations would have been dealt with internally by the railway company (see Chapter Four).[2]

Females were far more likely to be involved in persistent indecent behaviour (22% of persistent female offenders); apart from the obvious offence of prostitution (only three of our persistents appear to have been regularly prosecuted for this offence, see later) many were prosecuted for the use of obscene or profane language. This figure probably reflects public/private and male/female divisions, with more colourful language being present and tolerated within the private and almost exclusively 'male' employment contexts. Women swearing in the streets or in their houses where neighbours and passers-by, including police officers, could hear them were more likely to be censured. For example, the *Crewe Chronicle* reported a case on 6 July 1920, in which Edith Munty, one of our persistent offenders, was convicted for obscene language following the evidence of a constable who stated that she was shouting obscenities through a window in Lockitt Street, and that although he could not see her, he 'could recognize her voice'. It is also likely that police officers preferred to charge women who were fighting in the street (in one of the numerous neighbourhood fracas) with using obscene language rather than with breaching the peace or assault (this partly but not completely explains the high female figures in Table 3.1).

Although the percentage is somewhat lower than that of their female counterparts, for males the main offence was drunkenness. This accounted for almost a third of all male persistents' offending, with many of the habitual drunkards exhibiting a phenomenal rate and longevity of offending—witness James Newlands' prolific alcoholic career of over fifty court appearances in one decade. The second most prevalent type of offending among males was that of Education Act/Industrial School offences, with almost 20% of persistents failing to send at least one of their children to school, or not contributing to their maintenance in Industrial or Reform Schools. As head of the household, fathers were responsible for the education of their children, although in cases of neglect or the conducing of youthful offences by neglect both parents could be charged, as in the case of Wilbur and Sally Boswell, who were convicted in 1916 for contributing to their daughter's descent into prostitution at the age of fifteen.

---

[2] See Chapter Four for more on how the railway company dealt with criminality and delinquency.

Mothers were deemed to be responsible for most other aspects of the welfare of children. For example, the 1902 Licensing Act made it illegal to be drunk in charge of a child under the age of seven. It is interesting to note that this law was seen to relate primarily to women; on 10 January 1903 the *Crewe Chronicle* carried the by-line 'First Cheshire Case under the new Act: a warning to mothers'. It stated that 'to be drunk in charge of a child was now an offence against the law, and three appearances in a court rendered a person liable to be put on the black list [*and could be imprisoned for up to three years*]'. It was clearly assumed that mothers were in charge of their children, with no mention being made of a warning to fathers, although in law either parent could be charged. On 24 June 1903 Theo and Milly Flint (husband and wife, and brother and sister-in law respectively to Ellie Oldfield, our most persistent female offender) were jointly charged under the Act and sentenced to six months' imprisonment.

Age and Onset of Offending

Half of our sample of Cohort A persistent offenders were either not born in Crewe or were not living in Crewe prior to the 1871 census. With regard to the 21% of persistent offenders who had moved to Crewe by 1870, we have been able to trace their offending (if any) in the period 1870–1879 by consulting local newspaper reports. However, the vast majority of this 21% were not juveniles at the time they moved to Crewe and therefore we have been unable to establish if they offended as a juvenile.[3] For the 28% of persistents born in Crewe by 1871, we have been able to trace their entire offending careers whilst they lived in the town and found that over half (57%) had committed their first crime between the ages of eight and twenty; 44% started offending between the ages of twenty-two and forty; and 17% after the age of forty (11% were not classifiable).[4] The relatively late onset for Cohort A offenders is probably related to the fact that

---

[3] Much has been written on the subject of juvenile delinquency, ranging from Mary Carpenter's research in the 1850s to numerous present-day sociological and criminological research discussing cause and effect, punishment and reintegration. See for examples, Carpenter, Mary, *Juvenile Delinquents, their conviction and treatment* (London: W. & F.G. Cook, 1853); TNA HO45/16515 *Children: Juvenile Delinquency*: report by the Juvenile Organizations Committee, 1920; and Rosenheim, M.K., *A Century of Juvenile Justice* (Chicago: Chicago University Press, 2003).

[4] Once in Crewe, the majority of people seemed to stay there—64% of our persistent offenders are recorded as dying in Crewe, and the figure may be higher, as we were unable to trace the place and year of death of all 101 persistent offenders.

we rely entirely upon official records, and also because of their entry into the world of work. Offending related to employment initiated onset of a criminal career for 25% of Cohort A offenders aged twenty-two to forty (the single largest explanation for that age band), and 18% for those aged over forty-one (the second most common reason for the onset of a persistent offending career). For those aged twenty-one or under, the same figure was only 10%.

Persistent offenders tended to start offending at an earlier age than one-off or casual offenders (Moffat, 1993). From July 1909 (when juveniles' courts first began to run alongside adult courts, allowing juvenile offenders to be readily identified) to December 1940, of the total of 29,107 offences recorded in Crewe Petty Sessions during that period, some 3,036 involve juveniles between the ages of eight and twenty, accounting for 11% of the total.[5] This would suggest that there was some statistical justification for the contemporary concern that if someone started committing offences as a juvenile, they were far more likely to continue an offending trajectory, although, as our research on gangs shows (see below) most juvenile offending did not continue into adult life.

Family

Seventy (70%) of the persistent offenders in our sample married at some point in their lives. Sixty-two had children, and the average number of children in persistents' families was five. Persistent offenders who had convictions for not sending their children to school tended to have slightly larger families (averaging six children per family). However, although there was a mass of contemporary comment linking large families to crime, we found no such link in our study (see Chapter Five).

Socio-economic Status

The vast majority of our persistent offenders were manual labourers of one kind or another, with 42% of male offenders being employed at some stage of their lives within the Railway Works. This was fairly typical for Crewe at that time, although it does suggest that the criminal careers of our persistent offenders did not overly trouble the railway company (the exception obviously being

---

[5] These figures do not include any appearances in which the age of the defendant was not given, but the clerks were fairly assiduous at recording such details if the defendant was a juvenile; therefore any missing figures are likely to be low in number.

Table 3.2 Male employees at Works as a percentage
of male population of Crewe.

1871	42%
1881	46%
1891	44%
1901	36%
1911	32%

offences that resulted in a prison sentence, leading to automatic dismissal from the Works, see Chapter Four). Since the vast majority of the crimes for which our persistents were convicted were petty and low-level offences that did not result in custodial sentences, conviction did not result in dismissal (see Chapter Four).

Table 3.2 shows the number of Railway Works' employees as a percentage of the entire male population of Crewe, and reflects the fact that, as an elderly inhabitant of Crewe recorded in her memoirs in 1969: 'There was but one way of earning a living in Crewe [. . .] everything was dominated by the Railway Company' (Hodkinson).[6]

Of the eighteen female persistent offenders, only one-third are not recorded as being in paid employment, with the employed women working primarily as either domestic servants or seamstresses. Of the male offenders, some 15% were shopkeepers or market-stall holders (the size of these concerns varied greatly, from a small market-stall to a chain of grocery shops throughout the town); whilst three were farmers owning or tenanting land around Crewe. A couple of offenders were white-collar employees: an accountant and a railway clerk. Only one of the offenders is described as being a tramp ('tramps' in this study refer to local Crewe homeless people rather than peripatetic or itinerant workers 'on the tramp' around the region); all the others were either employed or working in the domestic sphere.[7] Our persistent

---

[6] Figures abstracted from census returns given in Chaloner, W.H., *The Social and Economic Development of Crewe 1780–1920*; and Drummond, D., *Crewe: Railway Town, Company and People, 1890–1914* (Aldershot: Scolar Press, 1995). These figures are somewhat artificially lower than reality, as the census figures include all male children as well as male adults; consequently the actual percentage of men working for the Works is likely to have been considerably higher.

[7] It should be remembered that vagrants and tramps were undoubtedly committing many offences, but they would not show up as prolific in our sample because they were itinerant and not resident in Crewe.

offenders then do not seem to fit the mid- and late-Victorians' view of the habitual criminal as invariably being a member of the 'undeserving poor'. Whilst several of the offenders were undoubtedly poor in both relative and absolute terms, very few of them seem to have been either work-shy or unable to hold down employment for often considerable lengths of time, and not many would fit the description of what Stedman Jones has called 'a small and hopeless remnant' (Stedman Jones, 2002: 320). Rather it would seem that the majority of our offenders enjoyed generally stable employment and seemingly integrated into wider society in much the same way as their non-offending counterparts: getting married, having children and staying within the town for the remainder of their lives.

Types of Crime

We turn now to an analysis of the types of crime committed by our Cohort A persistents in order to see what findings are revealed through their aggregated characteristics—see Table 3.3 below.

Three categories of offence constitute almost two-thirds of offending, with one offence dominating the crimes attributed to the peristents: that of drunkenness. It accounts for one-third of all the court appearances of our persistents and overshadows the next most frequent offence of Education Act/Industrial School infringements by a ratio of over 2:1. During the early part of the period under investigation, drunkenness was increasingly seen as a major

Table 3.3 Offences carried out by Cohort A offenders (%)

	%
Drunkenness	33
Education Act/ Industrial School	16
Work-related	15
Assault	5
Larceny	5
Vagrancy	5
Obscene language/indecency	3
Rates	3
Desertion of wife/family	2
Unlicensed/uncollared dog	2
Bastardy	1
Fraud	1
Public Health	1
Sexual violence	1
Unclassified	7
Total	100

social problem in Crewe. This is reflected in the following letter published in the *Crewe Chronicle* on 2 August 1879:

Sir, the increase in drunkenness has become very noticeable in our town, so much so that it is utterly impossible for any respectable individual to pass certain public houses about the hour of eleven on Saturday nights. It is pitiable to see poor wretches, maddened by their libations, endeavouring to complete each others' misery by spoiling each others' faces; then staggering home with the blissful prospect of black eyes, aching heads and empty pockets to greet them on the Sunday morning. But what astonishes me is how this sort of thing comes about. According to our laws, 'no intoxicated person shall be supplied with drink' thus effectively preventing drunkenness. Yet how is it we see such a vast number of men, aye, and women too, in a most beastly state of intoxication. How have they got so very drunk? To satisfy ourselves we have only to visit the different gin palaces of our town, where it is astonishing to see how openly and unreservedly the law must be violated.

There were certainly a considerable number of licensed premises within Crewe (Chaloner, 1950: 176). Chaloner remarks in his survey of the social and economic history of Crewe that 'between 1879 and 1905 improvements in the sobriety of Crewe followed a somewhat spasmodic course, and to judge from the statistics of convictions for drunkenness little real progress was made, especially as the police had a reputation for leniency. Only after 1905 did the work of the Licensing Committee begin to bear fruit.' (Chaloner, 1950: 177).

Chaloner put the subsequent decrease in prosecutions for drunkenness (see Chapter Two and below) down to a combination of shorter opening hours, reduced alcoholic content of beer, absence of men during the First World War and more sustained efforts by the magistrates, especially with regard to licensing outlets. It is clear that such changes had a considerable effect on the number of public houses; the ratio of inhabitants to licences had risen from 259:1 in 1889 to 645:1 in 1921.

The second most frequent type of offence committed by our persistent offenders was that related to education: notably non-attendance of school-age children and non-payment of Industrial or Reform school maintenance. Sixteen per cent of Cohort A persistent offenders were primarily convicted for these types of offence. The first nationwide measure to ensure a basic level of education for all children between the ages of five and ten was the 1870 Education Act (commonly known as Forster's Act), which set up a network of free secular primary schools. These ran alongside existing sectarian schools and attendance was not compulsory. This move seems to have been particularly opposed in Crewe, where 'clergymen, ratepayers and the Railway Company joined forces in a determined effort to keep elementary education on a voluntary and denominational basis in the town' (Geeson, 1969: 98).

By 1877, however, the town was forced to create a School Attendance Committee under the provisions of Lord Sandon's Act of the previous year. This committee imposed penalties on parents 'who persistently failed to send children to school, and on anyone who employed children below ten who had not yet passed a Standard IV exam or who had not made 250 attendances during each of five years' (Geeson, 1969: 115). This latter clause had caused problems for many people, as 'in Crewe [. . .] there had always been a tendency for boys to be tempted or obliged to leave school at an early age in order to take up junior apprenticeships in the Works' (Geeson, 1969: 115).

Peter Ranicar was appointed the first School Attendance Officer in Crewe and his detailed report of 15 December 1877 contained the following statistics: 69% of the total number of children on the various school registers actually attended a school; 843 children were not receiving any formal education; ninety-seven children were not being sent to school or receiving any form of education; the cost of attendance at denominational schools was 3d. per week (Geeson 1965: 116–17). Ranicar was a dedicated official, and issued sixty-two warning notices within three weeks of the publication of his Report. The first cases brought before the School Attendance Committee were heard in May 1878, when thirteen parents were each fined 2s. 6d. for not sending their children to school. By 1883, Crewe's school attendance record was averaging over 80%, being somewhat higher than the national average of 71% (Geeson, 1965: 121).

However, despite this impressive figure, certain individuals persisted in either not sending their children to school or not being in sufficient control of them in order to know if they were attending. Bert Poster was prosecuted five times for not sending his children to school. Indeed, in 1882 the School Attendance Officer was reported as stating that 'this was a family where the children did not attend school, but were allowed to run around the streets' (*Crewe Chronicle*, 30 September 1882). Bert was otherwise an upstanding citizen of Crewe, who in 1904 was presented with a trophy to mark

Table 3.4 Offending career of Wilbur Boswell senior.

Year	Life events	Employment and addresses	Offending and victimization events
1867	Born in Crewe		
1871		Living with his parents (Alice b. 1843 and John b. Middlewich 1842) at 64 Furber Street	
1874– 1880	Absent from school		
1881	Absent from school	Living at 18 Gladstone Street Apprentice slater working for his father	
1884			Assaulted by Charles Poole.
1886	Marries Sally Pryce	Breaks his apprenticeship with his father and tries to establish himself as a contracted slater	Father sues Wilbur for £10 unreclaimed wages. His father is described as illiterate and as never having gone to school.
1887	1st daughter Elizabeth born		
1888	1st son Wilbur Jnr born		
1889			Arrested by PC Booth and convicted for stealing tools from his employer, he was fined £1.00 or twenty-one days in default.
1890	2nd son James born		Drunk in Oak Street, no fine but must pay costs of the case.
1891		Slater living at 154 Henry Street	

Year		
1893	2nd daughter Beatrice born	Drunk in charge of horse and cart. In arrears for General District Rates.
1896	3rd son Donald born	Education Act x 7, prosecuted by GeorgePlant, School Inspector. Arrears of General District Rates. Arrears of Poor Rates.
1897	Living at 15 Audley Street, and working as a slater	Drunk in charge of horse and cart. Arrears of General District Rates and also arrears of water rates. Education Act x 2 (both charges were withdrawn).
1898	Self-employed master slater living at 19 Audley Street	Drunk and Disorderly in Audley Street. Education Act x 9, prosecuted by School Attendance Officers, William Thompson and Joseph Owen. Industrial School Arrears x 3. Ordered to pay 2s. 6d. weekly.
1899		
1900	Wilbur Jnr & James sent to Macclesfield County Industrial School for shop-lifting. Elizabeth sent to reform school at Stockport for two cases of larceny, and sending fraudulent begging letters to church.	
1901	4th son & 3rd daughter born (Henry and Eleanor). 19 Audley Street Self-employed master slater	

Table 3.4 (*Contd.*)

Year	Life events	Employment and addresses	Offending and victimization events
1902		15 Audley Street, slater	
1903	Elizabeth leaves reform school		
1904	Son Henry dies. Sons Wilbur jnr and James leave reform school		
1905			Education Act, prosecuted by William Whitley, fined 6d. Prosecuted under Street Making Expenses Act, for not paying for Audley Street to be paved, x 2. Ordered to pay by the courts.
1906		15 Audley Street, slater	Industrial School Arrears x 4, settled out of court. Malicious Injury against Education Officer, William Whitney. Neglect of 4 Children (with wife). He is bound over for a period of six months, but his wife is imprisoned for twenty-one days. Education Act (withdrawn).
1907	Sally (wife or sister) taken into Upton Asylum. Daughter Elizabeth marries Jerry H Coomber, a Nantwich bus driver		

Year		
1908	Daughter Eleanor sent to reform school	Arrears of General District Rates. Prosecution by Nuisance Inspector, William Urquhart (nuisance not abated).
1909		Industrial School Arrears.
1910	Unemployed slater, 23 Audley Street	Arrears for Poor Rates. Education Act. Industrial School arrears of £3.00. Obscene Language. Distress Warrant issued and court allowed to seize goods because fines have not been paid.
1911	Living at 25 Ludford Street	Industrial School Act x 2. Obscene Language, 10s. fine. Neglect of 3 Children (with his wife). Both are sentenced to 3 months hard labour. Prosecutes Terrence Olwins for malicious damage to a window—as a result of an attempted burglary when Wilbur lives with mother whilst his wife is in gaol.
1912	Living in Cemetery Road	Education Act. Industrial Schools Act.
1913	Daughter Eleanor leaves reform school	
1914	Living at 10 Grosvenor Street	Education Act.
1915		Obscene Language x 3, 10s fine for each. All in Grosvenor Street. Education Act. Reported as having 25 previous convictions.

Table 3.4 (Contd.)

Year	Life events	Employment and addresses	Offending and victimization events
1916	Daughter Eleanor in Rescue Home		Conducing by neglect (with his wife) Eleanor to solicit. Paid the fine of £2.00. Wilbur thought Eleanor was staying with a married sister. He had been working away a great deal, and he could not control Eleanor. 'The parents had drunken habits and at the house there were frequently drunken carousals day and night.' *Crewe Chronicle* 12 July 1916.
1917	Daughter Beatrice dies		
1918	Daughter Eleanor leaves Rescue Home		
1922	Son Donald marries Fanny Light. Son Donald dies. Daughter Eleanor marries Edward Evans		
1937	Death in Crewe		

his retirement as a postman after twenty-five years' service, and was described as 'one of the oldest and most respected postmen in Crewe' (*Crewe Chronicle*, 23 January 1904).

Similarly, Wilbur Boswell, the most prolific of all our persistent offenders, with over sixty reported offences to his name (see Table 3.4 for his offending career), was primarily convicted for not exercising parental control over his children; he received numerous fines for non-attendance of several of his children, and failed to pay Industrial School maintenance fees for those of his children who had been sent there as a result of their own misdemeanours. His most serious offence was the conducing by neglect of the prostitution of his fifteen-year-old daughter; it was reported that 'the parents had drunken habits and at the house there were frequently drunken carousals day and night' (*Crewe Chronicle*, 12 July 1916).

Many prosecutions resulted from work-related offences (15%). These ranged from shopkeepers obstructing the public footpath with their wares or carts, to the ill-treatment of working animals, unjust weights and measures, and lodging-house offences (such as renting out overcrowded and unsanitary rooms). From the mid-nineteenth century there had been an increasing body of legislation against such offences throughout the country, and Crewe was no exception. By 1900 Crewe had a panoply of officials concerned with public health and employment, including a Sanitary Inspector, a Markets Inspector, an Inspector of Nuisances, an Inspector of Weights and Measures, a Medical Officer of Health, an NSPCC Inspector, and an RSPCA Inspector. It is therefore perhaps not too surprising that some of our persistent offenders (who otherwise seem to have led 'respectable' lives) fell foul of this barrage of officialdom.

Perhaps the best example of this type of persistent is Edwin Heath, who was a prosperous grocer and shopkeeper, building up a chain of eighteen stores throughout Crewe and the surrounding district from 1885 onwards (Chaloner, 1950). He was prosecuted various times between 1888 and 1897 for cases that arose out of his grocery business (for adulterating food, not vaccinating animals against rabies, obstructing the footpath with carts and boxes, allowing his cattle to stray on the road, and employing children contrary to the Factories and Workshops Act). His offending history did not prevent him from being elected a Borough Councillor (and being offered the Mayoralty, which he turned down). Habitual offender legislation was clearly not aimed at prosperous members of the mercantile class such as Edwin Heath, nor would he have been labelled as a rough character in the same way as habitual drunks or street-toughs would have been, indeed, he had for a time, been a serious competitor for the Co-op. His offending career eventually came to a halt at the same time as his business empire diminished since he only committed work-related offences.

Other Types of Crime

The remaining 36% of crime committed by our Cohort A persistent offenders was of a varied nature, with no particular type accounting for more than 5% of the total. The types of crimes committed by our persistent offenders are irrevocably linked to social, technological and economic developments; for example, motoring offences (with cars and motorcycles) do not feature at all amongst our Cohort A persistent offenders due to the fact that the motor car was not widely available during the time they were offending. Admittedly the first motoring offence recorded in Crewe Petty Sessions was early; on 16 June 1903 Lionel Addington was fined £5 and costs for driving a motor car furiously, but there were only a further 860 motoring offences in the next twenty years. From 1923–1940 the number of traffic offences in Crewe increased almost five-fold.[8] However, the vast majority of Cohort A offenders were simply too old or poor to own or drive motor vehicles.[9]

The Impact of Gentrification on the 'Location' of Criminal Careers

The character and 'feel' of streets and locales change over time. Indeed, the gentrification or de-gentrification of areas has been noted by many criminologists, especially community safety theorists as a strong predictor both of levels of crime and fear of crime (Walklate, 1998). This may be due to physical changes, ie when commercial properties are turned into residential ones and the area becomes less busy and more settled; or when the demography of an area changes, ie when large properties are sub-divided into private

---

[8] *Report on Road Accidents in Great Britain involving Personal Injury (Fatal and Non-fatal) Year Ending 31/03/1937* (London: HMSO, 1938), quoted in *Crewe Chronicle* 12 March 1938.

[9] It is recognized that some working-class individuals would have appeared before the courts during the period in connection with motoring offences as a result of their employment as delivery van drivers, bus drivers etc.

rented accommodation, and people of low income stay for short terms, reducing stability in the area. We expected to find that the physical, demographic and cultural development of areas of Crewe between 1841 and 1901 (as evidenced by a study of census records) would affect or be affected by the same kinds of factors. In fact, the predominantly working-class character of Crewe meant that signs of gentrification were subtle and hard to discern. For example, we examined two streets that were often mentioned in trial reports in detail—Audley Street and Whitegates. From the time of their construction, both streets housed solidly working class residents—labourers, painters, fustian cutters, and so on—although by 1901 two engine drivers, and a railway clerk had moved into Audley Street, indicating it was considered a more respectable part of town. Between 1891 and 1901 Audley Street housed two prolific offenders (Bertram Varleigh and Wilbur Boswell) and ten non-prolific offenders. Three persistent offenders were resident in Whitegates for some part of 1881–1891 (Elspeth Hister, Peter Bates, Edith and James Munty) during which time they and members of their families committed forty-three offences. Overall, the number of offenders living in Whitegates fell between 1881 and 1901 (from twenty-one to twelve), and by 1901 there were no persistent offenders living in the street. So, were there criminal areas, and did they gentrify over time? Certainly there were streets in Crewe that had attracted reputations for being disorderly, but such connections made in the minds of police officers and magistrates were often illusionary, and that seems to have been the case here (as illustrated in Fig. 3.1. where the location of crime does not match the attendant reputation). The persistent offenders in our sample tended, like many casual offenders, to commit crimes (mainly of drunkenness, or drunken violence) in the public entertainment areas of town.

Cohort B: Characteristics

As shown in Chapter Two, crime trends were affected by social, political, economic and technological developments, and Cohort A was populated with offenders who committed their first offence early in the period we are studying. We wondered whether the persistent offenders in Cohort A would share the same characteristics as offenders committing their first offence in the middle of our period.

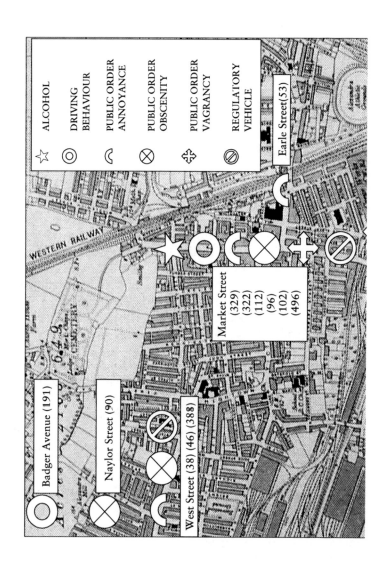

ALCOHOL

DRIVING
BEHAVIOUR

PUBLIC ORDER
ANNOYANCE

PUBLIC ORDER
OBSCENITY

PUBLIC ORDER
VAGRANCY

REGULATORY
VEHICLE

Earle Street (53)

WESTERN RAILWAY

Market Street
(329)
(322)
(112)
(96)
(102)
(496)

Badger Avenue (191)

Naylor Street (90)

West Street (38) (46) (388)

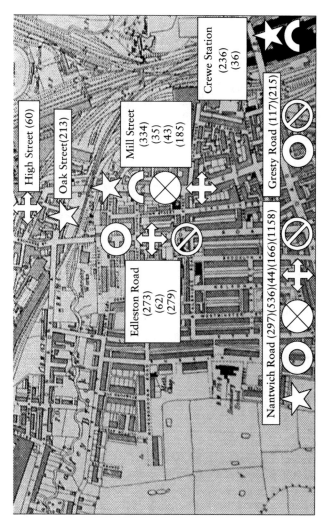

High Street (60)

Oak Street(213)

Mill Street
(334)
(35)
(43)
(185)

Crewe Station
(236)
(36)

Gresty Road (117)(215)

Edleston Road
(273)
(62)
(279)

Nantwich Road (297)(536)(44)(166)(1158)

Fig. 3.1 Map of Crewe (c. 1911) showing respective main locations for alcohol, driving behaviour, public order annoyance, public order obscenity, public order vagrancy and regulatory vehicular offences 1880–1940 (total number of each offence in brackets)

We therefore created another dataset of persistent offenders who committed their first offence in the period 1900–1910, utilizing similar methods to those used in creating the dataset of Cohort A.[10]

The total number of cases recorded in Crewe Petty Sessions for the period 1900–1910 is 11,034. This gives an average of 1,003 cases recorded per year, compared to an average of 430 cases per year in the period 1880–1890. So the number of petty sessions cases roughly doubled (233%), however, the population of the town had also increased at a roughly similar rate (184% from 1880–1910), suggesting that the crime rate remained fairly static in real terms. The 1900–1910 dataset of Cohort B persistent offenders consists of a total of 205 individuals who committed their first offence in the period 1900–1910. Of these 205 individuals, ten were the children of Cohort A offenders (see Chapter Five). The actual number of crimes committed by persistent offenders in each period is remarkably similar; in 1880–1890, Cohort A offenders were brought before the court for a total of 1,053 offences—an average of just over 10.4 crimes per persistent. In the 1900–1910 period 205 Cohort B offenders were charged with a total of 2,143 cases—again an average of just over 10.4 crimes per persistent. The amounts of offending in both cohorts therefore seems to remain constant, although the offenders in Cohort A and Cohort B are almost without exception not members of the same extended families. Persistent offending therefore seems to be more of a 'bubbling cauldron' effect than a 'ripple' effect, with individuals throughout the entire 1880–1940 period persisting in their criminal careers and their family name then disappearing from the ranks of persistent offenders, to be replaced by new persistent offenders, rather than several generations of the same family (see Chapter Five).

The figures regarding female offenders are less consistent and more ambiguous than those of persistent offenders overall. In Cohort A just under a fifth (18%) were female and in Cohort B a quarter were female. The types of offences brought before the court also changed dramatically in the two periods under consideration.

Of the offences that figured significantly in 1880–1940—drunkenness, larceny and public order offences—drunkenness fell

---

[10] This later period, 1900–1910, was chosen as it still allowed us to utilize two of our main sources: notably the 1901 Census (being the latest census currently available) and the Cheshire BMD (Births, Marriages and Deaths) online index.

markedly from 35% of the total number of offences in 1880–1890 to 18% of the total in 1900–1910.[11] The demise of alcohol-related offences continues throughout the entire 1880–1940 period, causing the overall total of such offences to fall to 12% of all offences. In the 1900–1910 period there are simply no persistents with a similar offending record to that of James Newlands (Cohort A), who has almost fifty appearances for drunkenness. Similarly, our most persistent female offender from Cohort B, Elsie Roberts, who notched up a total of almost thirty offences, was only arrested for drunkenness on seven occasions, being primarily found guilty of obscene language. Her relatively modest total of seven prosecutions for drunkenness is almost certainly due to changes in prosecutorial policy and practice. We have seen (above) that drunkenness appears to become less of a concern to the prosecuting authorities as the period progressed. Whilst it seems unlikely that Crewe offenders suddenly took the pledge en masse, it appears that there may well have been a decision made (it is not clear if consciously or sub-consciously) not to prosecute drink-related offences such as being drunk or drunk and disorderly so readily after the turn of the century; rather the offenders seem to have been increasingly prosecuted for offences such as street gambling (which escalated rapidly after legislation passed in the 1900s), criminal damage, obscenity and vagrancy, all of which could easily have been committed under the influence of alcohol.

This apparent concentration on public order nuisances (other than drunkenness) appears to have been relatively short-lived however; all Public Order offences fall again after 1910. Police resources after this time seem to have been used to prosecute the exponential increase in driving related offences, including driving behaviour such as speeding (or 'scorching' as it was known then); drunken or dangerous driving (7% of total crime for the 1880–1940 period) and the breaching of motoring regulations such as not holding a valid licence or having faulty brakes/lights (accounting for 10% of the total number of offences in 1880–1940).

Larcenies and thefts seem to have become less prevalent in the latter period, falling from 10% to 8% of total offences, but the

---

[11] This whilst other public order offences rose sharply from 5% to 12%. In fact, all categories of public order offences rose sharply: gambling from 0.5% to 5%, obscenity from 1% to 5%, and prostitution from 0.1% to 0.5%.

more serious acquisitional offences (breaking and entering houses, warehouses and retail premises; and burglary) increased markedly in percentage terms from 0.3% to 0.9%, although absolute numbers remained low. The reasons for this change remain unclear—perhaps the growth in the number of retail outlets during the period accounts for much of the increase in serious property offences, with there being a concomitant increase in the number of choices available to opportunistic burglars. The relatively small drop in minor property offences during 1900–1910 is more difficult to explain, and indeed the percentage figure rises again for the rest of the period, reaching an overall figure of 9% for the 1880–1940 period, suggesting that the figure for the period 1900–1910 may in some ways be atypical.

With regard to the fall in Education Act offences, as we have seen above with regard to the creation of the School Attendance Committee and measures to force parents to send their children to participate in basic education, it would appear that increasing governmental concern with the education of children paid dividends in relation to school attendance. There was undoubtedly some resistance to these measures from parents who argued that they simply could not afford to send their children to school because of straitened economic circumstances and this resistance continued for a number of years, perhaps being reflected in our figures—Wilbur Boswell being a prime example, with some twenty-five education-related offences to his account. By contrast, only sixteen of Cohort B persistent offenders appeared for education-related offences, and of these sixteen, only three appeared repeatedly for education-related offences.

For the purposes of our research, perhaps the most important development was the Education Act of 1902, which placed the responsibility for school attendance and education into the hands of Local Education Authorities, abolishing School Attendance Committees and School Boards. This measure was introduced with the express concern of increasing school attendance through stricter and more codified enforcement of the law, and seems to have been successful when our figures for the 1900–1910 period are compared to those of the 1880–1890 period. Of course, the diminution of the 'shock of the new' may have played some part in the decline in non-attendance, along with other factors such as a general increase in prosperity, resulting in less need for children to work; and the growth in children's welfare concerns expressed through bodies such as the National Society for the Prevention of Cruelty to Children (which first brought a case before the Crewe magistrates in October 1892).[12] From a perusal of the types of offences committed and the names of the persistent individuals involved in the two periods, it is clear that not only are the persistents in the respective periods usually totally different individuals from discrete families, but also that the nature of the respective persistents' offending careers is generally of a different nature in each of the periods.

Case Studies

We now move from the general to the specific in the form of three case studies drawn from the ranks of our Cohort A. These exemplify certain characteristics of our aggregated results, illustrating both the types of crime and individual present amongst our persistent offenders.

Elspeth Georgina Bispham

Born in Tranmere in 1833 she spent much of her early life in the town. She married Richard E. Bispham in Birkenhead in 1863 and had three children (one son and two daughters) by him. Richard died prematurely some time between 1868 and 1871 and Elspeth and her children are recorded in 1871 as living with her seventy-three year-old mother in Tranmere. Elspeth and her children moved to Crewe in 1879, where she found employment as a dressmaker. Within six months of moving to the town, Elspeth was generating newspaper by-lines as the result of her behaviour; the *Crewe Chronicle* carried an article entitled 'Captain's Widow in Trouble', in which she is described as middle-aged and well-known in Crewe.[13]

---

[12] The NSPCC was founded as the London Society for Prevention of Cruelty to Children in 1884 by Reverend Benjamin Waugh, at a time when the law could not intervene between parents and children unless death resulted from such abuse. The Society changed its name and became national in 1889, but it was not until 1904 that its officers were given legal power to take children into care on the authority of a magistrate.

[13] Despite considerable research, we have been unable to establish if Elspeth's husband was indeed a captain of any sort. It seems most likely that he was a captain in the Merchant Navy, rather than in any of the armed forces, as no records mention Elspeth receiving a pension from such sources.

She assaulted the landlord at the house she had been lodging in for six months. 'Owing to her keeping late hours and to the bad reports that were circulated about her, he had decided to give her notice, she said "she would see him in hell first" and spat in his face' (*Crewe Chronicle*, 27 September 1879). She then picked up a glass and hit him in the face with it. She is reported as saying that she had been persecuted ever since she had come to Crewe, and did not deserve one half or one quarter of what had been said of her. The newspaper reported that 'the magistrates remembered her once or twice, indeed the Mayor had very lively recollections of her'.

In the following year, Elspeth was charged twice with profanity and brought three prosecutions against various people for assault and malicious injury. In 1881 she was charged with being drunk, on two counts of obscene language and on two counts of assault. By this time Superintendent Leah of Crewe Police described her as 'the most troublesome woman in Crewe—in fact more troublesome to the police than all the people of Crewe together' (*Crewe Chronicle*, 30 April 1881). She in turn complained that her neighbours in Thomas Street were 'of bad character' (*Crewe Chronicle*, 19 March 1881). They had, she said, 'broken fourteen panes of glass in her house; they were wicked, used bad language, were always drunk and quarrelsome, while she was a "respectable captain's widow", and would be sorry to "mix" with such bad company, and treated them with contempt. She also spoke at some length about her "noble captain" and her dear children, and concluded by asserting her innocence of the charge imputed to her'. Despite this protestation of the love of her 'dear children', in another appearance before the court in April 1881 it is made apparent that her son and daughter in fact lodged in another house in Thomas Street for protection from their mother. In the census of the same year she is recorded as being in Knutsford Prison. Elspeth was undoubtedly wise to the ways of the court and the police; in September 1881 she failed to appear to answer yet another summons for assault, and Superintendent Leah remarked that 'the summons was not served personally, but pushed under the door of her house when no response was made to a knock. It was a trick of defendant's to lock her door if she had any knowledge of an officer approaching near. Mr Spekeman (the magistrates' clerk) said that the method of serving the summons was not just service, and the magistrates accordingly adjourned the case' (*Crewe Chronicle*, 11 September 1881).

This is the last that we hear of Elspeth in Crewe. In 1888 her son married in Preston, but his bride only lived a further four years, dying in Blackburn in 1892. Three years later her son, Rowan, remarried and enjoyed a successful career in the railway at Blackburn, rising from a railway agent in 1891 to a station master in 1901 (see Chapter Five). Elspeth died in the Wirral in 1897.

Elspeth's offending career in Crewe mirrors the aggregated findings that persistent females were often violent in their offending; she had three assault complaints lodged against her in as many years. Her case also illustrates some of the problems that we encountered in tracing persistent offenders. Her offending career in Crewe was short and prolific, and it is very likely that it continued after she left the town (and was probably well-established before she reached Crewe in 1879). Her offending could have been the result of a sudden life-crisis in the form of her husband's early death, leaving her to bring up three young children as a single parent. Interestingly, she did not commit any Education Act offences during her admittedly brief sojourn in Crewe (at a time when at least two of her children were of school-attendance age). Neither was she prosecuted for their neglect at any stage. None of her children were persistent offenders; indeed her son Rowan did extremely well for himself.

James Newlands

Born in Middlewich in 1835, James Newlands was one of the most prolific Cohort A persistent offenders, being charged with over fifty offences during the course of his offending career. He married in 1855 and spent many years living in Warmingham (near Crewe), where he was a butcher. By 1876 he had ten children and he moved to Crewe some time between 1876 and 1880. In 1879 he suffered the first of three life-crises that took place within two years. His daughter Margaret died at the age of fourteen, and in the following year he lost both his thirteen-year-old son and his wife. In 1880 he was charged with smoking in the market, where he had a butcher's stall. He seemed to have been fairly prosperous, being recorded as employing a housekeeper in the 1881 census. During that year he had no appearances before the magistrates, but in the following year he was charged on two occasions with being drunk.

Within the next decade he appeared before the court on over forty occasions for drunkenness, and was also charged with two Education Act offences and two counts of assault, including one against his sister-in-law. In 1887 he seemed to have lost his market stall, as he is described in the Petty Sessions as a former butcher. His heavy drinking continued, but in 1890 he boasted to the magistrates that he has been 'teetotal for a fortnight' (*Crewe Chronicle*, 18 January 1890). The magistrates replied, 'It is that cursed drink that brings you into trouble. If you would keep sober and respectable you would have plenty of friends.' His appearances for drunkenness continued throughout 1893, but for the last nine years of his life until his death in 1902 he was not charged with any further offences.

Newlands was in many ways the classic habitual drunkard, with a long offending career that plunged his career into a downward spiral. However, he did not appear to have been a violent drunk; he only appeared twice for assault and one of those charges was subsequently struck out, although in 1890 it was reported that 'he insists on stopping people and abusing them'—this was probably verbal rather than physical abuse (*Crewe Chronicle*, 28 June 1890). He did not appear to neglect his children, although he was prosecuted on a few occasions under the Education Act (probably for his son Andrew, see Chapter Five). A good case could be argued for the several bereavements that he suffered in the space of two years being a life-crisis that instigated his drinking, but as he did not move to Crewe until 1879–80, it is impossible to know whether or not he was a drunkard before these events. Similarly, it is striking that he appeared to suddenly desist from drinking from 1894 until the end of his life in 1902, and maybe ill-health overtook him.

Ellie Oldfield

Ellie Oldfield (née Flint) was born in Hawarden in 1865. She began her working life as a domestic servant in Wales but moved to Chester by 1881, where she married Jess Oldfield. By 1890 she had amassed 18 convictions for larceny and drunkenness in Chester. In the same year she and Jess moved to Crewe, although Ellie seems to have alternated between Chester (where her mother lived), Crewe and Northwich, appearing in all three town's Petty Sessions records in the last decade of the nineteenth century. Between 1891 and 1896 she appeared eight times for larceny and drunkenness. In 1896 she prosecuted her husband, John, a watercress seller for assault. The *Crewe Chronicle* reported that she had two black eyes and was lodging in Douglas's lodging house in Oak Street (*Crewe Chronicle*, 19 September 1896). Her husband accused her of taking articles from their home and pledging them without his permission. By 1899 Ellie featured regularly both in the court and in the *Crewe Chronicle*; on 12 August 1899 she was described as 'being rather too familiar with the inside of Crewe Police Court' and on 21 October of the same year, she was described as being 'equally as familiar with the inside of Crewe Police Station as she is with the inside of a public house'.

Her criminal career continued into the twentieth century, and on 26 May 1900 she was described in the *Crewe Chronicle* as 'the best candidate in the county for an Inebriates' Home'. Five months later on 27 October 1900 she was reported as appearing before magistrates for the fortieth time and promised to join the Salvation Army and sign the teetotal pledge. The *Crewe Chronicle* quoted Inspector Groghan of the Crewe Police as stating that he 'thought the age of miracles had passed. The only time she was sober was when she was in gaol'. The next year she appeared before the court on yet another charge of drunkenness and was sent to the Bristol Royal Victoria Home for Inebriates for twelve months.

Ellie returned to Crewe immediately after her sentence at the Home expired and was in trouble within three weeks of her return. On 22 March 1902 the *Crewe Chronicle* reported that she had stolen a cigar a foot long and two inches in diameter from a shop in Brook Street—Ellie was found in a public house sitting on the cigar. She expressed remorse saying that she had been teetotal for a year (which she probably had been, having been in the Inebriates' Home for that period). The chairman said 'You told us when we sent you to the Inebriates home twelve months ago that it would do you no good. You have proved your statement beyond doubt.' In the same year Ellie committed her most serious offence with the larceny of £20 from the lodging house in Oak Street, Crewe, where her daughter was celebrating her marriage. When arrested in Shrewsbury for the crime, Ellie pulled off her shoe and smashed ten panes of glass in the police station. She was sentenced to three years' imprisonment (which was commuted to two years' due to her good behaviour, indicating that she was much calmer without drink). In 1904, after her release, Ellie soon appeared before the magistrates yet again. The *Crewe Chronicle* carried a long report of her appearance on 26 September 1904:

Borough rate payers have paid £150 to send her to Bristol in 1901—she is incorrigible. No sooner has she come out of prison than she gets locked up again. She had not been in the town many hours from Portland [site of the Inebriates' Home] ere she was again in the arms of the law. This is invariably the case. The Crewe Police have tried leniency, but all to no avail. She has been humoured by her family, all of who reside in the town. This is the fifty-second time she has appeared before magistrates. The family were sick and tired of their mother and one of her sons was present in court. Ellie shouted 'Ha, it is all through him that I am here, and he will suffer for it as sure as there is God in Heaven'. The Mayor said it was very evident that Ellie was past redemption and that the town would be better off without her. After release from Inebriates' Home she had been drunk for a fortnight. After sentencing, Ellie said 'You have tried but you will never keep me away from my children. I shall come back again, and shall meet them again, and you too' pointing to her son. She has been before the magistrates thirty-four times, has paid nearly £7 in fines and in past ten years has spent 2,052 days in prison.

Ellie received a six-month gaol sentence. After serving this term, she disappeared from the Crewe records, probably moving back to Wales, as she died in Hawarden in 1911. Both of her brothers were well-known in Crewe courts with numerous convictions, and her partner in crime with regard to the larceny of £20 from the Oak Street lodging house, James Munty, was also a persistent offender. Ellie was a prolific persistent offender with over forty offences in under a decade. She was clearly an habitual drunkard and stole on a regular basis to feed her addiction. She was not uneducated—according to her prison records, she could read and write imperfectly—and did work intermittently as a charwoman, domestic servant and fish-seller. She was unable to desist from offending and neither prison nor rehabilitation seems to have had any effect on her. Her domestic and family life seems to have been unhappy; she separated from her husband and her two sons were often in trouble in Crewe.

Interrelationships between Offenders

As we researched the lives of our persistent offenders, it became clear that there was a surprising amount of interrelationship between them and other offenders. Fig. 3.2 below represents some of the most salient relationships between some of the most persistent families, individuals and social groupings in Crewe during the period we studied. Each individual is identified by their offending status (persistent, offender or non-offender) and where appropriate their familial relationships. Double-headed arrows indicate bilateral relationships (siblings, friends, marriage partners) and single-headed arrows indicate relationships of unequal power (eg parenthood, offender-victim dyad). Dashed lines represent family or friendship ties, solid lines represent offences that link the individuals to one another. What one can see is a mass of arrows between the individuals included in our diagram. Other relationships undoubtedly existed between them. What is clear, however, is that as well as the 'criminal fraternity' knowing each other, offending with and against one another, their connections went beyond the mere back streets and lodging houses of Crewe, for in the bottom-right-hand corner we find Edwin Heath.

As stated earlier, Heath was a larger retailer who had considerable economic power in Crewe, owning eighteen shops throughout the town. The Basing family also ran a number of stores in Crewe (see Chapter Four). Not in the same social bracket as Heath, the Basing family were marine store dealers who dealt in old goods, metals, rags, fat and bones.[14] As well as persistent offenders over two generations, they were embedded in a network of suppliers of stolen goods. Our persistent offenders also regularly stole from one another. Witness Ellie Oldfield stealing from the Scotts, the Scotts stealing from the Basings (who are also stolen from by Graeme Richards). Co-offending was common too—Amelia Dullace and Ellie Oldfield used to 'work' shops and lodging houses together, and Ellie was James Munty's partner in crime and probable lover. James himself used to steal with Wallace Munday, who later assaulted Moll Low (née Paisley) the wife of Casper Low who was almost certainly contracted by Jim Paisley to threaten his other son-in-law Adam Toshack, after Toshack had assaulted James' daughter Aurelia, who in turn stole goods from her husband when she eloped with Graeme Rowley, who was himself a persistent offender. There was clearly a farrago of strong, weak, familial and 'business' links which must have contributed to contemporary views on the existence of the criminal class (see Chapter One and the conclusion to this chapter). The other common form of interrelationship between offenders was gang membership (Shore, 1999). Our study attempted to trace the offending careers and interrelationships of young people involved in one juvenile gang in the 1890s; and another gang active in the 1930s.

---

[14] A marine store dealer was a rag and bone man and general tatter, usually working from a yard or shop. Magistrates and police officers often regarded marine store dealers as little more than fences for stolen property.

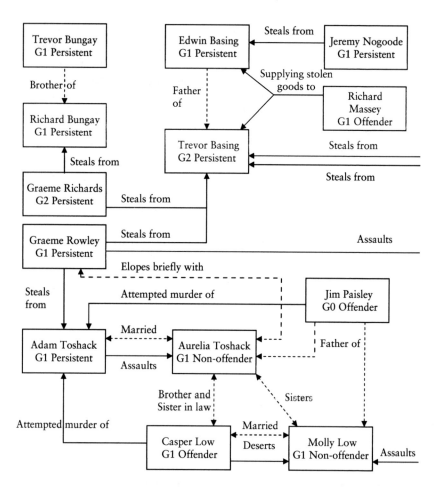

Fig. 3.2 Interrelationships between offenders: selected cases and selected offences only.

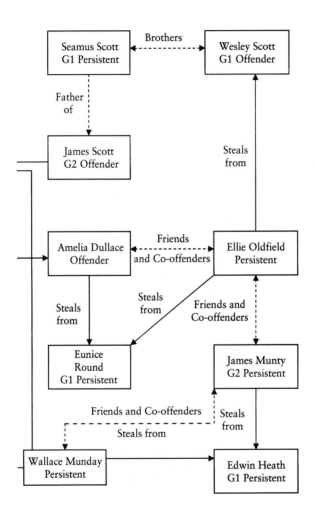

Gangs in Crewe

Crewe is not Los Angeles. The gangs that existed in Cheshire in 1880–1940 were similar to those that existed in many towns and cities throughout Britain.[15] They 'hung around' or 'colonized public space' (Godfrey, 2004), whistled at girls, clogged up street corners, and smoked cigarettes. They got drunk, swore and were boisterous, gambled in the street or acted as look-out for pitch and toss games; played football, cricket, and snowballing in the street—all of those offences in themselves; and usually attracting adverse comment from more established members of society:

I have the misfortune to traverse the High Street frequently in the evenings, and am sometimes foolish enough to imagine the footpath is intended for respectable persons, and not only for youths and girls to promenade; but I speedily observe my error by being jostled onto the roadway. Then in addition to this, I since heard language uttered by young women so foul and filthy that I felt ashamed to belong to the same sex, and this is an everyday occurrence.

Letter to the *Nantwich Chronicle*, 9 April, 1881

Occasionally young men congregated together to commit more serious crimes of violence or property offending. Stores such as Woolworths and Marks and Spencers were favourite targets for shoplifting because of their 'open' layout. One of the main crimes was the 'jemmying' of gas meters from unattended or empty houses, and, since these meters belonged to a vigorous prosecutor with its own detective officers—the L&NWR—these offences often reached the courts. Fights between gangs did not happen either because the neighbourhood areas were too tightly defined for 'turf wars', they were not treated seriously by the police, or they were never prosecuted in court. Youth crime in Crewe, therefore, mainly centred on property offending (See Table 3.5 below):

When prosecuting the spate of shop thefts described above, the police sergeant stated that 'the result of his investigations had been to

---

[15] Pearson (1983) has written on the nature of these gangs and the moral panics that accompanied them by reference to Victorian newspapers for whom these gangs held particular fascination, and Davies has deepened our knowledge by detailed study of the Manchester Scuttlers (Davies, 1999; 2000). Most large urban centres had their own gangs, indeed neighbourhoods could hold ten or twenty competing gangs of boys who fought over territory, prestige, and reputation as the toughest of the local 'mobs'.

Table 3.5   An 1890s gang: offences as juveniles and adults.

Wally Pritchard b. 1881	Geoffrey Roberts b. 1880	Jasper Digglebottom b. 1876	Joseph Stephens b. 1877	John Gray b. 1879	James Asquith b. 1879

1893
Shoptheft of biscuits and wine from Jacob William Walker
Shoptheft of twenty-nine watches, four chains, two lockets, two rings and one revolver from Beatrice Blower

Wally Pritchard	Geoffrey Roberts	Jasper Digglebottom			James Asquith

1893
Shoptheft of boots from Edgar Gilpin and Sons

Wally Pritchard	Geoffrey Roberts				James Asquith

1894
Pitch and Toss street gambling

think that the leader of these Jack Shepherds[16] was Jasper Digglebottom'. The defending solicitor defended Digglebottom, responding that he had been 'reading cheap Penny Dreadfuls and thought it was a fine thing to break into these shops and imitate Jack Shepherd.' He also pointed out that 'There was nothing against James Asquith who was fourteen years of age. His mother was a widow, and he assisted her to keep his six or seven small brothers and sisters. He had been a timekeeper employed by the L&NWR for eighteen months and that spoke of itself for his character. John Gray's father was a respectable man, and it was Geoffrey Roberts' first offence.' The newspaper does not record the court discussion around Joseph Stephens, but out of all these 'desperadoes', only he went on to offend in adulthood. In fact he was prosecuted a number of times, for a range of crimes. However, most of these offences were connected to his work-life (crying articles for sale in a public street; not controlling his cart horse, and so on; even the assaults he committed were against rivals in the fish-market). What happened to the other gang members? Wally Pritchard had moved out of Crewe by 1901;

[16] A notorious petty offender in the eighteenth century who managed to escape from many prisons, including Newgate.

Table 3.6   A 1930s gang: membership and activity.

Name	D.O.B.	1935	1936	1937	1938	1939		
Ernest Grimes	1925	breaking and entering			theft	theft		
Thomas O'Rourke	1927	breaking and entering						
Tony Baslow	1925		breaking and entering	theft	theft	theft		
Derek Baslow	1926		breaking and entering	theft	theft	theft		
Nigel Hooper	1925		theft	cruelty to sheep		theft	theft	indecency
Lionel Toss	1923		theft	theft				indecency
Dennis Wilks	1924			theft	theft			

Name	Date	Offences
Walter Wilks	not known	theft
Lionel Lees	1925	theft
Graeme Cutey	1924	cruely to sheep
Edward Downes	1926	theft
Kingsley Chopper	not known	theft
Richard Hall	1925	theft, theft, theft, theft, theft, criminal damage
Chas Hall	1926	theft, theft
Ernie Street	not known	theft, theft
David Pile	1925	theft, theft, theft, theft
Wes Cripps	1927	criminal damage

and the others seem to have drifted away from crime and became more bound into the social fabric of Crewe, often as a result of finding employment: Geoffrey Roberts became a labourer and committed no offences after 1894; John Gray and James Asquith both found employment in the Works; and there was no trace of Jasper Digglebottom and certainly he did not offend in Crewe after 1893.

1930s Gangs

On 22 January 1938, the following report appeared in the *Crewe Chronicle*:

Mrs Mosford Powell, Borough Bench, who said she had just had a most disappointing morning in the Juvenile Court dealing with young offenders, some of whom had been before the magistrates three times since July. They were charged with breaking into empty houses and stealing the money from electricity meters. They admitted having gone round the town, examining estate agents' windows and making a list of empty houses. The Police Superintendent told the Bench that it was the most appalling confession that he had heard from the children. One of the worst features of the affair was the attitude of the children themselves, who entered the court as if it was a cinema—hands thrust into their pockets and grins on their faces.

The four children in that case were part of a loose affiliation (so far as we can see from court records) of around ten juveniles who offended or made a nuisance of themselves towards the end of the 1930s. There were one or two others who were co-defendants but do not seem to have been regular members of the gang (see Table 3.6 above).

Table 3.6 has been arranged by time, with the earliest entry into 'gang' offences committed at the top and the later entrants towards the bottom of the figure. One can see, for example that the lengths of time and actual dates of engagement in this loose gang vary considerably. Tony Baslow's engagement lasts from 1935 until towards the end of 1937. Chas Hall's, on the other hand, does not start until 1938, ending in 1939. Some members only have one appearance (Thomas, Edward and Kingsley), whilst others (Tony, Nigel and Richard) rack up five convictions. What is clear, however, is that there is no clear gang leader (since no individual appears to dominate in terms of convictions) or indeed very much of a stable structure. Some are more intensively involved for brief periods (Richard, Derek and David, for example), but this appears to be a short-lived 'burst'. Perhaps most interestingly, the gang's offence profile reduces in seriousness over time too: from breaking and entering in 1935 then afterwards to theft and criminal damage (although two boys were found guilty of indecency in 1939).

The crimes committed by the 1930s gang were similar in nature to those committed by the 1890s gang, but the punishments imposed were somewhat different. For the offences outlined in Table 3.6 fines were imposed for six of the offences, seventeen offences were punished with 'bind overs' or probation orders (sometimes with a curfew), and for committing other offences, eight of the young men were in approved schools by the time the Second World War started.[17] Since the members of the 1930s gang were released back into the neighbourhoods in the years after our data set ends, we cannot see whether they re-offended. Neither, because the later censuses have not been released, can we determine whether they found work, or life partners, which affected their offending. Nevertheless, in our most detailed data-set, Cohort A, it is possible to see how many offenders managed to turn away from crime, and what factors appear to have initiated or assisted this process.

Desisters and Persisters in Cohort A

Four out of every ten of our persistent offenders (40%) ended their criminal careers before they died; 34% persisted in criminality for the entirety of their lives (we could not classify 26% of our sample as either persisters or desisters). We investigated the reasons why the forty-one offenders did stop offending, and these are shown in Table 3.7.

Because the offending of a majority of our Cohort A offenders was either work-related or associated with not sending children to school, the majority of Cohort A offenders stopped offending

---

[17] The courts bound over people to keep the peace for a certain length of time, commonly six months. If they did not they forfeited a set amount of money to the court. These were not convictions and the person in the dock had to agree to be bound over in this way. In practice magistrates used them in cases of domestic violence, or when they suspected the accused had committed a crime but did not think the evidence existed to prove it.

Table 3.7   Reasons for desistance in Cohort A offenders

	No.	%
Family related (children grow up/marital reconciliation)	11	27
Employment related (retired from work/career advancement)	6	15
Sudden stop	13	32
Physical decrepitude	9	22
Unclassifiable	2	5

when the children were no longer of school age, or when they retired from employment (together some 42% of Cohort A were in this bracket). For another 22% of offenders, their offending declined alongside their physical health. They desisted as they were no longer physically capable of carrying out the offences (ie fighting, burglary and so on). Those that preferred a type of offending which required little physical effort ie getting drunk, typically tended to continue their offending into old age (and to death). Those who just suddenly stopped offending (nearly a third of our sample) are harder to classify. There may be reasons which we cannot discern with our data, for example the influence of family persuasion; ill-health which prevented them leaving the house; a genuine reformation in attitudes towards alcohol, gambling, or offending in general, and so on (sudden cessation of offending is, of course, not unknown in the modern period). The part played by relationship-formation/marriage and employment is investigated in the following chapter.

Conclusion

The existence of a group of 101 offenders (admittedly with differing backgrounds, family structures and work situations) that committed disproportionate amounts of crime in one locale, inevitably takes us back to ideas of a 'criminal class' (see Chapter One). Was there a criminal underworld in Crewe?

Whilst there was undoubtedly a perception of the existence of a 'criminal class' throughout the nineteenth century, the likely reality is that there were relatively few hardened recidivists—Hay and Snyder state that with regard to the 1850s, 'the most precise calculations [. . .] using five or more indictable offences as a yardstick, could identify under 10,000 serious offenders in England and Wales', and this low level of persistence is reflected in our research for the period 1880–1940 (see Taylor, 1998: 191). It is more likely that the 'criminal' class, which in popular (ie middle- and upper-class) literate society consisted almost exclusively of idle, irresponsible and drunken males, was in fact a continually varying cohort of individuals with individual failings or desires, rather than an easily categorizable group of like-minded people, all hell-bent on undermining the cohesion of society. Our research has shown that even amongst the relatively small percentage of persistent offenders in Crewe there were often more differences than similarities; both in the individuals and in types of crime committed. With the exception of habitual drunkards, it has not proved easy to identify a particular 'type' of persistent. In one respect however, the existence or non-existence of a 'criminal class' was unimportant— it was a popular belief in its existence that fuelled so much of both the debate and the resultant actions in the field of crime and punishment during the decades surrounding the turn of the twentieth century. The idea of a hard core group of criminals plaguing society then, as now, is a hard one to shake off—erroneous as it may be.

4
Informal Social Control and 'Reform': Marriage, Employment and Desistance from Crime

'Informal social controls are far more effective than formal social control. The informal regulation of conduct in families, communities, friendship networks and voluntary associations is the pre-condition for law and order'

(Downes, 1997: 1)

Desistance from crime, that is to say the process of ending a period of involvement in offending behaviour, is something of an enigma in contemporary criminological studies. On the one hand it is the implicit focus of much criminological and criminal justice work. A good deal of the amount of research on probation, penality, and policing is aimed at encouraging people to cease offending either through rehabilitation or by deterring them. Yet in another respect desistance is an area that has been relatively neglected in terms of research. Although interest in the ending of the criminal career was largely ignored by criminologists (in favour of an understanding of why people *started* to offend), the last ten or twenty years have greatly extended what we know about the reasons why people *cease* offending. Early forays into the field, with a familiar and warranted sense of inevitability, have led on to more rigorous and sustained efforts at charting the processes and factors associated with desistance (for recent reviews of this literature see Farrall and Calverley, 2006; Laub and Sampson, 2001, 2003; and Maruna, 2001).

This chapter provides a short introduction to the literature on desistance. The review is skewed towards a consideration of the social factors that we have greatest ability to comment upon given the nature of the data at our disposal. Thus our literature review will focus on employment, partnership and family formation since those are the key life events that the UK census recorded during the period we are interested in. In this respect, we are unable to comment directly on these more nuanced 'internal' processes associated with desistance, such as regret, or changes in values. We shall also review the concepts used by contemporary criminologists to explore, 'make sense' of, and understand desistance.

Leaving Crime Behind: an Outline of Evidence and Theorizing

From the early twentieth century, which witnessed the development of interest in the reasons why people started to offend, through to the work of probation officers and the more recent innovations in situational crime prevention and sentencing, there can be traced a series of attempts to understand and deal more effectively with offending behaviour in such a way that it can be slowed down, reduced or halted altogether. Yet, despite this interest in understanding why people offend and how best to reduce the needs and opportunities associated with offending, the *systematic* investigation of desistance is a relatively recent development in criminology, much of the work in this field having been undertaken since the 1970s.

Desistance is usually defined as the end of a period of involvement in offending. Most researchers therefore think of desistance as meaning that an individual has given up offending permanently, rather than just ceasing to offend for a short while before continuing to commit further offences. As Maruna and Farrall (2004: 171) remind us, although it is true that most adult offenders exhibited many of the tell-tale signs of being delinquent children, the majority of juvenile delinquents do *not* go on to become adult offenders. For most individuals, participation in 'street crimes' (such as burglary, robbery, and drug sales) generally begins in the early teenage years, peaks in late adolescence or young adulthood, and dissipates before the person reaches thirty years of age (Holden, 1986, Barclay, 1990, Blumstein and Cohen 1987, Weitekamp *et al* 2000). Maruna and Farrall (2004: 174–5) argue that criminologists therefore ought not to be interested in short-term crime-free lulls (which they refer to as 'primary desistance'), but rather ought to preoccupy themselves with charting 'secondary desistance'—a process by which individuals often assume a role of non-offender or 'reformed person'. In many cases, but not all of course, this sort of change is associated with a reorganization on the part of the desister of 'who' they are and the sort of person they now wish to be, or become (Maruna, 2001; Farrall, 2005).

Factors and Processes Associated with Desistance

Drawing on the insights of earlier work on criminal careers, the corpus of studies into the termination of the criminal career has pointed to a number of correlates of desistance. The literature on desistance is commonly based on longitudinal data sets (eg Knight and West, 1975, Loeber *et al* 1991 and Sampson and Laub, 1993; Laub and Sampson 2003), or on one-off retrospective research (eg Shover, 1983; Cusson and Pinsonneault, 1986; Graham and Bowling, 1995). In a few cases (eg Leibrich, 1993; Burnett, 1992; Farrall, 2002) data have been collected by following the careers of persons after they have been made subject to criminal justice interventions. The research undertaken so far has shed light on the role of social and personal factors in desistance (see Adams, 1997; Farrall, 2000; Farrall and Calverley, 2006; Laub and Sampson, 2001, for outlines of this body of work). Below we outline the most salient of these for our own research.

Marriage and Family-Formation

One of the most common findings in the literature on desistance is that individuals cease to offend at about the same time that they start to form significant life partnerships (eg Laub *et al* 1998). One of the clearest statements in support of this line of reasoning came from Shover (1983: 213), who wrote that 'The establishment of a mutually satisfying relationship with a woman was a common pattern [. . . and . . .] an important factor in the transformation of their career line'. Cusson and Pinsonneault (1986) and Mischkowitz (1994) followed West (1982: 101–4) in arguing that what was important (in terms of facilitating desistance) was not marriage *per se* but rather the *quality* of the relationship and the offending career of the person whom the would-be desister married. The work of Laub *et al* (1998) supports this contention—as marriages became stronger amongst the men in their sample, so these men's offending began to be curtailed. A number of studies have suggested that the experience of becoming a parent is also associated with desistance from offending (see for example, Trasler, 1979: 315; Irwin, 1970: 203; Sampson and Laub, 1993: 218; Caddle, 1991: 37; Leibrich, 1993: 59; Jamieson *et al* 1999: 130; Uggen and Kruttschnitt, 1998: 355; Hughes, 1997 and 1998: 146; and Parker 1976: 41). Similar findings are reported by Brogden and Harkin (2002), who point to the role of family-members in helping ex-sex offenders from committing further crimes of this nature.

Despite the evidence suggesting that forming a life partnership may result in desistance, some researchers have questioned this rather simple 'cause and effect' model. Rand (1987: 137) tested the hypothesis that 'young men who marry are less criminal than those who never marry' and found no support for this in her data. Knight *et al* (1977: 359) found no significant differences (in terms of the number of subsequent convictions) between the married and unmarried groups from the Cambridge Study in Delinquent Development. Similarly, Mulvey and Aber (1988) reported finding no connection between partnership and desistance, nor were they able to find any firm link between parenthood and desistance. Rand (1987: 143) also found no support for the idea that men who became fathers were less criminal than those who did not. There is also, of course, the issue of domestic violence, which clearly calls into question the observed association between partnership and desistance. For a discussion of findings relating to desistance from domestic violence, see Fagan, 1989; Feld and Straus, 1989 and 1990; Tolman *et al* 1996; and Quigley and Leonard, 1996.

Employment

A number of researchers (eg Uggen and Kruttschnitt, 1998; Mischkowitz, 1994; Farrall, 2002) have provided evidence that desistance is associated with gaining employment. Meisenhelder (1977) noted that the acquisition of a good job provided the men in his sample with important social and economic resources, whilst Shover (1983: 214) reported how a job generated 'a pattern of routine activities [. . .] which conflicted with and left little time for the daily activities associated with crime'.

Similar sentiments were expressed by Robert Sampson and John Laub (Sampson and Laub, 1993; Laub and Sampson, 2003). They wrote that desisters were characterized as having 'good work habits and were frequently described as "hard workers"' (Sampson and Laub, 1993: 220). Farrington *et al* (1986: 351) reported that 'proportionally more crimes were committed by [. . .] youths during periods of unemployment than during periods of employment', a finding supported by the later work of Horney *et al* 1995. However, as researchers such as Ditton (1977), Henry (1978) and Hobbs (1988) have shown, full-time employment does not preclude either the opportunities to offend nor actual offending. Graham and Bowling (1995: 56, Table 5.2) found that for young males employment was not related to desistance, as did Rand (1987) when she investigated the impact of vocational training on criminal careers.

Although the precise mechanisms through which employment works to reduce offending have not been clearly specified in many studies, it is possible to distil a number of ways in which it might work. Farrall (2002: 146–50) notes that, in terms of its impact on an individual's life, paid employment has the potential to achieve the following: a reduction in 'unstructured' time and an increase in 'structured' time; the establishment of a daily routine which is focused away from offending; an income, which enables 'home-leaving' and the establishment of 'significant' relationships (Willis, 1984); a 'legitimate' identity; an increase in self-esteem; use of an individual's energies; financial security; daily interaction with non-offenders; for men in particular (see Wallace, 1986, 1987), a reduction in the time spent in single-sex, peer-aged groups; the means by which an individual may meet their future partner; and ambition and goals, such as promotion at work. In some cases, employment might also serve to take people away from situations in which they had previously got into trouble. Farrall (2002: 147–8) noted that the acquisition of employment encouraged sample members in his study to take a more responsible attitude to drug and alcohol consumption. In some cases, noted Farrall (2002), employment impacted upon an individual's relationship with his or her family. One of the probation officers Farrall interviewed for his study of desistance following supervision reported how, by starting work, one probationer's family no longer saw him as a 'druggie':

because he is now working and providing for the household, all his pressures [with his family] have gone down. He was on the verge of actually being thrown out, and [made] homeless, by them. And that has receded 'cause he is becoming—from their point of view—a productive and constructive member of the family, and therefore working with them instead of against them. Which is often the perception of families with drug addicts— 'no matter what they do, they still end up on drugs'.

Whilst the precise causal mechanisms through which employment influences desistance are many and varied, it remains one of the most consistent findings of research conducted into both why people stop offending, and into the relationship between crime and employment that during periods of employment an individual's engagement in offending is reduced or halted altogether. Of course, full-time education or voluntary work may also provide many of these features.

Other Factors

Various other factors have been identified which appear to be related to desistance. Amongst members of the Cambridge Study in Delinquent Development cohort, Osborn (1980) found that leaving London (where they had grown up) was associated with reductions in subsequent offending (both self-reported and official). Similar findings using alternative data sets have been made by Sampson and Laub (1993: 217) and Jamieson *et al* (1999: 133). The break-up of the peer group has been another, and more commonly, cited factor. Knight and West (1975: 49) and Cromwell *et al* (1991: 83) both referred to cases in which peer group disintegration was related to subsequent desistance (as did Warr, 1998). Experiencing a shift in identity (Shover, 1983: 210; Meisenhelder, 1982; Maruna, 1997 and 2000; Burnett, 1992; and Farrall, 2005) and feeling shame at one's past behaviours (Leibrich, 1993: 204 and 1996) have also been posited as processes associated with desistance.

An individual's motivation to avoid further offending is another key factor in accounting for desistance. Shover (1983); Shover and Thompson (1992); West (1978), Pezzin (1995); Moffitt (1993); and Sommers *et al* (1994) have all pointed to a range of factors which motivated the desisters in their samples. Burnett (1992: 66, 1994: 55–6) and Farrall (2002: 99–115) have both suggested that those who reported that they wanted to stop offending and felt they were able to stop offending, were more likely to desist than those who said they were unsure if they wanted to stop offending.

Others have pointed to the influence of the criminal justice system on those repeatedly incarcerated. Cusson and Pinsonneault (1986), employing data drawn from in-depth interviews with ex-robbers, identified the following as influential factors in desisting: shock (such as being wounded in a bank-raid); growing tired of doing time in prison; becoming aware of the possibility of longer prison terms; and a reassessment of what was important to the individual. Similar findings have been made by other researchers. Leibrich (1993: 56–7); Shover (1983: 213); and Cromwell *et al* (1991: 83) reported that desisters experienced a period of re-evaluation before coming to their decision to desist. Within a perspective heavily influenced by rational choice models, Shover and Thompson (1992: 97) wrote that 'the probability of desistance from criminal participation increases as expectations for achieving friends, money, autonomy and happiness via crime decrease'. Hughes' (1998) study of ethnic minority desisters living in the USA reported that fear of serious physical harm and/or death was cited by sixteen of her twenty respondents. Similar fears were reported by those interviewed by Sommers *et al* (1994) and Cusson and Pinsonneault (1986), and in Maruna's (1997) study of published autobiographies of desistance. Work by Meisenhelder (1977) and others (eg Shover, 1983; Hughes, 1998; and Burnett, 1992) has revealed that some of those repeatedly incarcerated say that they have become tired of prison and feel that they can no longer cope physically and emotionally with the experiences of prison life. In effect, some offenders reach a point in their lives when they can 'take no more' from the criminal justice system and 'burn out'.

The Age-Grading of Events

Following the findings of Uggen (2000) and Ouimet and Le Blanc (1996), which suggested that the impact of various life events upon an individual's offending is age-graded (that is to say, has a different meaning to and therefore impact upon on an individual depending on their age), criminologists have become increasingly attuned to the consideration of the age at which life events occur. Ouimet and Le Blanc (1996: 92) suggest that it is only (in the modern period) from around the mid-twenties that cohabitation with a woman was associated with desistance for the males in their sample. In a similar vein, Uggen (2000: 542) suggests that work appears to be a turning point in the criminal careers of those offenders aged over twenty-six, whilst it has a marginal effect on the offending of younger offenders. When findings like these are taken into consideration, the importance of structuring the enquiry by age is made apparent. As Flood-Page *et al*'s work (2000) implies, with respect to engagement in offending over the life course, age is also gendered. Of course, as we shall see presently, age and lifestyle are not reducible to one another, and need to be handled with sensitivity, and especially so in historical studies such as this. We are fortunate to be guided in our endeavours by a sound foundation of historical research, particularly studies of the life-course and peak age of conviction (see Barclay 1990, Hirschi and Gottfredson, 1983).

It was Peter King who noted that the peak age of property offenders was changeable in the last decades of the eighteenth century. The sharp male peak in the eighteen to nineteen-year-old bracket moved in 1791 to an equally pronounced peak at age twenty-one to twenty-two in 1821, whilst the less dramatic age profile of women moved from a peak at age nineteen to twenty-one to one at twenty-two to twenty-three (King, 1996: 65). Philips puts the peak age of conviction at age twenty-one to twenty-five by 1853–1855 (Philips, 1977: 161), and after the 1870s Education Acts made school attendance compulsory, the peak age of conviction became the year after school-leaving age, at least until the late twentieth century. In the early twentieth century the peak age for violent offences was later (between twenty-one to thirty for men) making it closer to the peak age of conviction today. Home Office figures (2004) show that the peak age of conviction for men is around eighteen, and the female peak between fourteen to eighteen. So, although the peak ages of conviction shifted back and forth over the last two hundred years, it is unsurprising that the peak remains in the lower age brackets. As King states:

> For both sexes, the often highly mobile period between the usual age of leaving home (mid teens) and the most frequent age at marriage (early to mid-twenties) was the key period of vulnerability to prosecution [. . .]. For various social and psychological reasons adolescents and young unmarried adults in many societies and periods have been perceived as both more likely to commit property offences and more likely to antagonize victims and control agencies and therefore more vulnerable to prosecution.
>
> (King, 1996: 61–90)

What is most noticeable, however, is that from the eighteenth century onwards, the divergence in offending between the sexes is most marked in the number of offences being committed in the age range twelve to twenty-one. During that adolescent life-stage, boys and young men outpaced young women in the judicial statistics to a considerable degree (Davies, 1999). Newspapers would have considered crimes involving violent young women to have been well worth reporting, and the lack of such reports superficially indicates a low number of trials involving women. However, the statistics collected by the police courts, forwarded to the Home Office, and published in the Chief Constables' Reports, provide a more reliable index.

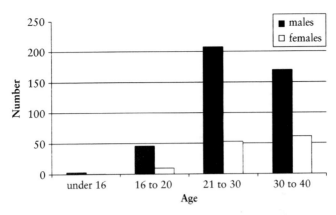

Fig. 4.1   Assaults, numbers of offenders, within age brackets, north-west English cities, 1900–1920.

As can be seen in Fig. 4.1, young men vastly outnumbered the young women caught up in the criminal justice system (particularly for violent offences). Whilst it is not possible to identify the age of every offender in our data set, the age of every defendant under the age of twenty-one was recorded, and we therefore identify all offences committed by juveniles. Moreover, because of the layering of data on offending, victimization and life events (employment and changes in employment of family members, changes of address, family formation, birth of children, and so on) we are able to comment on the relationship between age and the onset of offending.

Summary

To summarize, the desistance literature has pointed to a range of factors associated with the ending of active involvement in offending amongst those regularly involved in offending in the contemporary period. Most of these factors are related to acquiring 'something' (most commonly employment, a life partner or a family) which the desister values in some way and which initiates a re-evaluation of his or her life, and for some a sense of who they 'are'. Others have pointed to the criminal justice system as eventually exerting an influence on those repeatedly incarcerated. This body of work suggests that any attempt to investigate the impact of the criminal justice system on offending careers needs also to consider the role of various social processes, *viz.* employment, marriage, motivation and so on.

Theorizing Desistance

Let us leave, for the time being at least, the factors associated with desistance and turn our minds towards state-of-the-art attempts to explain desistance theoretically. We broadly follow Sampson and Laub's theorizing of the processes associated with desistance (see also Farrall, 2002; Farrall and Calverley, 2006) and which has received support from others (see Ezell and Cohen, 2004). Key to Sampson and Laub's theory of age-graded social control (1993) is the notion of the bond between an individual and society. The bond is made up of the extent to which an individual has emotional attachments to societal goals, is committed to achieving them via legitimate means, believes these goals to be worthy and is able to involve themselves in the attainment of such goals. Sampson and Laub's theorizing posits that engagement in offending is more likely when the bond between an individual and society is weakened or broken. In addition to this, they argue that at various points during the life-course, various formal and informal social institutions help to cement the bond between the individual and society. For example, for adolescents, school, the family and peer groups influence the nature of the bond between many young people and their wider communities, whilst employment, marriage, and parenthood operate in a similar way for adults. These institutions and the relationships between individuals that they encourage, help the formation of social bonds which in turn create informal social control. Thus avoidance of crime is the result of relationships formed for reasons other than for the control of crime. Changes, Sampson and Laub argue, in the individual's relationship with these various institutions are an inevitable feature of modern life, and, as such, are key to understanding engagement in offending over the life-course. Whilst much continuity in an individual's life can be observed, key events can trigger changes in an individual's bond to society and hence pattern of offending.

Similarly, because many relationships endure over time, so they can accumulate resources (eg emotional support between marriage partners, Laub et al, 1998) which can help sustain conventional goals and conformity. In contrast to Gottfredson and Hirschi (1990), who see low levels of self-control as the end of the matter, Sampson and Laub argue that levels of criminal propensity are open to influence, and that these influences are often the result of informal social control. Furthermore, unlike rational choice theorists who saw desistance as the result of a decision, Sampson and Laub's approach enables one to view desistance as the result of a process which stretches over time. Laub and Sampson (2003) updated their earlier study (Sampson and Laub, 1993) in that they follow members of the Gluecks' original sample through to the age of seventy. Although their book does not substantially alter their earlier theorizing on the relationship between informal social controls and patterns of offending over the life-course, they do take the time to respond to various criticisms and observations relating to their earlier work. In a nutshell, they argue that a number of informal social controls (such as employment, marriage, community groups and peers) as well as formal control agencies (such as the police, prisons and probation) greatly influence the nature of many people's criminal careers during their life-course (see above and Sampson and Laub, 1993).

A number of critics had suggested that the relationship between desistance and marriage is spurious, as the men who 'decide' to marry are likely to have had different criminal career trajectories anyway. Work by Laub et al (1998) suggests that many of the classic predictors of onset and frequency of offending do not explain desistance, nor the effects of marriage (Laub and Samspon, 2003: 44–5). Furthermore, Johnson and Booth (1998) suggest that personality and interactional styles in relationships are malleable, and as such a 'good' marriage can alter the behaviour of 'bad' actors. Similarly, employment and the relationships and attitudes which come with it are malleable (Uggen, 2000), something which the case studies from an earlier study suggested also (Farrall, 2002: 146–52 and 177–8).

Bottoms et al (2004) refer directly to the fabled 'American Dream' and propose a similar 'English Dream' for working-class children and adolescents. Such a dream consists of a safe job as an employee of a stable firm, 'enough' money, consumption of certain desired products and services (clothes, meals out, cars and so on), a steady romantic attachment and the likelihood of parenthood (2004: 384). This, of course, as Bottoms et al acknowledge, is only one form of one dream—doubtless there are other dreams which draw their precise configuration from cultural, ethnic, class and other considerations. A similar set of aspirations held by members of the Victorian (and Edwardian) working class can be distilled from a number of publications (White, 1986; Benson, 1989;

Vincent, 1980; Thompson, 1988).[1] We return to the subject of the 'English Dream' in the conclusion of this book.

Marriage, 'Romantic Attachment' and Crime

We found that the married amongst our sample (n = 70) had, in total, slightly more convictions than the unmarried (10.49 compared to 10.07), although when this was calculated as a rate of years in married life for years lived, the reverse was true (.2045 compared to .2767). Neither of these figures were significant, however. Amongst the married, we found that convictions went up after marriage (from a rate of .06 to a rate of .22, paired-sample T-test, sig = .001). The rates of conviction for the married group after their marriages ended also went down (from .24 to .13, although this was just outside the range of significance, p = .071). As such, it would appear that marriage per se or the processes associated with being in a state of marriage did little to reduce convictions. In part, this was due to offences relating to failing to send children to school, although this does not fully account for our null findings, since not all unions resulted in parenthood, not all parents with children were convicted for absenting their children from school, and even those who were, were also convicted of a range of other offences such as larceny, drink-related offences, assaults and offences relating to their employment. What then accounts for the null finding with regards to marriage and desistance?

As noted above, marriage, partnership and cohabitation have all been argued to be, in some way or another, related to desistance from crime. The explanation commonly given for this relationship

---

[1] David Vincent, in his groundbreaking article *Love and death and the nineteenth-century working class*, illustrated the problems of trying to extrapolate working-class attitudes (in this case towards marriage and romance) from what remains a paucity of sources. His research synthesized accounts from the 104 autobiographies of working-class men and women from the period 1790–1850; this number accounts for the vast majority of known records (Vincent, 1980). A recent article by Mike Savage (2005) has re-evaluated several such classic qualitative studies. See also White (1986) or Benson (1989). Middle- and upper-class attitudes and aspirations have been better served (probably as a direct corollary of there being more detailed surviving sources). Wiener (2004) discusses the changing attitudes and patterns of the aristocracy, whilst Kidd and Nicholls (1998) contains several articles dealing with middle-class aspirations.

is that there is something inherently 'civilizing' about the 'love of a good woman' (as Maruna, 2001 characterizes it) and that this changes men for the better. Evidence in support of this line of thinking has not always been readily available (see the review above), but it is commonly accepted that family formation is associated with desistance. Some have suggested that this is because family formation is a key step along the pathway to maturity (Graham and Bowling, 1995), whilst the work of others can be read as suggesting that processes similar to identification are at the root of the transformation (see Gadd, 2006).

However, all of the above is premised on an image of marriage and families as being institutions that stem from and are intimately wrapped up in romantic love. Romantic love—that is the longing to be with another individual because of the pleasurable feelings which they engender in oneself and which are reciprocated—is the bedrock of this tenor of explanation. However, marriages are not simply about romantic attachments. Numerous authors (Goffman, 1963 for example) have reported how partners are also able to provide practical assistance to one another. In addition to this, marriage had an economic aspect. Although the family as 'social unit' and 'social actor' has been questioned (cf Davidoff *et al*, Hammerton, 1992; Harris, 1995; Meacham, 1977; D'Cruze, 1998), in the course of our research we found evidence to further support the view that during the late nineteenth century and early twentieth century marriage was sometimes, for the general population, as much about economic or practical necessities as it was about romantic feelings.

In all, there were eight men from our group of 101 persistent offenders whose wives died before reaching the age of forty. These wives almost always left behind them young children, and often babies, as some of these deaths occurred during childbirth. What is notable is not that half of these men remarried (since remarriage following spousal death is common), but rather the *speed* with which they remarried. Take, for example, the case of Horace Higgsworthy. Horace, a butcher by trade, was born in Crewe in 1850 and married his first wife (Serena Browne) in the autumn of 1868. Their first child was born the following year and they produced seven more children between 1871 and 1882—around one every other year. In 1884 Serena died in childbirth. Horace remarried the following year (1885) to a woman called Marcia Feathers, daughter of a ship-broker and owner. They had no children of their own (Marcia was also socially disadvantaged as she was a widow with four sons from a previous relationship). Horace, who previously had not been in any trouble that we can detect, was before the magistrates six times in the following six years. All of his offending appeared to be related to drinking, and included assaulting a police officer and other citizens. After this, Horace and Marcia (who stayed together and remained in Crewe) appear to have resolved any differences they may have had and Horace did not appear in court again. Our interpretation of this case is that, faced with eight children aged between two and thirteen years old, Horace did what was 'logical' for a man in his situation at that time. Devoid of informal support (his parents were already dead by that time) and without the assistance provided by the modern welfare system, he married the most suitable and available person he could find in order that he might continue his life as before as much as was possible. As it turned out, his constant drinking suggests that his second marriage, or at least the first few years of it, was not a happy one.

If Horace's was just an isolated case, one might be forgiven for arguing that we had drawn interpretations from our data which could not be empirically supported. However, it was not. Take, as a further example, the case of James Benson. James was a farmer living at Wells Green, near Crewe. Born in 1836 he married Edith in 1867. Their marriage did not produce any children, however. James' farm was, even by those days, a considerable undertaking. In 1861 (when it was still being run by his father, Stephen) the farm was of 118 acres. In 1871 as well as James and Edith living at the farm they housed four servants, and in 1881 they had three servants and a nephew living with them. In 1883 Edith died, and in 1885 James, then aged in his late-forties remarried a twenty-year-old called Fran. Over the next twelve years they produced six children. The same year as James and Fran married, we see James start to appear in court for drinking-related offences (previously his offending had been limited to one case of driving furiously in 1881). In 1890 the *Crewe Chronicle* reported that he had had 'beer for breakfast' on the occasion that he was again found guilty of furious driving and also being drunk and disorderly. Again, we argue that James married Fran not out of romantic attachment, but out of necessity—he had a large farm to run and needed domestic, female support in order to continue this. Whilst their marriage produced several children, judging from the sudden onset of drinking convictions in Crewe, we suggest that (at least initially) they did not enjoy a happy marriage.[2]

This suggests to us that marriage in the late nineteenth and early twentieth centuries may not have acted as the brake on male offending that it is currently held to act as. Marriage in the contemporary period (with the increased emphasis upon romantic love) may act as a mechanism for reforming men who wish to please or win approval from their spouses. We must remember that, despite any financial inequalities that exist in the late twentieth and early twenty-first centuries (and these undoubtedly *do* exist), women in the period that we are discussing were in a far worse position. Few had access for very long periods of their lives to independent sources of income, few had a livelihood outside of marriage, few were in a position to leave a marriage if they wanted to, those who refrained from marriage were often dealt with suspicion and *none* had the vote (until 1918). During periods in which gender inequalities are less pronounced than they were in the late nineteenth and early twentieth centuries, females may be able to exert (willingly or otherwise) a greater degree of control over their men-folk. Hence the marriage-desistance nexus may be as much an artefact of historical shifts in wider social, economic and political inequalities that take decades to emerge, as it is about romantic love. In other words, this mechanism for producing desistance is open to influence by those structural and cultural forces in vogue at any particular time in the society under consideration (see the concluding chapter to this book).

Employment, Desistance and the L&NWR Works

The Groups in Our Study

Let us leave one sphere of Victorian (and indeed contemporary) life and turn to another: employment, and more specifically employment at the L&NWR Works. As noted in Chapter Two, the L&NWR Works at Crewe represented both the largest single

---

[2] See also John Tebay (who remarried three years after his first wife died, leaving him with six children aged seven to twenty-three years old to look after). Also the case of Adam Toshack who remarried two years after his first wife died leaving him two young boys aged five and eight to look after.

employer in Crewe and the surrounding area for some considerable distance, and one of the most advanced engineering plants in the world at that time. As Drummond (1995:75) notes, by the early 1880s the Works had become the norm for men seeking employment in Crewe—there were simply few other employers in Crewe at that time. The Works, over time, established a series of workshops with specialist and dedicated roles in the production of locomotives, carriages and associated railway paraphernalia. Sons often followed their fathers into not just the Works, but the same workshop (Hudson, 1970: 58), in which the men often ate and drank together rather than walk to the company-provided dining rooms. In this way a strong sense of camaraderie was instilled in individual workshops (Drummond, 1995: 65–6)—a sense of camaraderie which the L&NWR was itself keen to promote via the formation of various sporting teams (the Crewe Alexandra stadium was designed to accommodate every workman employed at the Works at the time when it was built). By fostering friendly rivalry between workshops, the L&NWR hoped to increase production. Boys starting at the Works (some would have started when they were twelve years old, but many were aged fourteen at the commencement of their careers) were quickly introduced to life in the Works and all that it entailed. Employment in the Works provided a strong source of identity, ascribing with this a set of duties and obligations that formed a powerful gendered-moral code. Craftsmen and foremen would instil in young boys and apprentices models of their own future masculine identity (Drummond, 1995: 80) via example-setting and lessons in particular aspects of the trade into which they hoped to enter. The Works also ran a series of very basic welfare schemes for their employees, which extended to pensions, schools, an orphanage and insurance. Whilst clearly not in the same arena as 'total institutions' such as the armed forces, mental institutions, prisons or workhouses, the Works represented an extremely important feature of the lives of not just its employees, but also of their families and of those who worked in arenas of the local economy ancillary to the Works and those who worked there. Local shops, public houses, hostelries, and manufacturers owed their economic survival to the Works as much as any of the Works' employees did.

In this way, but not only this way, the Works exerted a considerable form of control over the individuals and populous of Crewe at this time. Drummond (1995: 153) writes that even by 1890 the

L&NWR 'controlled practically every level of politics [. . .] through the level of economic influence it exercised in the new town'. The L&NWR became the 'de facto government' (Drummond, 1995: 153). The railway company, via its own police force, also in effect became the de facto agency of social control for its workforce and their families (see also Hudson, 1970; Godfrey, 2002). Gatekeepers were special constables by as early as the 1870s with the power to search and arrest men leaving the Works. Detectives working for the Works' police force had the right to enter Works' men's homes, undertake searches of those properties, inspect these homes for cleanliness and the residents for moral probity (Hudson, 1970: 62). Works rules were published in booklet form and notices described them further. Punishments were regulated, carried out and could be harsh. Despite the culture which surrounded the furnace men's use of alcohol at work (they sent their sons out to buy beer from a local public house, Drummond, 1995: 78) there was a general disapproval of being 'in drink' either at work or in Works' time. Such behaviour, if detected, in theory brought instant dismissal, however in practice such individuals were often just suspended for some period of time. Similarly, fighting at work, or amongst employees outside of work as the result of a dispute initiated at work, resulted in informal punishments. Theft (of any sort, related to the Works or otherwise) was not tolerated and it almost always resulted in dismissal. Attendance at the Works at the correct time of day was also closely monitored, and lateness, idling or leaving early dealt with by way of fines, suspensions or, if repeated too often, dismissal.

The Works were, without a shadow of a doubt, a very dangerous place to be employed. Of the 137 employees whose records we collated (and which were biased towards offenders who worked at the Works and who, as we shall see, often did not work for long there), one was killed in an accident at the Works (a further employee and Cohort A offender died in 1914, poisoned by the lead paint he used in his work in the carriage works). Around a fifth of our sample left the Works through incapacitation, often the direct result of their labours.

Using staff records made available to us by Bombardier Transportation UK Ltd. (the current owners of Crewe Works) we were able to view the disciplinary and accident records of hundreds of workers (approximately two-thirds of those employed between 1853 and 1922, with a predominance of those working between

1880 and 1920). We sought to advance our knowledge about the role of employment in helping people to stop offending by answering the following questions: Did employment, career progression, and/or promotion at the Works impact upon the offending careers of employees? Did an offender's conviction impact upon their employment career vis-à-vis the Works, ie were they the ones selected for dismissal when reductions in the workforce were required? Lastly, did persistent offenders have different discipline and injury records from non-offenders?

We constructed a database (described more fully in the methodological appendices) that contained information about each individual's employment (promotions, disciplinary events, injuries, rates of pay, reason(s) for leaving and character assessments) for the following groups of employees: those of our 101 persistent offenders who worked for any period of time at the Works (n = 35); a randomly-selected group of Works employees who had between one and four convictions (n = 48, mean n of convictions = 1.4) and whom we refer to as occasional offenders; and a group of Works employees who had not appeared in court (n = 56). As with other chapters, we supplement our quantitative data analyses with life-histories of specific individual cases.

We commence our exploration with a consideration of the general characteristics of the groups outlined above. In terms of their dates of engagement at the Works, each of these groups saw engagement in the period shortly after the Works was moved to Crewe. The earliest start date was for a non-offender (December 1843), but this is something of an outlier, the next start date for this group being April 1851.[3] In terms of the trades which our sample occupied at the time of the creation of the records, some twenty-eight were fitters, twenty-four were labourers, seven were turners, six were strikers, five platers, five rivetters, five smiths, five moulders, the remaining forty were the likes of shunters, spring makers, stores men or apprentices and there were fourteen cases who were unclassified.

---

[3] The earliest start date for a persistent was June 1853, and for the occasional offenders the earliest was October 1857. The latest leaving date for the non-offenders (all leaving dates are truncated by data availability) was 22 March 1922. For persistent offenders this was 22 December 1922. For occasional offenders the latest leaving date was 29 November 1929, but this was again an outlier, the next latest being 1 September 1927.

Table 4.1 below reports on seven characteristics of our three groups: the average length of time that each group was employed at the Works; their final rate of pay; the total number of times that they were injured; the age at which they commenced employment at the Works; their character; their ability and their timekeeping. The last of these three are the scored assessments recorded for each man upon leaving the Works (probably entered by the respective departmental foremen). From these scores we constructed a five-point scale from 'feeble' to 'excellent/superior'. As one can see, our group of persistent offenders scored significantly below both the non-offenders and occasional offenders in terms of their length of service. The persistent offenders worked, on average at the Works for 5,102 days (just under fourteen years), whilst non-offenders and occasional offenders respectively clocked up 11,372 and 10,254 days (or over thirty-one and twenty-eight years respectively).

Table 4.1 Basic characteristics of Works' sub-groups.

Variable	Group	No.	Mean	Significance
Length of Service	Non-offenders:	50	11372	
(days)	Occasionals:	43	10254	
	Persistents:	23	5102	***
Final Salary	Non-offenders:	56	33	
(weekly, in shillings)	Occasionals:	46	30	
	Persistents:	20	22	**
No. of times injured	Non-offenders:	56	1.23	
(events recorded)	Occasionals:	48	1.08	
	Persistents:	24	.17	**
Age starting work	Non-offenders:	56	22	
(in years)	Occasionals:	48	26	
	Persistents:	18	23	NS
Character	Non-offenders:	47	3.06	
(recorded	Occasionals:	44	3.02	
by Works)	Persistents:	19	2.58	**
Ability	Non-offenders:	47	2.94	
(recorded by Works)	Occasionals:	44	2.89	
	Persistents:	20	2.55	*
Time keeping	Non-offenders:	14	3.57	
(recorded by Works)	Occasionals:	18	3.56	
	Persistents:	5	2.80	NS

ANOVA *p <= .05, **p <= .01, ***p <= .001, NS = not significant.
Games-Howell test of significance used.

The relatively shorter period of employment experienced by the persistent offenders probably goes a long way in accounting for their lower average final salary of 22s. Non-offenders again came top of the earnings score in this respect (at 33s.). Occasional offenders earned slightly less, at 30s. The shorter periods of employment experienced by persistent offenders also probably accounts for their having fewer recorded episodes of injury (less than a fifth of a day on average, compared to over a day each on average for non-offenders and occasional offenders). There appeared to be no statistically significant differences between these three groups in terms of their age at commencement at the Works. Our persistent offenders were also rated as having slightly poorer characters and to be of slightly less ability than either of the other two groups. In terms of time keeping, our three groups appeared to differ little, although it ought to be noted that sample sizes for this data dropped significantly.

Table 4.2 summarizes a series of crosstabulation tables that again explore the differences between the three groups of employees. More of the non-offenders (54%) and the occasional offenders (38%) were promoted than of the persistent offenders (25%). All groups showed signs of having troubled periods of employment (indicated by the requirement to repeat their apprenticeship or journeymanship or being fined, suspended or dismissed for poor behaviour at work). Despite their shorter average careers at the Works, it appears that the persistent offenders were almost as likely to have been in trouble at work as those who worked there twice as long.

Persistent offenders were more likely to have been dismissed from work (this being dismissed for poor conduct, laid off during times of recession or discharged for illness). There was no evidence,

Table 4.2 Further characteristics of Works' sub-groups.

Variable	Non-offenders		Persistents		Occasionals		Significance
	%	No.	%	No.	%	No.	
Promoted	54	30	25	6	38	18	*
Troubled employment	55	31	46	11	69	33	NS
Dismissed	9	5	57	13	29	13	***
Dismissed at reduction	8	4	0	0	0	0	NS
Sample size	50–56		23–24		43–48		

*p < = .05, **p <= .01, ***p <= .001, NS = not significant.

however, that persistent offenders were selected ahead of other groups when the Works was laying off staff (referred to as dismissed at reduction). For none of the other data available to us could we find any statistically significant differences between our three groups of employees.[4]

This initial exploration of the general characteristics of our three groups of Works employees provides an answer to one of our research questions. It would appear that persistent offenders did *not* have different discipline and injury records when compared to non-offenders or occasional offenders, although one has to bear in mind their generally shorter periods of engagement at the Works. In other words, the data suggests that persistent offenders were more troublesome than other workers for the time they were employed.

Offending and Works Employment

We come now to the main part of our enquiries, the impact of employment at the Works on offending by its employees. Following the literature on the relationship between employment and desistance, which generally suggests that employment and progression in that employment will become associated with less offending over time, we make a number of propositions: first, that employment at the Works 'controls' behaviour, such that offending should stabilize or reduce upon commencement at the Works; second, that progression in employment terms at the Works ought to be associated with a decline in offending; and lastly, that after leaving the Works, especially so if dismissed, offending ought to increase. Set against this, in order to temper the 'work cures all ills' tenor of the above, we additionally propose the following: that employment, especially within 'heavy', male-dominated, working-class cultures of the Victorian era such as the railway Works increased the chances for offending via wages which were spent on alcohol, leading to drunkenness and disorderly behaviour (see Chapter Two on the number of public houses in Crewe).

Table 4.3 reports on our sample of employees as a whole group, and compares number of offences and rates of offending committed

---

[4] This data included: nature of behaviour that resulted in disciplinary action, reasons for leaving the Works, and nature of injuries sustained whilst employed at the Works.

Table 4.3 Impact of employment at Works on offending (all cases).

A Comparison	Mean no. of offences (T1–T2)	No. of cases	Significance
Before engagement—During engagement	0.50–0.86	121	NS
During engagement—After engagement	0.78–1.43	122	NS
Before engagement—After engagement	0.44–1.36	118	*
Before promotion—After promotion	1.63–1.25	24	NS
During engagement—After dismissal	0.83–4.83	23	*

B	Mean rate of offending (T1–T2)	No. of cases	Significance
Before engagement—During engagement	0.0197–0.0320	109	NS
During engagement—After engagement	0.0308–0.0328	71	NS
Before engagement—After engagement	0.0238–0.0322	71	NS
Before promotion—After promotion	0.1289–0.1256	16	NS
During engagement—After dismissal	0.0764–0.1118	12	NS

T tests. *p <= .05, **p <= .01, ***p <= .001, NS = not significant.

before, during and after engagement at the Works, before and after promotion (including successful completion of apprenticeship), and during employment after dismissal from the Works for those sacked.[5]

As Table 4.3 shows, for the sample taken as a whole, there was no statistically significant impact of engagement upon the number

[5] An unfortunate side-effect of using data relating to rates is that for the calculation of rates to be possible, the exact year of entry/promotion/departure had to be known, and unfortunately this was not the case for those men who we could not find in the Works' records. For the simple count (discussed above) it was possible to assess this roughly using census data and reports of social circumstances from the newspapers. For example, imagine an individual listed as a farmer in the 1871 and 1881 censuses, but as a labourer in the Works in 1891 and as a farmer in the 1901 census. During the period 1874–1880 he is convicted of six offences, all of which can be attributed to the time before he started at the Works (after 1881 but before 1891).

of offences committed (row 1). If anything, the average number of convictions went up (from .50 to .86). Leaving the Works (row 2) did appear to have an impact (the number of convictions rose from .78 to 1.43), but again this was not statistically significant. A comparison of the number of offences committed before and after engagement at the Works (row 3) does find statistically significant results—after men left the Works the number of their convictions appears to go up (from an average of .44 to 1.36). Promotion at the Works (row 4) did little to discourage offending (although the average number of convictions did fall slightly). Dismissal from the Works (row 5) was associated with a dramatic increase in offending—the average number leapt from .83 during employment at the Works to 4.83 after dismissal.

Of course, given that not all men would have been employed at the Works for the same length of time, we produced a yearly rate of convictions for each man for the same time periods. Table 4.3 (B) reports on this. As can be seen, the actual rate at which men were convicted appeared to change very little as a result of their employment at the Works. Promotion and dismissal similarly had no effect when rates of offending are considered.

How did this vary for our different groups of offenders? It is, by definition, impossible to compare the offending before engagement or during engagement for non-offenders, so the following analyses rely on only our two groups of offenders (Tables 4.4.and 4.5).

Table 4.4 suggests that for occasional offenders, after engagement in the Works their offending increased from an average n of .04 to 1.11 (the opposite of what one might expect, row 1). Similarly (row 2), as they left the Works, their offending declined (from 1.09 to .33). The overall effect was to increase their offending (row 3). Promotion appeared to have no impact on their offending (row 4), and neither did dismissal (row 5). These patterns are supported by a consideration of the rates at which the occasional offenders were convicted. The rate of conviction leapt from .00 to .04

If a further conviction in, say, 1895 resulted in a newspaper report which described the man in question as 'recently of the Works', it is possible to count these convictions and all subsequent convictions towards the post-Works employment offending count. However, because the calculation of rates requires more precise data, this case would not be available for use in the rates analyses. This accounts for the reduced number of cases that we are able to rely upon when dealing with rates.

Table 4.4   Impact of employment at Works on offending (occasional offenders).

A Comparison	Mean no. of offences (T1–T2)	No. of cases	Significance
Before engagement— During engagement	0.04–1.11	46	***
During engagement— After engagement	1.09–0.33	45	**
Before engagement— After engagement	0.04–0.33	45	*
Before promotion— After promotion	0.31–0.88	16	NS
During engagement— After dismissal	0.75–0.75	12	NS

B	Mean rate of offending (T1–T2)	No. of cases	Significance
Before engagement— During engagement	0.0000–0.0394	40	***
During engagement— After engagement	0.0366–0.0114	24	*
Before engagement— After engagement	0.0026–0.0091	30	NS
Before promotion— After promotion	0.0241–0.0260	11	NS
During engagement— After dismissal	0.0356–0.0269	6	NS

T tests. *p <= .05, **p <= .01, ***p <= .001, NS = not significant.

on commencement at the Works, and similarly declined after they left. Again promotion and dismissal appeared not to affect rates of offending.

Turning to the persistent offenders, one sees a slightly different set of figures (Table 4.5). Their offending went down (row 1, but only slightly and not significantly) on arrival at the Works. After they had left the Works, which, as one would expect, acted as a regulatory force, their offending went up (from an average of 1.80 to over 6, row 2). This result was statistically significant. Promotion (row 4) appeared to reduce their offending, although this did not reach statistical significance. Dismissal (row 5) dramatically increased their rate of offending—on average convictions whilst employed at the Works but before dismissal stood at 0.91, after

Table 4.5   Impact of employment at Works on offending (persistent offenders).

A Comparison	Mean no. of offences (T1–T2)	No. of cases	Significance
Before engagement— During engagement	2.32–2.12	25	NS
During engagement— After engagement	1.80–6.24	25	*
Before engagement— After engagement	2.17–6.30	23	*
Before promotion— After promotion	4.25–2.00	8	NS
During engagement— After dismissal	0.91–9.27	11	*

B	Mean rate of offending (T1–T2)	No. of cases	Significance
Before engagement— During engagement	0.1129–0.1077	19	NS
During engagement— After engagement	0.1093–0.1713	12	NS
Before engagement— After engagement	0.1464–0.1838	12	NS
Before promotion— After promotion	0.3552–0.3489	5	NS
During engagement— After dismissal	0.1259–0.2136	5	NS

T tests. *$p <= .05$, **$p <= .01$, ***$p <= .001$, NS = not significant.

dismissal from the Works this rose to 9.27. When we consider the rates at which our persistent offenders were being convicted, we see little signs of employment at the Works having made any impact upon them (rows 6–8). Again promotion and dismissal when rates of offending are considered are not statistically significant.

What ought we to make of these data? Let us discuss the findings that when rates, rather than the raw counts, are used, statistical significance is harder to achieve. We suspect that this is partially the result of simply having too few cases upon which we could rely for accurate information concerning the timing of entry, promotion and departure from the Works (see footnote five). We feel, however, reasonably confident that employment in the Works, for the persistent offenders, appeared to stabilize their offending. The number of convictions recorded against them after they commenced at the

Works stayed at around two, and the rate went down slightly (from .1129 to .1077) although this did not reach statistical significance. On the other hand, for the occasional offenders, employment appeared to be associated with the onset of their (brief) troubles with the law. Occasional offenders saw their convictions rise from almost none to slightly over one. This dropped back after they left the Works.

If we examine the sorts of offences which the occasional and persistent offenders committed, we find little difference in general in the nature of the offences committed. However, if we examine the nature of their offences and the *timing* of them, an interesting trend emerges (Table 4.6).

Looking at the persistent offenders we see that, over time, more and more of them are found guilty of drunkenness (Table 4.6). Before they commenced employment at the Works, a mere 7% of them had been convicted. This rose during the time that they were employed, to 27%, and after they had left the Works over half of them were convicted at least once for an act of drunkenness in Crewe. When we turn to the occasional offenders we see a different pattern. None of them had been convicted for drunkenness before they started at the Works, but whilst they were working for the L&NWR at Crewe, almost a fifth of them were convicted of drunkenness. After they left the Works however, and it must be remembered that a vast majority would have spent the greater part of their working lives at Crewe and so would have been quite old when they left (two-thirds left after they were aged fifty), a mere 4% were convicted of drunkenness. Thus a significant proportion of the occasional offenders appeared in front of the magistrates at Crewe for acts of drunkenness during their working lives. However, these acts were limited in frequency (occasional offenders had committed no more than four offences it must be remembered, and many had committed a good deal fewer, with an average n of

Table 4.6 Drunkenness: before, during and after engagement at the Works.

	Before	During	After	N
Persistent offenders	7 %	27%	56%	25–30
Occasional offenders	0 %	19%	4%	47–48

convictions of 1.4) and temporally, the bulk being whilst they were employed at the Works.

We can draw a number of conclusions from the above. It appears that for the persistent offenders amongst our sample, employment at the Works had the effect of stabilizing their offending. Their offending did not increase dramatically after they entered the Works (Table 4.5), but rose dramatically in the period after they had left, especially so if they were dismissed (Table 4.5). Promotion reduced their offending quite dramatically (by more than half) but this did not reach statistical significance. Of the thirty-five persistent offenders who were amongst the Works employees, eighteen appeared to have offending histories that suggested that their employment at the Works was associated with a reduction in their offending. There were a further ten whose histories suggested that their engagement at the Works coincided with an increase in their offending. Seven cases were unclassifiable (almost always because their records could not be found amongst those held at Crewe Works or the National Archives and the precise period of their engagement at the Works could not be determined from the available censuses).

When we look at the occasional offenders, we see an initially perplexing trend: engagement in the works was associated with an *increase* in offending behaviour (Table 4.4), whilst leaving the Works was associated with a decline in such behaviour. However, as demonstrated by Table 4.5, this was probably the result of the group of offenders' immersion in a culture in which heavy drinking was common.

Let us now turn to another of our research questions. Did those found guilty of crimes in court leave the employment of the Works for different reasons than those who did not have any convictions recorded against them? For example, were they selected for dismissal when reductions in the workforce were required? As Table 4.2 above demonstrated, persistent offenders were more likely then either non-offenders or occasional offenders to have been dismissed from the Works, however, this appears to have been as a result of their own actions, rather than as a result of their being 'weeded out' when the Works looked to reduce the size of its workforce more generally.

Aside from the quantitative data analyses, which suggest that, by and large, employment in the Works had a beneficial impact upon the offending careers of many of the men employed there (with the proviso that it appears that some of them diverted a not inconsiderable portion of their wages towards some of Crewe's many public houses), what else can be detected from an examination of the employee and petty sessions databases?

Did an offender's conviction impact upon his employment career in any way? By and large the answer to this question is a qualified 'yes—it ended it'. For example, James Hough (born 7 August 1845), a one-off offender, started work at the Works on 1 April 1875. He rose to the post of fitter. Twenty years later, at the end of September 1895, James was found guilty of the theft of fifty-four high-denomination postage stamps from the Crewe Co-Operative Society (of which he was the Vice-President). The *Crewe Chronicle*—perhaps as an unwitting agent in a strategy of social control—noted that he had been employed at the Works. His Works records refer to his conviction for theft as the reason for his dismissal two days after his conviction.

Similarly, Silas Mawsley, a machinist who had previously worked for J. Eardley of Market Drayton, was dismissed after twelve years of employment at the Works after being imprisoned for an assault. Silas had commenced work on 10 May 1893 (being promoted to a machinist a year or so later). He had been already convicted for being drunk on Edleston Road in March 1893, which did not appear to hinder his engagement at the Works. However, when he was found guilty of assault in September 1905 he was imprisoned for over a month in lieu of payment of a fine of £3. Walter Smith was convicted in court three times. He had started at the Works in September 1881, and in November 1892 was dismissed for fighting with another worker. There then followed his three court appearances (in 1900 for a breach of the peace and an assault and in 1902 for a further assault). These cases confirm the general rule identified by Drummond (see above) that men found guilty of fighting or theft were dismissed from the Works (see also Locker, 2004; Locker and Godfrey, 2006; Hudson, 1970; Drummond, 1995).

On the other hand, there were a number of cases where it is clear that the Works disregarded offending, although one might have believed that they would have taken a keen interest in such offences. There were two cases (Harold Hughes and William Potts, two occasional offenders) who were dismissed for being drunk at work, but for whom previous convictions for drunkenness had been ignored.

Hughes started at the Works in 1864, and was convicted of being drunk in March of 1884. However, it was not until he reported drunk for work (in November 1894) that he was dismissed. Similarly, Potts started at the Works in March 1894 and was convicted of being drunk in 1904, although was not dismissed until 1907, when he reported drunk for work. The reasons why the Works turned a blind eye to such behaviours when committed out of Works' time, but which had such obvious consequences for those individuals and the people they work with, is probably related to cultural and economic factors. There may have a tacit approval (or at the very least tolerance) of 'the working man's right to get drunk', for example, and this spirit of toleration may have been greater in times of labour shortage (Godfrey, 1997). See for example, the following remarks by a railway foreman:

I am continually bothered with my men. Some design to emigrate, some get drunk and are discharged, and others are hurt. There is a difficulty in obtaining strong fellows who read and write [. . .]. It is fast becoming to this, and if John Porter gets drunk, instead of dismissing the honest fellow, I shall have to say 'why, John my boy, you've had a little beer. If you feel ill in the morning you need not hurry.

(entry for 18 August, 1853, Turner, L. (ed) (1891)
*Fifty Years on the L&NWR, and Other Memoranda of
the life of David Stevenson*, Crewe, Turner)

In the end, the need for a workforce may have outstripped the Works' desire for a 'respectable' (or sober) workforce, and again it would appear that a certain level of tolerance was exercised when it came to the effects of drunkenness amongst the men. This general tolerance may, as we have indicated above, account for the rather surprising rise in convictions for drunkenness amongst men of previous 'good character' upon commencement at the Works.

Work-related Offending in Non-railway Trades

As stated above, the Works was the main employer in Crewe, but there were also a range of small industrial and retail employers. Amongst these, two types of retail trader—the self-employed market-stall-holder and the scrap-metal dealer—appeared frequently in court records. There were eight persistent offenders in Cohort A in these trades (responsible for 147 offences between them) of whom Peter Court has a typical offending profile. He was born in Dublin in

1853 and moved to Crewe in 1880, working as a market fishmonger. His offending career was closely related to his occupation; in the early 1880s he assaulted, and was assaulted by, a number of fellow market traders on several occasions. He also appeared before the magistrates for not cleansing his market stall properly, failing to pay the General District Rate and the Water Rate, and on one count of larceny. He appeared for several more work-related offences until 1888, when he clearly began to have problems with at least one of his four children; between 1888 and 1891 he was charged six times with Education Act offences. The long-running feud continued with fellow market stallholders, with further allegations of assault being heard in court.[6] In 1894 and 1897 he was charged with selling bad fish (*Crewe Chronicle* 14 July 1894). In 1901 he was charged with threatening Wallace Hamble in the Cheese Hall Vaults. In his defence Court was reported as stating that 'I have never hurt man, woman or child and don't intend to do so' (*Crewe Chronicle* 17 August 1901). The following year his wife died, and he was also charged with letting his chimney catch on fire and leaving a cart in the highway. In 1903 he was found guilty of being drunk and disorderly, being described as 'one of the most conspicuous members of society in the town' (*Crewe Chronicle* 11 July 1903), and his last recorded offence was in 1905 for obstructing the highway with his fish cart (he died the following year).

The most persistent offender of Cohort B was Fred Briggs, a market-hall fruiterer whose offending profile of almost fifty offences committed between 1910 (for playing football in the street) and 1938 (refusing to pay court imposed fines for other offences) consisted largely of public order offences including nine cases of obscene or abusive language, and eight assaults, but only one offence of being drunk in charge of a vehicle. Court and Briggs both

---

[6] Peter Court's protagonist and fellow fishmonger Alphonse Cressy himself fell foul of the Market Inspector on at least two occasions. The involvement of Alphonse Cressy's brother, Adam Cressy (a butcher) in fights with Peter Court seems to suggest that there was a degree of planning in the confrontations, as Mrs W. W. Hodkinson recalled in her memoirs that the fish market was a separate entity from the rest of the market. She also gave a brief description of Thomas Barr, the Market Inspector from c. 1900–1909, describing him as being 'much in evidence in those days in a dark blue uniform with a peaked cap. [. . .] He had a very sharp eye for scavengers and short shrift they got from Mr Barr.' (Hodkinson [née Roberts], W.W., 'Crewe—as I once knew it'), p. 21.

exemplify the offending careers of people employed at the margins of society. They were both primarily convicted of work-related offences, but remained in the same occupation for at least twenty-five years and appeared to have a stable family relationship with their wives and children, none of whom were themselves persistent offenders. Similarly, self-employed old-metal dealers like Wesley Ingthorpe (approximately twenty prosecutions for work-related offences), worked in an environment which lacked formal structures of supervision or informal social controls that come with larger workforces. There were many people who worked in similar work-structures, and who did not go on to offend. The difference seems to be that market traders and old-metal dealers worked on very low margins in a very competitive business which relied on their using sharp practice (between 1880–1940 there were 144 offences of adulterating food with cheaper materials or selling food past its best; and ninety-eight offences of giving false measures) or using illegal markets (receiving and 'fencing' stolen brass and lead, for example). For men such as these, work was criminogenic (see also Hobbs, 1995).

Despite being witnesses to and victims of crime on many occasions, publicans did not make it into Cohort A in great numbers. Many publicans were prosecuted for serving alcohol to drunks, serving alcohol outside of legal licensing hours, and many were the victims of drunks refusing to quit their pub, theft from tills, criminal damage caused by drunk people, and so on. There were some pubs and entertainment areas where offending was prevalent. For example, Market Street and Nantwich Road saw more than their fair share of disorderly behaviour (see Table 4.7).

Table 4.7 Number of offences committed in Market Street and Nantwich Road Public Houses, 1880–1940.

Red Bull	53 Market Street	19
Adelphi Hotel	60 Market Street	6
Blue Cap Dog Inn	68 Market Street	13
Masonic Arms	94 Market Street	3
Nags Head	157 Market Street	4
Egerton Arms	38 Nantwich Road	10
Robin Hood	55 Nantwich Road	9
British Lion	58 Nantwich Road	9
Brunswick Hotel	71 Nantwich Road	4
Crewe Arms	Nantwich Road	3

The publicans who managed these premises obviously were 'involved' in offending, but not to the extent that they could be considered persistent offenders, possibly because they were not in their jobs long enough to rack up too many offences. However, two publicans (Trevor Round, Prince of Wales, 120 West Street, c.1885–1911; and Wilbur Cuthbert, Lion and Swan, West Street, c.1885–1915) were in post long enough to commit between them thirteen work-related offences (thereby placing them in Cohort A).

One other occupational group featured significantly in Cohort A, and could hardly have done otherwise—prostitutes. There were three prostitutes in Cohort A, who, aside from the offences of their trade—soliciting and indecent acts—were also prosecuted for public urination, and vagrancy (sleeping out in back yards, back alleys and outside 'privies'). Theirs were miserable lives, being subjected to violence by 'pimps' and clients; being constantly moved on by the police and making a living in very difficult circumstances. Each of the Cohort A prostitutes died relatively young. Jemima Strang, the deaf and dumb daughter of a labourer, died at the age of thirty-six; Fanny Morris (alias 'Simpson') appeared in court twenty-six times during her brief twenty-four years of life; and Minnie Valler died as a homeless woman aged forty (see Chapter Five wherein we discuss intergenerational patterns of offending). As far as can be determined only one of the three prostitutes worked in any of the established brothels in Crewe (see Table 4.8), and perhaps the sex workers in those establishments were responsible for some of the 168 prosecutions for prostitution between 1880 and 1940.

Table 4.8   Brothels in Crewe.

Address	Year when prosecuted
Beech Grove	1907
Cross Street	1908
Warren's Row, Sydney	1909
Fareham's Row	1910
Frank Street	1910
Lockitt Street	1912
Clarke Street, off Lockitt Street	1914
Naylor Street	1916
Orchard Place, off West Street	1916
Co-operative Street	1916
Mill Street	1918
Heath Street	1925

Conclusion

In this chapter we have considered those factors associated with the desistance amongst our sample of both persistent offenders and those who were employed at the Railway Works. Naturally, we were constrained to considering only those factors that we had access to data about, and these, of course, were 'social' (rather than psychological or psychosocial) in nature. Marriage and having children, as modern commentators have found, appear to act as mechanisms for reforming men who wish to please or win approval from their spouses or who generally accept the responsibility that parenthood brings. We suggested that in times when gender inequalities are less pronounced than they were in the late-nineteenth and early-twentieth centuries, females are able to exert (willingly or otherwise) a greater degree of control over their boyfriends and husbands (and for that matter, maybe over their fathers and brothers too). However, our data led us to conclude that marriage in the late-nineteenth and early-twentieth centuries may not have acted as the brake on male offending that it does today. This clearly alters our understanding of the role of informal social controls. Informal social controls cannot, of course, ever be fully divorced from processes of formal social control. The role of females (as wives) in processes of desistance and reform is—in part—influenced by their structural position, institutional practices and the social, cultural and political status ascribed to them. Similarly, social mores surrounding drinking and employment (and whether the two are compatible at the same moment) greatly influence, we feel, the nature of the 'trouble' in which some of our sample found themselves.

Turning to consider employment at the Works, we are reasonably confident that such employment stabilized the offending of persistent offenders. The number of convictions recorded against them after they commenced at the Works steadied, and the rate at which they were convicted went down slightly too. When persistent offenders left the employ of the Works, their offending increased, especially so if they had been dismissed. On the other hand, for the occasional offenders, employment at the Works appeared to be associated with the onset of their (brief) contact with the criminal justice system. Offending receded after they left the Works. Why was this? Our explanation rests on an understanding not of employment as simply an economic activity, but also as a social activity. Work formed a similar function for the employees of the Works too, and, as today, many of these activities involved a combination of socialising and alcohol. When we looked at the persistent offenders we saw that the nature of their offending was closely related to their life-stage as it related to their employment. When we turned to the occasional offenders we saw a slightly different pattern. A significant proportion of the occasional offenders appeared in front of the magistrates at Crewe for acts of drunkenness during their working lives. However, these acts were limited in frequency—the bulk being whilst they were working at the Works. The engagement at the Works for the 'essentially law-abiding' was associated with an increase in offending behaviours, probably, we feel, the result of the group of offenders' immersion in a culture in which heavy drinking was common. For the persistent offenders, on the other hand, it was promotion at work that reduced their offending quite dramatically (by more than half).

This suggests a number of points to us. First, that the same process can produce different outcomes for different groups of people—encouraging one type of offending for one group and suppressing offending for another—and it is therefore the quality of the process which must be considered. Second, that an understanding of the local culture of an organization is required before one can think through the ways in which this may affect the individuals who find themselves—via their own choices or through other means—operating within it. Organizations in the late nineteenth century may, on the surface, appear to be very similar to those in the modern period. However, their practices and institutional norms may differ greatly, and in so doing may alter trajectories of offending.

5

Families and Crime: the Intergenerational Patterns of Offending in Crewe

We need far earlier intervention with some of these families (from Hell), who are often socially excluded and socially dysfunctional. That may mean before they offend; and certainly before they want such intervention. But in truth, we can identify such families virtually as their children are born [. . .] If we are not prepared to predict and intervene far more early then there are children that are going to grow up in families that we know perfectly well are completely dysfunctional [. . .] The kids a few years down the line are going to be a menace to society.

Prime Ministerial address on 'Our Nation's Future', 7 September 2006

The investigation into the intergenerational patterns of offending has been a marginal area of research (Smith and Farrington, 2004: 230), but the studies there have been in this area consistently suggest a strong relationship between parental offending and the behaviour of their offspring (Farrington, 2002: 670). Studies conducted from the 1950s (Glueck and Glueck, 1950; Ferguson, 1952) have found that offenders frequently have parents—and especially fathers—who have been convicted. Farrington *et al* (1996) found that 63% of boys in the Cambridge Study of Delinquent Development who had convicted fathers were themselves convicted of an offence. It seems a common finding that (at least for males) a father's offending was the most important of the family-related variables in predicting sons' offending (Farrington, 2002: 671).

Several longitudinal research projects and projects which have compared parental offending with offspring's offending have established that there is a 'social transmission' of offending between generations of the same family (Farrington *et al*, 1998; Robins, 1979; McCord, 1977; Wilson, 1987; and West and Farrington, 1973). For example, Farrington and his colleagues reported that around three-quarters of convicted parents themselves had a convicted son or daughter (1998: 86), and that fathers' offending was strongly related to sons' offending, but less strongly related to daughters' offending (and vice versa for mothers who offended). Most of the evidence in this area suggests that this is not the result of parents and siblings co-offending, that is to say that the offences committed by parents and those committed by their offspring relate to different incidents (Farrington, *et al*, 1998). Ages of onset of offending between generations were not strongly correlated, although ages of onset within generations *were* strongly correlated.

Smith and Farrington (2004: 237–9), using data from the Cambridge Study of Delinquent Development report the following key findings: having a convicted father is a risk factor for their children having early childhood troublesome behaviour and adolescent antisocial behaviour; men with early histories of conduct problems were no more likely to have grandchildren with conduct problems than those men without early histories of conduct problems; almost two-thirds of antisocial fathers (61%) did not have children who displayed misconduct problems. Of the 338 men in the study, 133 (39%) had at least one child over the age of twelve who had had a conviction recorded against them. Convicted grandfathers were also more likely to have grandchildren with conduct problems than non-convicted grandfathers.

However, Smith and Farrington (2004: 242) report that whilst there was a suggestion of continuity in offending across three generations of families, these relationships did not reach statistical significance. They summarize by pointing to three findings that stand out: continuity in antisocial behaviour spans three generations; parenting mechanisms appear to play a strong role in this; finally, continuities cannot be predicted from childhood and discontinuities may shed light on the processes by which transmission is disrupted.

Farrington *et al* (2001), using data from the US (Pittsburgh) report that offending was highly concentrated in families—if one relative had been arrested there was a high degree of likelihood that another had been also. For example, 53% of arrested grandmothers of their sample also had arrested husbands (ie grandfathers of sample members). Similarly, 79% of the aunts of sample members had arrested husbands (ie uncles of sample members), whilst 82% of sample members' mothers had arrested husbands (2001: 584–5). In terms of the intergenerational influences, three-quarters of the sample who had arrested grandfathers also had arrested fathers.

Similarly, 44% of sample members who had arrested fathers were themselves petitioned to appear in court.

Explaining Intergenerational Patterns of Offending: Individual-level Explanations

Several attempts, dating back to the late-nineteenth and early-twentieth centuries' eugenics movement, have been made to account for the strong relationship between parents' offending and that of their children. Generally speaking (see Smith and Farrington, 2004: 231–2; Farrington 2002: 670–1 and Farrington *et al* 2001: 593–4), these explanations can be grouped into a number of schools of thought.

Biological or Genetic Factors

As McCord (1991: 213) and Hahn Rafter (1997) have noted, biological explanations of the relationship between crime and generations of the same families have progressed little since the eugenics movement of the early twentieth century. The mechanism of transmission adopted by this school is the hereditary influence of the gene. Farrington (2002: 671) cites a study by Grove *et al* (1990) employing identical twins (some of who were reared apart, others not) and which found that heredity influences accounted for 41% of the observed differences for childhood misconduct and 28% of adult antisocial behaviour today. However, the sample size of thirty-two leads to inevitable questions about how far the conclusions of the study can be extended. There are in any case very few studies of the role of genetic factors in the intergenerational transmission of offending.

Assortative Mating

Another explanation is that when selecting partners, people often select people similar to themselves (ie homogenous assortative mating). Two possible mechanisms exist under this school of thought. First, that the drivers behind this are social (in that there are known to be strong social and geographical forces behind with whom people socialize). A second possibility would be that individuals consider each other's personality and behaviours and make selection on these bases. Rowe and Farrington report that assortative mating did indeed appear to be one explanation of transmission from parents to offspring (1997: 195). They suggest that this is the result of parents choosing partners who are similar to themselves, rather than because marriage partners tend in general towards selecting a mate from within a homogenous social group (which would, in this case, lead to offenders selecting other offenders as mates). Historical studies assert that the damage done by a criminal conviction to a woman's reputation would lead her to consider mates that she would not otherwise have considered suitable. In bald terms, this would also lead female offenders to 'select' or 'end up with' offending husbands (or husbands who were violent to their wives). However, modern research by Johnson and Booth (1998) suggests that both personality and interactional styles in relationships are malleable, and that relationship formation and interactions are not as mechanical and deterministic a process as some suggest. They suggest that a 'good' marriage can alter the behaviour of previously 'bad' actors. So, whilst selection effects may be present, the possibility of changes to both the behaviour of those individuals who form the relationship and to the dynamics of the marriage 'itself' is possible.

Parenting and Socialization Practices

A further explanation is that offenders make 'bad parents' and that poor parenting leads to early misconduct amongst the children of offenders and that this in turn leads to more entrenched criminal careers amongst the children of offenders. Nineteenth-century commentators (see Cox and Shore 2002: 14–17) routinely ascribed bad behaviour by children to the faults of their parents (particularly working mothers). However, the suggestion that parenting and socialization practices (such as poor supervision, inconsistent discipline, parental conflict and lack of affection) may contribute to subsequent criminality on the part of the offspring has received mixed results in modern criminological literature. West and Farrington (1973: 117) failed to find any evidence to support this line of reasoning (although do provide several caveats to their work). Nagin *et al* (1997) represent one team who did find evidence to support the socialization practices model. They report that for the children of young (ie under age twenty-one at time of birth) mothers, poor parenting and role modelling appeared to be one of the best explanations for offspring involvement in crime. Against this, Hennessy *et al* (1978, cited in McCord, 1982) found that there was no relationship between 'broken homes' and crime for middle-class children, suggesting that the relationship might not be as clear-cut. More recent reviews (eg Smith and Farrington, 2004: 232) report that in general the evidence to support this theory is consistent and strong, citing several studies that have found links between parents, their socialization practices and offending by their offspring.

Intergenerational Exposure to Risk

The geographical concentration of lower socio-economic groups in the sorts of areas with multiple risk factors which endure over time, and which would tend to produce generations of offenders, is another explanation for the strong relationship between parental and child offending. In this explanation, the intergenerational transmission of offending is simply part and parcel of a much wider process of deprivation and marginalization. Disadvantages in terms of poor educational provision, poverty, and disrupted neighbourhoods are more likely to lead to offending, and, given the geographical and social concentration of these problems and generations of the same families, the intergenerational transmission is therefore somewhat spurious. Nagin *et al* (1997) found that for the children of young (ie under age twenty-one) mothers, poor or deprived resources appeared to be one of the best explanations of offspring involvement in crime (along with poor parenting, from which it could not be fully assessed independently as the two models are very close to one another). On the other hand, using the same data set, Rowe and Farrington (1997) found that there was little evidence of a family environment effect when they explored the familial transmission of offending across two generations. We explore these issues in greater detail in Chapter Seven.

The Imitation Thesis

A further explanation for the strong relationship between offending within families in general is that individuals within families tend to imitate one another. Support for this thesis is clear amongst siblings (Rowe and Farrington, 1997), but the same data set failed to find any convincing evidence that imitation worked between generations (West and Farrington, 1973).

Bias in Criminal Justice Operations

Finally, the relationship between parental offending and the offending of their offspring could be caused by biases known to exist within the criminal justice system. The habit of 'rounding up the usual suspects' might extend from known (or suspected) offenders to their offspring, hence yielding a strong relationship between fathers and sons, for example, via the prejudices of the police, especially prior to the twentieth century when detective methods seldom strayed from questioning all strangers and all known offenders (Cox, 2006). However, current thinking (eg Farrington, 2002: 671) is against this possibility. When examined in detail by West and Farrington (1973) the confluence of convictions of fathers and sons owed much to their tendency to offend more than the operation of any police bias.

Explaining Intergenerational Patterns of Offending: Structural Explanations

Another tradition in the investigation of the relationship between parental and child behaviours has focused on the structural factors that may influence offending. Hagan (1988) outlines a power-control theory of class relations in the family and the delinquency of the children of that family. Hagan argues that one of the most immediately recognizable consequences of industrialization was the movement of production out of the household (1988: 163). This shift saw men, older male children and often also older female children starting to need work outside the home in order to contribute to the household income, whilst mothers predominantly remained tied to the domestic space. This emerging social trend created not just a social and physical separation from the world of work for women (and led to the creation of a women's sphere of operation in the form of child and home care) but also created an *ideological separation* from the world of work. Adult males became 'breadwinners' associated with production and public life, whilst adult women became proto-housewives associated with consumption and domesticity (Laslett, 1983; Hall, 1992; Davidoff and Hall, 1987; Lown, 1990). Of course, with this came a reorganization of power within families and consequently of the informal social control exerted over family members. Hagan argues (1988: 166) that patriarchal families (ie those in which the adult male worked outside the home and the adult female was preoccupied with the domestic sphere) reproduce this gender divide through a gendered-division in the control of their children. This operated such that female children were socialized and controlled to become risk-averse (since risk-taking is the antithesis of domesticity) and as such were less likely to become delinquent (Godfrey 2004: 21–41).

On the other hand, male children experienced lower levels of control in this manner, and hence were more likely to develop preferences for risk-taking and hence become delinquent. In contrast to this, argues Hagan, were more egalitarian families (ie those in which both parents worked and experienced similar levels of authority at work, the male experienced no authority at work and the female derived authority at home, or those that were headed by lone females). Egalitarian households were less concerned with reproducing female domesticity, and as such produced daughters whose experiences of informal social control were similar to that of their brothers, leading to similar levels of delinquency between the genders.

Using Canadian data from the late 1970s, Hagan does indeed find that in patriarchal families mothers are more involved in the control of the children than are fathers, and moreover that mothers, more than fathers, exercise more restrictive control of their daughters than their sons (1988: 191). The exhaustive data analyses reported by Hagan find general support for his thesis.

Another structural model of family processes and patterns of offending is provided by Sampson and Laub (1994). Sampson and Laub argue that there are direct relationships between overly-harsh discipline and lack of supervision on the part of parents and the delinquency of their children. Such parenting often leads to the breaking of bonds of respect and trust between parents and children, making subsequent child rearing all the harder. However, over and above these factors (which are essentially individual-level processes) Sampson and Laub cite more structural influences, such as family poverty and community disadvantage as further encouraging childhood delinquency. They cite Rutter and Giller (1983: 185) who report that 'serious socio-economic disadvantage has an adverse effect on the parents, such that parental disorders and difficulties are more likely to develop and good parenting is impeded'. Communities that are disadvantaged, in short, do not allow good parenting the chance to develop: parents are either under too much stress themselves and are less well resourced than (for example) middle class households. Such circumstances help to perpetuate delinquency as poor parenting is itself associated with anti-social behaviour and leads to a diminishing of the parents' ability to control their children.

Using data on males born between 1924 and 1935 in Boston, Sampson and Laub (1994) find support for their theoretical model. They conclude by arguing that 'poverty appears to inhibit the capacity of families to achieve informal social control, which in turns increases the likelihood of adolescent delinquency' (1994: 538). Furthermore they argue that by focusing their interest in the structural factors as well as the direct causes, they are able to uncover the role played by poverty in mediating the relationship between parenting style and childhood delinquency.

Summary of the Literature

Where, then, does this leave us with regards to the various explanations of the intergenerational transmission of offending? With regards to the individual-level factors, it would appear that there are three explanations that we can discount almost immediately. The 'imitation thesis' and the suggestion that biases in the criminal justice system would appear to be unsupported by the available evidence. The suggestion that biological or genetic factors are the cause of the relationship also appears dubious to us, partly because of the small sample size of some of the studies employed. There is some (albeit patchy) evidence that intergenerational exposures to risk may be operating as suggested, however, as Nagin *et al*'s (1997) work suggests, this is mediated by the formation of the family and its ability to protect itself from the risks posed to it and its members. There appears to be a good level of support for the suggestion that individuals select partners who are like themselves, and that this leads to children who are genetically similar to their children. The style of parenting and socialization practices has, of late, faired well in the various assessments of it.

Turning to the structural factors, it is clear from Hagan's work that the make-up of families and their relationship to wider social forms influences not just whether children from any one family offend, but also which children are most likely to do so. Hagan's work embeds the family in wider social, economic and historical processes and highlights the role of such factors in influencing delinquency and crime across generations of the same family. Although not inspired by the same Marxian framework as Hagan,

Sampson and Laub highlight the role of both structural factors and individual/family level processes in determining childhood offending. Their model, which draws together community, family and individual factors also seeks to embed families within wider socio-economic processes.

Methodological Considerations in Generation Studies

There are a number of issues of a distinctly methodological nature that require comment. Smith and Farrington have noted that there are few studies of the intergenerational transmission of offending that have relied upon self-reported data (2004: 231). This is partly because of the difficulties and costs associated with maintaining contact and cooperation with respondents (Smith and Farrington, 2004: 231). Hence very few studies manage more than about twenty years of data (Smith and Farrington, 2004: 231). In addition, few studies have considered more than three generations of families. There are again understandable reasons for this. Respondents can become fatigued by repeated interviews over the course of several years, not to mention the decades that are required to investigate intergenerational aspects of human life. In addition, longitudinal research is still a relatively recent development in criminology (there were few longitudinal projects prior to the end of the Second World War, for example), and so criminologists have not had the time in which to develop such data sets.

However, there are a number of qualities to which intergenerational studies ought to aim. Smith and Farrington (2004: 232) suggest that researchers ought to aim for the following: two or more generations at comparable points in the life span; comparable and valid measurement across generations; correct temporal ordering between causes and effects; and multi-agent measurement. Therefore the data set that we collected is in a position to be able to address some of the deficiencies experienced by existing data sets. Naturally enough, it also has some limitations. Here we outline what we perceive to be our study's strengths and limitations. We start with the limitations.

Because of the time that has elapsed since our subjects were alive and offending, our data set is limited to only those offences that appeared in the Petty Sessions Court at Crewe. We are not limited to convictions, however, since we also recorded cases that were dismissed (6.5% of total cases); withdrawn or settled out of court (10%); cautioned (0.5%); and those cases (0.7%) that were committed for trial at higher courts (Quarter Sessions or Assizes). In addition to this there were a number of court actions or decisions which to a modern researcher do not have the feel of 'crimes': proceedings for suicide attempts or for 'lunacy' (632 cases or 1.3% of the total) and decisions over bastardy/maintenance arrears (1,698 cases or 3.5% of the total), for example, which society today no longer sees as criminal offences. There are also those structural biases that may have operated in ways that inhibited or disinclined some sections of society from reporting what they felt to be crimes.[1]

We rely on official and quasi-official data for not just our measurement of offending and victimization, but also for our measures of other aspects of our subjects' lives. Where our sample members were living, with whom they lived and the nature of their employment are drawn from a range of data sets (the 1851, 1861, 1871, 1881, 1891 and 1901 censuses; newspaper reports of their appearances in the Crewe courts; and the records of their employment at the L&NWR Railway Works). Whilst this can provide us with a staggering array of information, we are unable to comment directly upon micro-processes such as spousal relationships, parenting styles, parent-child disciplining procedures and so on. Similarly, attitudinal data are also largely absent from our analyses. Also, we are unable to comment directly upon biological and genetic influences. Nevertheless, Sampson and Laub provide some compelling arguments against the influence of biological and genetic factors. They write (1993: 69):

We argue that parents who commit crimes and drink excessively are likely to use harsh discipline in an inconsistent manner or to be lax in disciplining their children. A central characteristic of deviant and criminal life styles is the rejection of restrictions and duties—especially those that involve planning, patience, and investment in the future [. . .]. Parenting is perhaps the most demanding of conventional roles, and we expect that deviance in the adult world will manifest itself in disrupted styles of child socialization.

---

[1] Domestic abuse, spousal rape (which in any case was not a crime in England and Wales until the case of *R v R* [1992] 1 AC 599, formalized in section 142 of the Criminal Justice and Public Order Act 1994) and many cases of child abuse are therefore likely to be under-represented in our data set. That said, there were numerous cases of domestic abuse brought to the attention of the magistrates in Crewe.

Namely, supervision and discipline will be haphazard or nonexistent, and the parent-child/child-parent attachments will be tenuous. *According to this conceptualization, there is little, if any, need to introduce biological theories of heredity if the direct effect of parental criminality on delinquency is null and instead is mediated by social processes of family functioning.* (Our emphasis added).

We are able to infer some of the processes of family functioning described above from court reports of cases of child neglect, failure to send children to school, or to have children vaccinated (in other words, evidence of neglectful parenting), and other structural level processes from census records, newspapers reports, employment records and petty sessions data.

There is a remarkably high level of residential stability within Crewe amongst our sample members (63% of Cohort A offenders lived for over thirty years in Crewe, over half of these were born and died in Crewe). Whilst moves of home *within* Crewe are common, and whilst some spend periods living away from Crewe, the vast majority of our sample members reside within Crewe for many years of their lives. Because all of our data comes from one locale, offenders and their brothers, sisters, sons and daughters, and so on, who left Crewe and who appeared in magistrates' courts outside of Crewe, were not recorded in our data set.

What, then, of our strengths? Because we have collected sixty-one years of data (from 1880 to 1940) we are able to explore intergenerational patterns of offending across more than the three generations that other studies have focused on. We have been able to trace the offending of: our persistent offenders in Cohort A (which in this chapter will be referred to as generation one or G1); their fathers and mothers (G0); the children of G1 (G2); and the grandchildren of G1 (G3). In some cases we have also been able to trace a fifth generation (G4).

Whilst official data inevitably contains some biases and is deficient at some levels, it ought to be remembered that self-reported data (the other main technique for assessing individual-level offending and victimization) also has certain biases associated with it. For example, many studies of the intergenerational patterns of offending have relied upon the respondent for information regarding the offending of proximal others (mothers, fathers and siblings). However, this is based on the assumption that the respondent is aware of the offending of these individuals. In the case of parents and offspring this is a reasonable assumption, but as some (Farrington *et al*, 2001: 592) have noted, more distant relatives (grandparents, aunts and uncles) may have offences about which the respondent is unaware. Over and above this, self-reported data can contain various omissions (deliberate or otherwise). There are also perennial biases in non-response.

Another problem associated with self-report studies (and also identified by Farrington *et al*, 2001: 592) concerns the issue of who was living with whom at various crucial points in the life course. The unravelling of the relationship between parents and the offending of their children is based on the assumption (again, not unreasonable) that they live together. However, family break-up and reformation is not uncommon and presents an array of potential influences on the child's offending. By tracing our sample members and their parents and offspring in seven censuses we have been able to assess the extent to which certain individuals were living together at various points in time.[2] Finally, unlike some of the more established longitudinal studies, we have not limited ourselves solely to male subjects, and are able therefore to consider female offenders and the patterns of offending associated with their offspring.

The Data Set and the Research Questions

To recap, our data set includes the offending patterns of all individuals who committed more than five offences between 1880 and 1940 and whose first offence was committed between 1880 and 1890. These individuals we refer to as Cohort A G1 (generation one). Because of the availability of the censuses for 1851, 1861 and 1871, we were in some cases able to identify the parents of these individuals (we refer to G1's parents as G0). The total number of offences committed by G0 was also recorded. The total number of offences by G2 individuals (ie the sons and daughters of G1) was similarly recorded. Due to technical constraints (namely the difficulties of identifying and isolating specific individuals after 1901, the last point at which census data is available at the individual level) we limited ourselves to only those G3 offenders who had committed

---

[2] When crimes were reported in the newspapers, we have been able to record the addresses of offenders between censuses. This has greatly assisted our determination of the composition of offenders' households.

more than five offences and whose G2 parents had also committed five or more offences. By using this dataset we were able to address a number of questions: To what extent was offending transmitted between generations of the same families living in Crewe between 1880–1940, and for how many generations? Were there differences in the rate of transmission conditioned by gender? Which life factors are in place when transmission occurs, and what disrupted transmission? We provide answers to these questions relying upon both quantitative and qualitative data analyses.

To what extent was persistent offending transmitted between generations of the same families living in Crewe between 1880–1940? We were able to trace the parents (G0) for sixty-eight of our 101 G1 offenders (see Table 5.1). In most cases (forty-one) these individuals were resident in Crewe for all of some of their lives. Some twenty-seven of our G1 offenders had parents who were residing outside of Crewe at the time of the 1861 and 1871 censuses.

In some cases we were able to infer that they had died by that time (given the age of G1 and the assumption that many G0s would not have lived beyond their seventieth birthdays). However, in the majority of G1 cases where we could not identify G0, this was because, despite searching the censuses it was impossible to identify their parentage with any degree of accuracy.

Given that all of our G1s were persistent offenders who had committed at least five offences, we explored not merely whether there was a transmission of offending behaviour from G0 to G1, but also whether there was a transmission of 'persistent' offending (Table 5.2).

As can be seen from Table 5.2, of the thirty G1s who committed between five and ten offences, twenty-two (73%) had parents who

Table 5.1   Offending amongst G0s.

	No.	%
Found: Non-offender	27	26
Found: Offender	14	14
Found: Not living in Crewe	27	27
SUBTOTAL FOUND	68	67
Dead by 1861 or Not Found	33	33
TOTAL	101	100

Table 5.2 Patterns of offending G0 and G1.

G0	Non-offender	Offender	Total
G1			
5–10 Offences	22 (73)	8 (27)	30 (100)
>10 Offences	4 (40)	6 (60)	10 (100)
Total	26 (65)	14 (35)	40 (100)

All figures are no. (row %). Chi sq = .056.

Table 5.3 Sons, daughters (G2) and offending.

	No.	%
G1 had a son	28	28
G1 son was an offender	16	57
G1 had a daughter	34	34
G1 daughter was an offender	11	33

were non-offenders, whilst eight were the children of offenders. On the other hand, of the ten G1 offenders who committed more than eleven offences, four had non-offending parents, whilst six had offending parents. Despite the clear evidence that amongst our sample persistent offenders were more likely to have had offending parents, these differences did not reach statistical significance (in any case, due to small expected cell sizes which in one case fell below five, the findings would have to be treated with extreme caution).

Let us now turn our attention to the sons and daughters of G1 persistent offenders (G2s). There were thirty-four G1 cases who had children who offended at least once. Table 5.3 reports descriptive data on sons and daughters and their offending. As can be seen from Table 5.3, twenty-eight G1 members had at least one son, of which sixteen had at least one son who was found guilty of at least one offence. When female G2s are considered, despite there being more G1s with female G2s (thirty-four) far fewer (eleven, 33%) were found guilty of an offence.

Excluding nieces and nephews who lived with G1 offenders for some period of their lives (a smattering of cases) in all there were 318 G2 individuals (165 being female and 153 male). Of these, the vast majority (77%) were not found guilty of any offences (see Table 5.4).

Table 5.4   Amount of offending amongst G2s.

	No.	%
No offences	244	77
One	24	8
Two to Four	25	9
Five or more	16	3
SUBTOTAL IDENTIFIED	309	98
Impossible to identify	9	2
TOTAL	318	100

Only sixteen G2s were found guilty of five or more offences at court. In all, G2 accounted for 263 offences, 186 (71%) of them being committed by the sixteen persistent offenders who had been found guilty of five or more crimes. Of these sixteen, only one (Andrew Nolde) had a child (John, G3) who had been found guilty of more than five offences. None of the G3 persistents had their own children who committed more than four offences. Hence, when persistent offending is the object of the enquiry, intergenerational transmission does not appear to be that common, or at least not amongst offenders between 1880 and 1940.

As noted above, there were thirty-four G1 offenders who had G2 sons or daughters who offended. In this section we report on the analyses of the processes by which offending was transmitted. These analyses entailed a reading of each G1 offender's life history (as documented amongst the 1861–1901 censuses, court reports, newspaper trial reports, employment records for those who worked at the railway Works, and other records) and attempting to extract the crucial episodes and processes that either led to transmission or inhibited it. Table 5.5 reports on the reasons for transmission as gleaned from the life histories.

The explanations are not necessarily exclusive, as some G1 persistent offenders had more than one son or daughter who offended and the reasons for this may have been different (hence the total does not sum to thirty). In Table 5.5 the codes relate to the causes of G2 offending. In six cases, the father and child worked in the same trade, and their business practices were strongly related to their offending (see below). In another six cases it appeared that the parent was struggling to cope with looking after a large number of

Table 5.5   Reasons for transmission (G1 to G2).

	No.	%
G2 of impressionable age (5–10)	9	19
G1 and G2 both violent	4	8
G1 and G2 in same trade	6	13
Too many children to control	6	13
G2 engaged in G1's offending	6	13
Poor parenting	9	19
Coincidental	6	13
Transmission unclear	2	3
TOTAL	48	100

children (five or more). Often this followed the bereavement of G1's spouse (see Chapter Four). In some cases it was clear that G2 had been encouraged or coerced into offending by their parent(s). Instances of poor parenting were inferred from the life histories, and included a range of evidence from G1 James Newlands who neglected to vaccinate his G2 son Joseph to G1 Wilbur Boswell whose fifteen-year-old daughter was found soliciting. It was reported that Wilbur had no idea where his daughter was residing at the time.

In some cases the offending of G1s and G2s appeared not to be related to one another in any way. Take for example the case of Cyril Long (G1) and his son Arthur (G2). Cyril racked up eleven convictions between 1888 and 1899, after which he committed no further offences. One of these offences (in 1892) was for not sending Arthur to school when he was thirteen years old, the others being for Arthur's brothers and sisters. Arthur was convicted just once during his lifetime—in 1905 for a chimney fire. It is hard how to see how the two episodes are directly related to one another. A similar case concerns another Cyril, this time Cyril Eastman (G1), who was found guilty of sixteen offences ranging from theft from a young girl when he was aged eleven years old to assaulting a police office and damaging his uniform whilst drunk at the age of thirty. His son, Jeremiah (G2) was convicted of theft in 1914 when he was aged seventeen and again in 1937 (aged forty) for riding a bicycle without a light. This too was unconnected to the offending of his father, since his father had left the family home in 1905, when Jeremiah was eight years old. Below we explore particular case studies in greater detail.

Case Studies of the Intergenerational Transmission of Offending

Transmission through Business Ownership

Edwin Basing was born in Ireland in 1844. We found the first trace of him living in England in the 1861 census, when he was living with his brother Michael and his family in Whitchurch, Shropshire. Edwin was working as a marine store dealer at that time. In 1868 Edwin married Hilary Russell in Nantwich (the town adjacent to Crewe). Their first son (John, G2) was born in 1870, and they had ten further children at roughly two-yearly intervals thereafter until 1889.

The 1871 census recorded Edwin living with his wife and son John in the High Street, Sandbach (again, near Crewe), and working as a general store dealer. By 1880 his family had increased (Ernest, b. 1872, Marian, b. 1874, Joseph, b. 1876, Alice, b. 1878 and Trevor, b. 1880) and he had moved to Crewe. At this point we find him first recorded in the Crewe petty sessions, when he was convicted for having unjust weights and measures in his store in Market Street. The 1881 census had him living in Market Street and working as a general store dealer. Two further sons (Frank, b. 1883 and Graeme, b. 1885) and a daughter (Florence, b. 1886) followed, and in 1887 Ernest (G1) was found guilty of receiving stolen brass from Richard Massey (a boy who was then sent to reform school) and of having an unmuzzled dog. He was again listed as a marine store dealer. In 1888 his fourth daughter (Dora) was born and he and his dog were back in court—this time for a Rabies Order. 1889 saw the birth of Jemima (his fifth daughter), and in 1890 he and his dog were yet again in trouble (again a Rabies Order was made).[3]

In 1891 the census listed him as a general dealer living at 74–6 Market Street and the 1892 *Crewe Street Directory* listed him as a draper in Market Street. 1896 saw Edwin's wife Hilary (G1) in court for assaulting Gerry Nott. In 1900 Graeme (Edwin's son) was convicted of throwing snowballs, and Edwin (G1) died that year aged fifty-seven.

In the following year's census Hilary was listed as a widow working as a draper, shopkeeper and milliner at 74 Market Street.

---

[3] There were a number of acts passed to attempt to prohibit rabies spreading throughout the UK. People who fell foul of this legislation could be dealt with in the magistrates' courts. Britain has been rabies-free since 1922.

All of their children except John were living at the same address, and Ernest (G2) was listed as a general dealer. 1901 also saw Hilary convicted of two accounts of purchasing lead in less quantity than was authorized by law.[4] She also appeared before the magistrates for failing to pay her General Domestic Rate (the historical equivalent of the Community Charge).

A few years rolled on by: Graeme, G2, was convicted of riding a bicycle without lights, Hilary again failed to pay her General Domestic and Water Rates, the family dog was back in trouble for being 'dangerous' and an order was made for it to be destroyed. After Hilary died in 1904, Trevor (G2) advertised himself in the *Crewe Chronicle* (21 May, 1904) as a 'Bone, Fat and Skin Merchant' in Bright Street, and he was successfully prosecuted for his failure to abate a nuisance due to the awful smell at his business address. The *Crewe Chronicle* of 21 May 1904 reported that his yard 'was full of maggots', and that 'it was a trade that the young man had been brought up into'.

In 1905 Frank (G2) was found guilty of not paying his General Domestic Rate and in 1906 he was also convicted of cruelty to animals, not paying the Poor Rate, Water Rate and General Domestic Rate. He also allowed his horses to stray. In 1909 it was Graeme's turn (G2) to appear before the magistrates—this time for obstructing a footpath (which usually meant a poorly parked cart, or that goods for sale were spilling onto the street). Things settled down for a few years, and it was not until 1916 that Graeme (G2) was back in court for a breach of the Public Health Act. The case is brought by the Inspector of Nuisances, Mr. Richard Henry Lewis. Graeme was listed as a marine store dealer in Earle Street. It was a further ten years before Graeme was in trouble again. In 1926 he was found guilty of two charges: buying old iron from an under-sixteen-year-old and failing to keep a record of such purchase. In 1927 Graeme's own son (G3) was found guilty of receiving stolen goods.

In all, of (G1) Edwin's ten children three were persistent offenders. These three (Trevor, Frank and Graeme) appear to have been the most heavily involved in the running of the family business

---

[4] This was an offence which was drawn up to make the sale of small quantities of lead illegal. This was an attempt to make the small-scale theft of lead from roofs and guttering less attractive.

(a mix of general store dealing and rag and bone trade). Ernest (G2) seems initially to have joined the family business too, but he does not appear in court for any offences and we cannot trace him past 1901. Another son, Joseph, was listed as a medical student in the 1901 census, suggesting that he probably escaped the rigours of the family business. None of Edwin's daughters appeared to have offended (cf Hagan, 1988). Interestingly, Hilary's offending appeared to be related to the firm too—purchasing lead and the keeping of a yard dog to guard the premises being typical of this line of work. She, of course, was only convicted for these offences between the death of her husband and the family business passing to her sons. In this way, then, the intergenerational transmission of offending was partly the transmission of control of slovenly-run businesses and the continuation of some 'shady' practices. Those who were not eligible for employment in the family business, such as female children and younger sons (John, Ernest and Joseph) who would have had to start their own businesses before their father died, avoided 'inheriting' his dubiously-run firm. This is confirmed by the fact that it was Graeme and Frank's sons who inherited the business and also became involved in illegal trade practices.

Another case involving the passing on of a business or business knowledge involved James Newlands (G1) and his son Andrew (G2). James was born in 1835 in Middlewich. In 1855 he married Alice Carpenter and they begin to start a family (Wallace, b. 1857, Molly, b. 1859, Andrew, b. 1861, Margaret, b. 1865, James, b. 1867, Carl, b. 1869, Joseph, b. 1871, Arnold, b. 1873, Stephen, b. 1874 and Lillian, b. 1876). In the 1861 and 1871 censuses James (G1) and his family were shown as living in Warmingham (a village near Crewe) where he worked as a butcher. In 1879 James' daughter Margaret died, followed by his wife and son James in 1880. This year saw the first of his fifty-two convictions (for smoking in the Market Hall in Crewe). In 1881 the census listed him as living at 13 White Lion Lane in Crewe, and from 1882 he was persistently convicted each year until 1893 for being drunk. In 1888, for example, he was before the magistrates seven times, whilst in 1889 he was there eleven times. In 1890 he received eight convictions for drunkenness.

His son Andrew (G2 persistent) along with his brothers Joseph and Stephen, became a butcher, and being the eldest son, appeared to inherit his father's business. In 1881 Andrew, then aged twenty, lived with his father in White Lion Lane and was described as a butcher, whilst Joseph and Stephen were respectively eleven and eight years old. Joseph and Stephen eventually opened a butcher's shop together at 171 Ford Lane.

We can only identify for certain that Andrew (G2) came before the magistrates. Both his brother and his son were called Joseph and both could be before the magistrates for what look like offences that could be related to their work (being drunk in charge of a cart and driving a horse and trap furiously). However, what we can say for certain is that in 1883 Andrew (G2) was convicted for selling diseased meat. He was then convicted in 1897 for failing to pay his Water Rates and his Poor Rate. In 1901 (when he was again listed as a butcher in the census) he was found guilty of being drunk in charge of a horse and cart in Earle Street and for not sending his son Joseph (G3) to school. He was convicted of straying cattle once in 1902 and twice in 1905 (the year his wife Emma, died). He was convicted of neglecting to vaccinate Joseph in 1906 and of furious driving in Middlewich in 1910; and 1917 saw a further conviction for allowing a horse to stray. He died in 1935.

James Newlands (G1) seems to have started to drink after the death of his wife and children in the late 1870s and early 1880s. The vast majority of his convictions were for drunkenness (with the odd one or two for failing to send his children to school or assaulting his sister-in-law). Importantly, none were for public health or for keeping unclean stalls, yards etc. His offending appears to have been as a result of his personal tragedy. Andrew (G2), however, appears to have been convicted of offences relating to his line of work. From the start of his career (he is twenty when convicted for selling diseased meat) until near the end of it (he was sixty when convicted of malicious damage to the pasture fields) he appeared to have been a somewhat careless butcher (the cattle in his care stray frequently). We interpret this as signs not simply of the transmission of offending between father and son, but rather the failure to transmit good practice in the butchery trade between father and son. This process, we contend, was disrupted because James (G1) was in all probability too drunk or hungover to either be at work, or to teach Andrew (G2) the ways of the trade.

The Precedence of Parental Offending?

Most of the literature in this field, quite reasonably, makes the assumption that G1 offending precedes temporally and therefore causally G2's offending. The case of Edith Munty, however, demonstrates the ways in which G2 offending can precede G1's offending. This case study also demonstrates the importance of sudden events in the initiation of offending careers and the salience in the timing of such events in the lives of young men and women. Edith Munty (G1, née Mountjoy) was born in Antrim, Ireland in 1849. In 1861 she was living in Durham with her parents and her brothers and sisters. We are not sure when, where or how they met, but in 1871 Edith married James Munty in Crewe. James was a soldier who was barracked in several towns in England and further afield, and it could be that they met in Durham. Alternatively, given that they were married in Crewe and that the 1871 census lists Edith as living with her parents-in-law in Crewe, it could be that Edith and her parents moved to Crewe between 1861 and 1871 (her father was a locomotive fireman, and so may have moved his family to Crewe in search of work, or have been transferred from another company location). In 1874 Edith and James had their first child (Wilbur) in Chatham, Kent. A second son (James) was born in 1878 in Faisalabad (which produced some interesting spellings by census enumerators, and by 1891 James was listed as simply being born in 'York'). In 1880, a third son (Ernest) was born in Devonport, Devon, and the 1881 census listed the whole family as living at the New Infantry Barracks, York, where James (G1) was a Private. 1882 saw the birth of their last child (Margaret, born in York). In September 1883 James (G1) died in Birkenhead. From here, the family's fortunes took a distinct turn for the worse. They appear to return to Crewe, for in 1884 the eldest son (Wilbur, G2, now aged ten) was charged in Crewe for threatening co-lodgers with a stick. Three years later, Wilbur (G2) was birched for larceny and in 1889 James (G2, then aged eleven) was birched six strokes for stealing a jacket. In 1890 Wilbur (G2) was convicted of being drunk in West Street on two occasions. He was listed in the petty sessions records as living in Ford Lane, which is supported by the fact that in the 1891 census, he is not listed as living with Edith.

Until this point, Edith had not been convicted of any crimes in Crewe (nor had her by now late husband James). Both Edith and James appeared to have spent significant periods of their lives in Crewe and so it seems likely that had they been prosecuted, they would have been prosecuted in Crewe. However, in 1897, Edith made the first of her appearances in court at Crewe. She was convicted twice for being drunk on the High Street, and stated that she was having trouble with her children and that this is why she was drunk. In 1899 she was convicted for being drunk on Oak Street (a street notorious at that time for lodging houses, pubs, and drunken behaviour). In 1900, James (G2) spends fourteen days in Stafford prison for stealing 60lbs of lead from Edwin Heath (a Cohort A persistent offender). He later spent a further fourteen days in the same prison for the theft of an iron mattock (pick-axe). He rounded off the year by being convicted for drunkenness.

Edith (G1) does not appear in the 1901 census, but we know that she was still resident in Crewe as she appeared in court for being drunk and disorderly in Market Street and for being vagrant in Sandon Street in that year. (Her daughter, Margaret, G2, was in service in Chester according to the census). In 1902, Edith (G1) was convicted of wilful damage to a glass window belonging to Elly Jones (her sister-in-law). In this same year, James (G2) was convicted with Ellie Oldfield (Cohort A offender) for the larceny of £20 from Elizabeth Haslop (the daughter of a lodging house keeper who rented rooms to many Cohort A and B offenders). In 1903, Edith (G1) was drunk in Sandon Street. This was her last conviction before she died in 1906. Both of her sons Wilbur and James were convicted in 1903. James was convicted for breaking a window, whilst Wilbur was convicted for being drunk and disorderly in Market Street and for aiding and abetting prostitution in Middlewich Street (the girl involved, Molly Blake, was sent to Miss Wright's Rescue Home in Chester).[5] In 1905 both brothers were convicted for being drunk in the Egerton Arms, Nantwich Road. James' last convictions occur in 1906 when he was found guilty of the larceny of 50lbs of lead, and received three months' hard labour in Stafford prison, and, finally, in 1914 when he was found guilty of being drunk and disorderly in Mill Street. We can find no trace of him after this. Similarly, Wilbur's last conviction (for being drunk on licensed premises) also occurred in 1906, and again we can find no trace of him thereafter.

Edith's offending appears to commence with the death of her husband in 1883. Thereafter the two eldest boys (Wilbur, aged nine at the time of his father's death and James, aged five) are repeatedly in trouble. The two youngest children, Ernest (aged three when his father died) and Margaret (about one at that time) do not appear in

---

[5] Miss Wright was subsequently appointed a probation officer.

court. We believe that Edith, through no fault of her own, was simply unable to cope with looking after all four children. With a babe-in-arms and a toddler she would have been hard-pushed to care for Wilbur and James too. Unsupervised as they probably were, they appear to have become involved in petty offending (a ten-year-old threatening adults with a stick is hardly a serious threat) which escalated into more serious and sustained offending (theft and drinking). Edith appears to have followed her sons into crime, becoming a drunk in the last ten years of her life—a period when her two youngest children (Ernest, aged seventeen and Margaret, aged fifteen) may have left home, Margaret to go into service and Ernest to we know-not-where. The transmission of offending between generations of the same family would appear to be, in Edith's case, the transmission of misfortune (James' death) and to vary for subsequent generations in terms of the outcomes. The variations in outcomes appears to us to be age-graded—when such events take place in the timing of a life is as important as whether or not they occur at all.

What are the Processes by which Transmission was Disrupted?

Why did the social transmission of criminality not take place? Finding the answer to these questions again entailed a reading of each G1 offender's life history (as documented amongst the 1861–1901 censuses, court reports, newspaper trial reports, employment records for those who worked at the railway Works, and other records) and attempting to extract the crucial episodes and processes that inhibited transmission. Table 5.6 reports on the reasons why transmission did not occur as gleaned from the life histories.

Again, most of these codes are readily understandable; however, we shall explain a few of the more unusual ones. In five cases G1's offending was over by the time that G2 had been born, or at least by the time of their fifth birthday. In some cases, G1's offending was either at the very end of their lives and associated with an illness (infirmity due to old-age which resulted in failures to pay rates, for example) or occurred after the child was fifteen years old, and as such may have been less under the influence of their parents. Sometimes G1's offending was due to a specific event (such as the

Table 5.6   Reasons for non-transmission (G1 to G2).

	No.	%
G1 offending is employment related	10	22
G1 offending is alcohol related	7	15
G1 offends before G2 birth/5th year	6	13
G1 offending related to a specific event	6	13
G1 offends towards end of life/G2 child over 15yrs when G1 offending starts	4	9
G1 does not live with G2	3	6
G2 escapes poor background	3	6
G1 offending is Ed Act only	2	4
Influence of 'good' G1 parent	1	2
Unclear why not transmitted	4	9
TOTAL Responses	46	99

death of a spouse which was then associated with a brief period of drunkenness before a return to a non-offending life style). In two cases, G1 and G2 did not live together, hence there was little opportunity for the transmission of values associated with offending, of if they did, this was rectified by the influence of a better G1 role model. In three cases the G2 individuals managed to escape the poor circumstances of their parents. Nine G1 persistent offenders failed to pass on their offending to their children as their offending was related to their line of work, and their children either pursued other lines of work or were girls who 'married out' of the family (and perhaps the offending environment) (cf Hagan, 1988).

In seven cases it appeared that G1's offending did not lead on to G2 offending as G1's offending appeared to be related exclusively to drunkenness (either recreationally or as an alcoholic). This may have had a number of effects on children: they may have been largely absent from their lives or they may have become such an obviously poor role model that the G2 children turned their backs on their parents.

Case Studies of the Intergenerational Non-transmission of Offending

In this section we explore some of the ways in which offending was not transmitted between G1 and G2. Some of these case studies are relatively short, reflecting the lack of offending by G2 sons and daughters.

The Death of a Spouse

Six G1 persistent offenders experienced isolated events which led to their offending. In almost all cases these related to the death of the spouse. In Chapter Four we described the life and offending history of Horace Higgsworthy, whose offences of drunkenness appear to have been attributable to the grief he experienced after the death of his first wife. Unlike James Newlands (see above) who also lost his wife, Horace seems to have been able to eventually regain control over his drinking, or to limit his drinking to his home environment, where it was not so problematic for society. The part played by his second wife in his offending can only be guessed at, but nevertheless, his offending is limited to drunkenness for around six years, and seems not to have influenced his children at all.

The Good and Bad Influences of Parents?

The life events and offending history of Elspeth Georgina Bispham were described in Chapter Three. It was only possible to trace her son, Rowan, in the censuses (her daughters may have moved out of Crewe and married outside of the area). Indeed, Rowan also married out of the area (in Preston) in 1888, and in 1891 was working in Blackburn as a railway agent. His first wife died in 1892, but he remarried in 1895 and in 1901 was, according to the census, the Station Master at Blackburn (a very prestigious and well-paid job). It would appear that Rowan had managed to escape the rather dire circumstances that his upbringing had presented him with (a parental death at around age six years, relocation to a new town and a mother in reduced circumstances). It is noteworthy that like many who seek to leave troubled beginnings behind them, he moved away from the original sites of this trouble (Birkenhead and Crewe).

Two other G1 persistent offenders 'failed' to transmit their criminality to their G2 offspring in ways which emphasized the difficulties in researching this topic without the advantage of a density of qualitative data. In both of these cases, it appears that G2 represented a child with some difficult behaviour, the results of which were visited upon their parents. Jonathan Downmaker (G1) for example, was convicted six times for failing to send his child Toby (G2) to school between 1890 and 1893. Eventually Toby was sent to Bradwall Reformatory School, at which point Jonathan was also prosecuted for failing to pay for Toby's upkeep there. Jonathan himself had no other convictions and lived in Crewe from at least 1868 until his death (at the age of sixty-seven) in 1900. None of his other children (and there were five of them, two girls and three other sons) were in trouble with the courts at all. Toby returned to Crewe after his spell in Bradwall, and was working as an Iron Founder in 1901. He does not appear in the Crewe courts thereafter.

In another case it appeared that the influence of the father protected the children against the influence of the mother. Minnie Valler (née Dolan and also known as 'Slasher') was born in 1849. She married Christopher Valler (b. 1838), a platelayer for the railways, in 1870, and their first child (Catherine) was born in 1871. In 1872 Minnie was involved in a peculiar episode. It seems that a neighbour ran into Minnie's house screaming that her husband was trying to kill her. A police constable (probably not in uniform) arrived quickly and separated the couple who were now fighting in Minnie's back-yard. The constable fell over a ladder, trapping and breaking his leg. As soon as the resounding crack of his leg echoed around the yard, Minnie and the fighting couple ran into the house, only to emerge fifteen minutes later, and only then called a doctor. When the case came to court, Minnie alleged that her neighbour was in the habit of getting drunk and kissing men (including the attending police constable). It also appears that this constable stopped off on his beat at Minnie's house as well to 'light his pipe'.

The following year a second girl was born to Christopher and Minnie and in 1875 Minnie was found guilty of being drunk and disorderly. The case attracted the interest of the *Crewe Chronicle*, which reported that, in a raid on 'disorderly houses' (brothels) a police inspector 'found Annie Ball and Jessie Hoddle, who acted as her 'bully',[6] Minnie Valler, alias Slasher, Jerry Britol, and three children aged between three and eight on some rags in one corner of the room, altogether, and all undressed'. The newspaper noted that 'prostitutes from the potteries[7] came nearly every Friday and Saturday and stayed with the prisoners' causing 'great rows going on at night'. The inspector reported that he had been through some of the lowest places in London, Liverpool and Manchester, but he

---

[6] A man who protects or 'runs' a prostitute.

[7] The potteries are a collection of towns around the modern city of Stoke-on-Trent where pottery was manufactured.

had never seen anything so bad as that house in Blackberry Street. 'Minnie Valler', the article reported, 'was drunk on the kitchen floor with four men, who said they were there "for a bit of a game". It went on: 'There was no glass in any of the windows and they could not sleep for people throwing stones and bricks through the windows. The house was in a most beastly state and the stench was very bad. About six weeks previously, the prisoners lived at a house in Cross Street, and for two years had kept a brothel there'. Minnie was described as 'a prostitute', who said she was twenty-nine years of age, and her husband and children were then in Nantwich Workhouse. She said that she had supported them for some time by washing and charring. Neighbours, the *Crewe Chronicle* reported, 'could hardly sleep at night owing to the dreadful rows and quarrels going on between the men and women; shrieks of 'Murder!' and other cries were frequent. The language used was very obscene'. Jessie Hoddle and Annie Ball were subsequently committed to Quarter Sessions.

However, this was not the last time that Minnie was in trouble with the courts. The very year following (1876, in which her third child, Emily was born) she was charged with murder, although the charge was dismissed at the Assizes. It appeared that Minnie and Sarah Pound, the wife of a platelayer, were arguing over their children. The *Crewe Chronicle* again takes up the story: 'Minnie hit Sarah's child and the women tussled. They rolled over on the ground, and Pound never got up. Her face was black and foamed around her mouth. It seemed to have been a fit.' However, it was impossible to say with certainty that the fight had brought on Sarah Pound's fit and the Grand Jury threw it out.

Following this, Minnie's life settled down to one of drunkenness, vagrancy, and prostitution. This continued from 1887 until her death in 1889. During this time, her husband and family continued to live in Crewe with her and a further daughter (Emma, b. 1879) and two sons (Christopher, b. 1885 and Gerald, b. 1887) were born. Her vagrancy (associated with her prostitution) took place in many of Crewe's then more notorious streets (Cross Street, Mill Street, Oak Street, Edleston Road and High Street). Christopher (G2) appeared not to be involved in any of Minnie's offences (he is not referred to in any of the newspaper reports about Minnie and is never a co-accused with her). He appears in court only once: the year after Minnie's death he was found guilty of failing to send one of his children (probably Emma) to school. Christopher continued to work in Crewe as a railway labourer, and in 1891 was living with his two sons, whilst two of his daughters were in service. In 1901 he was living with his second daughter, Alice, who was married by now, and her family in Crewe. He died in 1913 with no further offences to his name.

It would appear that Christopher's avoidance of engagement in offending (as measured by criminal convictions) was a contributory factor in his children avoiding offending. Despite their mother's wayward behaviour, they appear to have been a close-knit family (Christopher lived with his family members in each census). This closeness, together with a good male role model, may have been sufficient to protect the children from engagement in crime (see Chapter Four for more discussion about the lives of prostitutes).

The Production of Heroes

In 1851 Bertrum Varleigh (b. 1838) was lodging with a butcher in Coventry. Between then and 1861 he appears to have married Lesley and become a watchmaker in Bath Street, Coventry. They had a child (Eleanor) in 1862, before his wife died in 1864. Two years later he remarried, this time to Ester Wilkie, and they moved to Hackney where they had children (Sally b. 1869; Bruce b. 1870; Ester b. 1872; Alice b. 1874). In 1881 Ester and all of the children were recorded as living in Coventry, but she describes herself as 'a widow'. There is no record that we could find of Bertrum dying between 1874 and 1881, but in 1884 a Bertrum Varleigh, born in Coventry, and of the right age, married Isabella Dorset in Crewe. At this time he seems to have added a second surname and was known as Bertrum Varleigh-Roberts, watchmaker, born in Coventry. Isabella gave birth to twins Harold and Jim in 1885. Under the name of Bertrum Varleigh-Roberts, his former name of Varleigh, and also as Bertrum Roberts, he was prosecuted for drunkenness twice in 1888; three times in 1889; and twice more again in 1890. Ester Varleigh is recorded as a widow living in Coventry with three children in 1891, and Bertrum is living alone (still recorded as married) in Audley Street (next door to extremely prolific offender Wilbur Boswell). He was now calling himself Bertrum Roberts. His wife joined him in the 1901 census living at the same Audley Street address. The twins, Jim and Harold were very active in the Sunday Schools and Methodist Church as youths, and both found employment at

Crewe Works after their father died in 1912. In the years immediately before the First World War they both trained as medical assistants in the Naval Reserve in their annual Works holidays. It was on one such training 'holiday' that war broke out, and the twins joined up as volunteers. They did not have a chance to return to Crewe before joining HMS *Formidable*, though they wrote letters of explanation to their mother (remembering to reassure her that they had managed to keep attending church services). HMS *Formidable* was sunk by a torpedo within weeks and the boys were found washed up on the beach near Lyme Regis, wrapped in each other's arms. This was not only a personal tragedy, but had a huge impact on the town of Crewe. The boys received a large funeral procession, lead by a colour-sergeant, and thousands of the town's population attended (see Potts and Marks, 2004).

Their father went under a few different names, may have had a bigamous marriage, a problem with alcohol, and a concomitant number of criminal convictions, yet his sons are amongst Crewe's war heroes. The Varleigh-Roberts twins remain our starkest example of the production of 'good' children from difficult circumstances and a problematic parent.

Structural, Family, Parental and Individual-level Processes in the Reproduction of the Intergenerational Transmission of Offending

Of our 101 G1 persistent offenders, sixty-four had at least one child, making, in all 318 G2 children. An unfortunate effect of each family having more than one offspring, is that, in theory at least, most normal statistics are unsuitable for use with such data. This is because such statistics make a number of assumptions about the data at hand, including that observations about one case are independent of observations about another in the same data set. With siblings included in the data set, it is clear that the data about each is partly determined by the data about the other (in that they share certain characteristics by virtue of sharing the same parents). This situation violates the assumption of independence of observation (see Appendix A). A number of possible solutions to this problem exist:

First, one could select one G2 from each family and run analyses on these cases only. However, this reduced the sample size to around 64 and resulted in no statistically significant differences, something which we found surprising given the frequent findings that parental factors influence offspring's behaviour.

A second possible solution was to turn to Multi-Level Modelling (MLM). MLM allows one to explore relationships amongst variables in data sets such as ours in which cases are 'clustered' together by virtue of the fact that they share membership of a super-ordinate group (such as children in the same class at school, or employees in the same company).

An initial exploration of the data set suggested that there was, in fact, *no* family effect, and as such, the data were perfectly safe to use with ordinary tests of statistical significance (see Appendix B). In short, we were able to revert to basic analyses using all 318 G2 cases as if they were unrelated to one another. The assumption has still been violated, but to no effect. This is similar to a driver passing a red light at 3 a.m. when no one else is around: technically a crime has been committed, but with no ill-effects or detection.

From a series of crosstabulations, it appeared that a number of variables were related to offending amongst G2 (see Table 5.7 and

Table 5.7 Summary of crosstabulations of variables associated with G2 offending.

Variable	Category	Percent (no.) G2 offender	Statistical Sig
Gender of G2	female	7 (12)	***
	male	36 (53)	
G1 assault spouse	assaulter	44 (8)	*
	non-assaulter	20 (53)	
G1 convicted of Education Acts	convicted	26 (41)	*
	not convicted	19 (24)	
G1 from rural area	from rural	25 (44)	*
	not from rural	16 (21)	
G1 was violent	violent	26 (39)	*
	not violent	17 (26)	
No. G1 parents with alcohol problems	0	20 (22)	*
	1	19 (35)	
	2	44 (8)	
G2 gang member	gang member	92 (12)	***
	not gang member	8 (53)	
No. of family moves	0–1 family moves	24 (10)	*
	+2 family moves	14 (55)	

No. = 304–310. All tables based on 2 x 2 tables with 1 degree of freedom, except no. of parents with alcohol problems, which was a 3 x 2 table with 2 degrees of freedom. *p = <.05, ***p = <. 001.

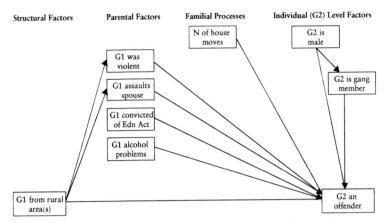

Structural Factors   Parental Factors   Familial Processes   Individual (G2) Level Factors

All paths have been explored using crosstabulation tables and were found to be significant at the 0.05 level or greater. See Table 5.7.

Fig. 5.1   A theoretical model of transmission of offending from G1 to G2: structural, parental, familial and individual-level processes.

pictorial representation in Fig. 5.1). This table, which summarizes a series of crosstabulation tables, suggests that if G1 had assaulted their spouse, been convicted of child regulation offences, grown up originally in a rural area or been violent, so their G2 offspring had an increased chance of being convicted. Similarly, if G2 was male or had joined a gang, these factors were associated with their being convicted. If G2 had two parents who had alcohol problems, so they too were more likely to be convicted.

These variables were entered into a logistic regression model, the output of which is summarized in Table 5.8. Our final model suggests that G2's gender, their active presence in gangs, their parents' rural origins and the number of home moves made by the family whilst living in Crewe were key in determining whether or not G2 was convicted. Males, those in gangs, those with parents who came from rural areas and those who lived in families which moved home frequently were more likely to be convicted. Our model therefore suggests that a number of levels of influence were at work in determining whether or not the offspring of persistent offenders were convicted themselves. Structural factors, here measured by whether or not G1 came from a rural or an urban area, influenced G2 offending. As the wider economy changed, leading to social

Table 5.8 Summary of logistics regression model of variables associated with G2 offending (all cases).

Variable	B	S.E.	Wald	DF	Sig
G1 from rural area	.693	.344	4.049	1	*
N of family moves	.845	.434	3.791	1	*
Gender of G2	1.897	.369	26.471	1	***
G2 gang member	3.996	1.117	12.792	1	***
Constant	1.477	2.344	.397	1	NS

No. of cases = 304. Corrected predicted cases: 82.2%, No. = 250.

changes amongst the population, which became increasingly urbanized, so the effects of this were felt amongst the children of persistent offenders. Persistent offenders who had migrated from a rural area were more likely to have children who would be convicted themselves (see Bourgois, 1996a and 1996b). Familial processes seem to be at work too. Families who made frequent changes of address were also likely to have children who would be convicted. At the individual level, G2's own gender and their involvement in gangs or not were also important variables in determining whether or not they were convicted.

Like others (eg Sampson and Laub, 1994; Hagan, 1988) we have developed a model which accounts for the transmission of persistent offending between two generations of the same family which draws upon both individual-level factors and family and structural level processes. What this suggests is that transmission is affected by, not simply, individual-level characteristics (such as some of those listed above at the start of the chapter), but is mediated and shaped by both changes at the societal level (ie the rapid social changes which were brought about and caused by the move from the countryside to the growing urban areas, such as Crewe). This drives us back towards historically-informed sociology models of transmission, and away from the models seemingly favoured by psychologists and psychiatrists. In line with other studies of the resilience of families over time, our data suggests that, in the long run, even families which have experienced quite severe traumas sustained over considerable periods of time have a remarkable capacity to 'come good' in the end (see also Elder and Pellerin, 1998).

From the children of all 101 G1 persistent offenders, sixteen were G2 persistent offenders. This represents a transmission rate from G1 persistence to any one G2 member being a persistent offender of 16%. These sixteen G2 persistent offenders had, in turn, three G3 persistent offenders, a transmission rate of about 19%. These analyses suggest that the rate of transmission did not change greatly between G1/G2 and G2/G3.

Conclusion

This study suggests that the transmission of intergenerational patterns of persistent criminality exists only in the short term and does not persist over longer periods of time. It would appear that in the late nineteenth and early twentieth centuries short term transmission was reasonably common, longer term transmission was a rarity—the commonly held belief that there are generations of people within 'criminal families' is erroneous.[8] No doubt offenders appearing in court who shared the same surname (which may be a local name, originating from a common occupation or geographical feature in the area) were often assumed to be related. However, whilst we had many offenders who appeared to be part of a large extended family, in fact, they were not related or not closely related. Instead, our data suggest that whilst patterns of persistent offending may exist over the short term within families, after the third generation this petered out considerably—or, as we summarized it in Chapter Three, there was a bubbling cauldron rather than a ripple effect.

Like the assumed transmission of other undesirable characteristics (eg marital discord, see Hetherington and Elmore, 2004) it would appear that at least in the late-nineteenth and early-twentieth centuries there was no 'automatic' transmission of persistent involvement in crime between parents, siblings and grandchildren. These processes are gendered, influenced by social structure and, in part, elective (in that some choose to join gangs). Certainly it would appear not to be a foregone conclusion that 'criminal' parents produced 'criminal offspring'; at least not for the period that we studied.

---

[8] Magistrates still routinely regard people with the same surname as being from the same extended family, see Cox and Godfrey, 2005, 71–2.

6

Victimization and Offending

Insufficient attention [has been] paid to the complexity of criminal victimization; all too often the use of the label 'victim' is underpinned by the assumption that it may only be applied to members of relatively powerless groups, or that it describes a state of being which itself induces powerlessness. [. . .] We have moved so far [from 'victim precipitation' theories] that victims are conceptualized as individuals who have no experience of crime as offenders.'

Newburn and Stanko, 1994: 153

Historical Research on Victims

When individual victims are mentioned in historical research, they are very much the supporting actors in case studies of offenders. Victims of crime in the bulk of historical research are an abstract group, providing not much more than a backdrop (Kearon and Godfrey, forthcoming). As George Rudé said in 1985, 'What do we know about the characters or attitudes of victims? The answer is very little' (Rudé 1985: 76). However, nineteenth-century victims of crime have been examined in studies of the use of the criminal law by particular social groups (King, 1984 and 2000; and Storch, 1975 and 1976), and also in research on domestic abuse and violence against children. There is also one aspect of historical research which does deal, if obliquely, with the victim/offender overlap—treating some offenders as victims of the criminal justice system—juvenile delinquents suffering cruelty and humiliation as part of the reformative process, for example (see Godfrey and Lawrence, 2005), or women alcoholics locked up in inebriates' homes forced to conform to a concept of femininity they could never adhere to (Morrison, 2005).

We hope to address head-on the victimization of our persistent offenders, and therefore add a new aspect to debates on the victim/offender overlap. We are aware, however, that our dataset only allows us to consider prosecuted crime, and this may under-represent the levels of victimization experienced by offenders. Below, we illustrate one example of this under-counting of victimization by reference to a murder committed in Crewe in 1890.

The Murder

At midnight on 25 January 1890, Richard Davies, aged fifty-one, a well-to-do tailor with premises in Victoria St, Crewe, was murdered on his way back home at Hough (some two miles away). His attackers had apparently stopped him and his two sons, Richard aged twenty, and George aged sixteen, brutally killed him using an axe (indeed he had been virtually decapitated). His sons reported the crime, but were arrested about a week afterwards, charged with parricide at Crewe magistrates' court, and committed to Chester Assizes for trial. There was considerable sympathy for the victim who had not had a cross word with anyone in the neighbourhood, and also for his wife, who would be compelled to testify against her own sons. The pathos was increased when the funeral procession passed through the spot where he was murdered en route to Haslington cemetery, and when mourners were forced to wait in the rain because the grave had been made too small.

The Factors that Emerged During Trial

The judge's notes for this case document the evidence presented in the trial.[1] We will not rehearse either the evidence or the cross-examination. However, it was clear that the boys had been responsible for killing their father (a heinous crime at any time; in the Victorian period only regicide was considered a worse crime). What also became clear during the case was that Richard Davies Senior had committed a number of cruel and violent acts against his own family, none of which had ever been reported to the police (or apparently even to neighbours and friends). His children, some of whom were very young, were compelled to work at their father's shops for seven days a week and were not permitted to take time off to attend church or Sunday School. The older boys worked very long hours (from 8 a.m. to 9.30 p.m.) and received board and

---

[1] HO144/541/A51374/1. We are grateful to Rachel Tilly for a copy of these notes. As this case received national publicity, we have not anonymized the names of the participants.

lodgings in return rather than wages—sometimes they worked so late that they slept at the shop rather than come home for a few hours' sleep before starting work early the next day. Richard Davies Senior always ate alone, and enjoyed better food than he allowed the family. His wife never reported domestic violence to the authorities, but disturbing stories emerged during the trial. On one occasion it was alleged that he had held a loaded revolver to her head threatening to kill her; on another occasion whilst drunk he had deliberately set fire to her nightdress—he was indeed 'a domestic tyrant of the worst kind' (*Daily News* 5 April 1890).

The Verdict and its Aftermath

After forty-five minutes of consideration, the jury brought in a verdict of guilty on both boys, but recommended mercy (ie that the sentence of death be respited and a lengthy prison sentence be served instead).[2] The plea for clemency was bolstered by a widespread public campaign (petitions, questions asked by the local MP, comment by local and national newspapers). For example, *The Daily News* of 5 April 1890 commented that 'It is scarcely possible that the Home Secretary can intend to leave these two boys to the gallows. The jury did their duty in finding them guilty of the wilful murder of their father, but they recommended them to mercy on grounds of their youth.'

The night before both boys were due to be executed, word was indeed received from the Home Secretary that George would be reprieved on grounds of his youth. He served a long period of imprisonment and afterwards emigrated to Australia. There was no reprieve for Richard, and he was hanged at eight o'clock the next morning.

The Unprosecuted Offender

The two boys and their mother were victims of crimes, but only ended up in courts as defendants and witnesses and never as complainants. There are vast numbers of offenders and therefore victims that never reach the courts (particularly with violence within the family, see Godfrey, 2003; D'Cruze, 1998; Stanko, 1985). Our research examines those that did end in court proceedings, but we are aware that there may be a high level of victim/offender

---

[2] It was common practice for the judge to take note of such directions—indeed prompt them—and for the Home Secretary then to consider each case on its merits.

relationships which cannot come to light because no official action was taken. This is similarly the case with revenge attacks and vigilantism which persistent offenders may have carried out or alternatively have been victims of. Storch stated that acceptance of the police as a legitimate force in working-class communities came when people realized they offered a better (or at least alternative) option for solving neighbourhood disputes (Storch 1975 and 1976). Out of all the people in Crewe, the police were least likely to help our persistent offenders, and therefore they may be over-represented in vigilantism (or more probably in disorganized ad hoc episodes of revenge). Even when the police *were* involved, there may be hidden acts of violence. For example, the eleven-year-old daughter of one of our persistent offenders, Peter Court, a man who had several convictions for violence and threatening behaviour (see Chapter Five), was raped by another of our persistent offenders, Joshua Tinker (see Chapter Two). We think it likely that Peter would have exacted some kind of physical justice for his daughter if the police had not caught up with Tinker first (or perhaps he did and Tinker never bothered to report it?). Oral history studies have tried to examine 'crimes' which never reached the courts (see Godfrey 2003), and other criminological researchers have also been important in developing this area, and the history of their efforts are described below.

A Brief History of Victimology[3]

At first glance, modern criminology, particularly victimology, would appear to have come a long way in the fifty or more years since von Hentig published *The Criminal and His Victim* in 1948. However, in another sense victimology appears *not* to have come very far at all. Despite realist and critical critiques of 'conventional' victimology; despite the introduction of concepts like repeat victim-ization into the debate; and despite the obvious policy-related interest; one is still left with the feeling that victimology has not yet fully got to grips with one of the most consistent findings in its own field: the overlap between 'offenders' and 'victims' (Walklate, 1992: 104, Fattah, 1993: 230–3). This situation has led Newburn and Stanko to conclude that 'in much recent victimological literature,

---

[3] This section draws upon Farrall and Maltby, 2003.

victims are characterized as helpless and vulnerable' (1994: 154). Recent research on the emotional responses to criminal victimization has suggested that victims may actually be less passive than previously thought (see Ditton *et al*, 1999).

'Conventional' victimology (as described by Walklate, 1992) was focussed upon the risks faced by various social groups, concepts such as 'proneness', 'precipitation', 'vulnerability' and 'attractiveness', and with the situations in which victimization might occur. This style of victimology suggested that incidents of victimization were fairly rare, and that lifestyles greatly influenced the extent to which an individual became victimized (eg Hindelang *et al*, 1978). The focus of the research at this time was very much on developing typologies of victims (and their lifestyles), the measurement and identification of 'victimizable' individuals, and to exploring public rather than private victimization (Walklate, 1992: 105–6). This research agenda left conventional victimology open to a number of criticisms, which have resulted in it having been attacked for the following: failing to consider the 'home' as a dangerous place; overlooking the possibility that gender and race were associated with increased victimization as a result of sexism or racism; failing to extend knowledge much beyond what could be gleaned from official statistics; and ignoring the reality of the experiences associated with victimization (see *inter alia* Newburn and Stanko, 1994; Stanko, 1988; and Walklate, 1992).

Whilst the victimology of the 1970s was fundamentally conservative, the victimology that emerged to challenge it was based on a broadly leftist political agenda. Left realism was a broad criminological enterprise which attempted to theorize from real-life situations and episodes (especially as women, the elderly and ethnic minorities experienced them). This entailed an 'accurate victimology' (Young, 1986: 23) that was to be produced via local crime surveys. Yet, as others have been at pains to point out, realist victimology was unable to escape from the worldview that 'victims' and 'offenders' are separate groups. So, despite coming from a more politically, epistemologically and methodologically informed position, the left realists did little better than those who had gone before them.

Ultimately, realist victimology may be remembered not for its accurate victimology (*sic*), but for its inability to: perceive men as victims; uncover in greater detail the experiences associated with victimization; or, accurately record the extent to which victims and offenders were the same individuals—in other words, for failing to get to grips with some of the complexities surrounding the victim/offender overlap. As Newburn and Stanko note (1994: 161) a fully realist victimology needs to acknowledge and explore the fact that there are not simply 'victims' *and* 'offenders', but rather people who are *both* victims and offenders.

Critical victimology, a more recent development, seems to be unclear over what the focus of its endeavours should be. Some, such as Miers (1990) and Holstein and Miller (1990) suggest that critical victimology should focus upon the ways in which labels such as 'victim' are applied, how such concepts are defined and who has the power to apply such labels. Sandra Walklate (Walklate, 1996, 1992; and Mawby and Walklate, 1994) proposes a different, but still 'critical' approach to exploring victimization. This was a call for empirically-based research, an integration of quantitative and qualitative methodologies, and comparative and longitudinal studies which are able to explore those social processes that 'go on behind peoples' backs' (1996). Such an endeavour would ultimately seek to understand how power relations impacted upon the victim/offender relationship, attempt to chart the extent of corporate crime, and explore the processes associated with victimization in such a way that their socio-economic and cultural contexts were acknowledged (Walklate, 1992, 1996). This represents a more useful set of ideals for approaching the exploration of victimization. However, like left realism, critical criminology also fails to refer to one of the most consistent findings produced by victimologists: the strong association between having offended and having been victimized. It is unclear why this should be the case. It would appear that whilst left realists and critical victimologists are content to accept that such a relationship *does* exist, this tremendously empirically and theoretically exciting observation remains virtually unresearched.

Offending, Victimization and Lifestyles

In recent years, a number of studies have started to undermine the belief that 'offenders' and 'victims' form distinct groups in society (see for example Singer, 1981; Fagan *et al*, 1987; and Lauritsen *et al*, 1991). Such studies, usually based on survey research, have suggested that engagement in offending behaviour is one of the strongest correlates of victimization and vice versa (Van Dijk and Steinmetz, 1983; Gottfredson, 1984; Hartless et al, 1995; and Ballintyne, 1999).[4] Such research has produced a number of salient findings. For example, that violent offenders are the most likely to experience violent victimization (Singer, 1981; Fagan et al, 1987; O'Donnell and Edgar, 1996a and 1996b; and Wittebrood and Nieuwbeerta, 1999) and that an individual's lifestyle is a significant factor in mediating the nature of the relationship between their offending and victimization (Gottfredson, 1984).

One of the earliest studies that established a link between offending and victimization was that by Singer (1981). Using data drawn from a follow-up study of the Philadelphia cohort (Wolfgang et al, 1972), Singer highlighted the significance of victimization in explaining the seriousness of offending careers. Singer's results suggested that victim experience was a major predictor of offending behaviour, particularly in the case of serious assault, where offending behaviour—he argued—was learnt through either repeat victimization or exposure to offending. In a similar vein, Van Dijk and Steinmetz's analysis (1983) of Dutch juveniles echoed Singer's findings, and suggested that offending following victimization was contingent upon the victim having the *opportunity* to offend. As with Singer's findings, Van Dijk and Steinmetz highlighted the significance of lifestyles that increased both the *opportunity* for offending, and the *exposure to risk* of victimization.

Chief among the British studies that noted the importance of lifestyle was Gottfredson's (1984) analysis of the 1982 British Crime Survey. Gottfredson suggested that the social processes that contributed to high rates of offending corresponded with those that contributed to high rates of victimization. As such, where people lived, where they spent time and with whom they associated were highly predictive of both offending and victimization (1984: 17). From this, Gottfredson concluded that the lifestyles which were conducive to offending were also conducive to victimization. Peelo et al (1992) threw further light on these relationships by suggesting that the situations that offenders placed themselves in were precisely those which exposed them to greater risks of victimization.

---

[4] See also Mayhew and Elliott (1990: 92) who find only partial support for this 'overlap' in their data.

Building upon the earlier work in this field, Fagan *et al* (1987) suggested that the social processes that contributed to offending were actually quite different from those that contributed to victimization. They suggested that although there was a relationship between being an offender and being a victim, this relationship varied between offence and victimization types. For example, violent offenders were more likely to experience violent victimization (1987: 600)—often as a result of their own offending. On the other hand, petty offenders were more likely to experience victimization randomly, and which was less directly the result of their own offending (1987: 607–8). The relationship between violent victimization and offending has been further supported by a study which reported that being a victim of violence was associated with re-conviction (May, 1999: 20), and by the work of O'Donnell and Edgar on victimization in prisons (1996a and 1996b).

Like many other areas of research, the establishment of precise causal relationships has, thus far, proven hard to establish. A few studies have, however, been able to shed some light on this issue. Lauritsen *et al* (1991) found evidence to support the proposition that offending behaviour had a direct influence on increasing the risks of victimization, and that experiences of victimization increased involvement in delinquency (1991: 286). Peelo *et al* (1992) supported many of these findings with qualitative data. They noted that, with regard to petty theft (in particular), victimization may actually *lead* to offending as the 'victim' attempted to replace lost items.

Farrall and his colleagues (Farrall and Maltby, 2003; Farrall and Calverley, 2006) reported on the victimization of almost 200 men and women serving probation in England and Wales. Farrall and Maltby (2003) found that, when compared to a similarly aged random sample of people drawn from a nationally representative household sample, probationers were statistically much more likely to have been victimized. Furthermore, the nature of their victimizations was far more 'nasty' and non-routine than many people's victimization experiences (and included credible death threats, abduction, drugging and gang-rape). In a follow-up of this same group, Farrall and Calverley (2006) found that even when these individuals appeared to cease offending, they still experienced approximately the same levels of victimization as continuing offenders. The apparent explanation for this appeared to be entrapment in adverse neighbourhoods (where crime was prevalent) and the influence of their own lifestyles which left them at greater risk of victimization. These aspects of their lifestyles included who they knew and associated with and a certain element of carelessness on their own part.

Data Sets and Research Questions

With the exception of Peelo *et al* (1992) and Farrall's studies, all of the investigations undertaken have employed exclusively survey-based methodologies. Several of these studies have relied upon either household surveys (Van Dijk and Steinmetz, 1983; Gottfredson, 1984; Mayhew and Elliott, 1990; and Lauritsen *et al*, 1991) or samples drawn from schools (Hartless *et al*, 1995; and Fagan *et al*, 1987). The effect of this style of sampling procedure is to produce a sample which is likely to be drawn from those in stable accommodation and/or who regularly attend educational institutions. However, research has suggested that those living in hostels, temporary accommodation or with no fixed abode are particularly likely to be victimized (Peelo *et al*, 1992: 6–7) and that those that do *not* regularly attend school are amongst the most likely to offend (Farrington, 1992: 129, Table 6.1).

Additionally, most of the studies undertaken so far have focussed their attention on the young (for example, Hartless *et al*, 1995 studied eleven to fifteen year-olds, Fagan *et al*, 1987 studied those of school age as did Lauritsen *et al*, 1991, whilst Van Dijk and Steinmetz, 1983 relied in part on data from a survey of twelve to eighteen year-olds). Whilst adolescents are undeniably amongst the most delinquent groups in society, as Moffitt and others (1993 and 1997) have demonstrated, engagement in offending for the majority of young people is limited to no more than a few years. Because very few people manage to pass through life *without* either offending or becoming a victim, criminologists should waste little time with one-off petty offences or victimizations. A certain amount of offending *and* victimization is inevitable, and as such our attention should instead be drawn to those people who have high rates of engagement in offending and victimization.

Despite evidence of a relationship between offending and victimization, few studies have established a causal ordering. Whilst Singer (1981) suggested that victimization led to offending, he did so only with specific reference to serious assault, and maintained the need for other factors to be explored. Similarly, Van Dijk and Steinmetz (1983) suggested a direct causal link between victimization and offending but only when the situations which allow for adequate offending opportunity existed. The reliance upon survey methodologies is, perhaps, in part to blame for this situation. Survey research undoubtedly provides an excellent basis for developing knowledge about some of the most common regularities in criminology (for example, the age-crime curve). However, survey research is not *always* the best medium for explaining the causes of these relationships.[5]

The data we have to hand for our study, whilst not being able to address all of the theoretical and methodological problems referred to above, is able to tackle at least some of them. Because we have an almost complete run of petty sessions data for over sixty years, we are able to explore the extent to which persistent offenders were more victimized than one-off offenders; the causal ordering of victimization and offending (which comes first? In what ways are they related to one another? Does the termination of one result in the end of the other?); and the ways in which the relationship between victimization and offending change over the course of an individual's life-span. We explore these questions by using data about the 101 persistent offenders identified in the Crewe Petty Sessions database. Our analyses rely upon both quantitative interrogations of this data set, as well as individual case study analyses. Alongside our 101 persist offenders, we collected a roughly equal number of one-off offenders who appeared in the Crewe Petty Sessions database between 1880 and 1890.

Were Persistent Offenders More Victimized than One-off Offenders?

Of the 101 persistent offenders, twenty-three had experienced one or more victimizations, and, of our ninety-nine one-off offenders, seven had been victims of crime (see Table 6.1).

---

[5] Qualitative methodologies, conspicuously absent from the investigation of the offender/victim overlap, offer a potentially fruitful avenue in the attempts to explain this relationship.

Table 6.1   Victimization and offending.

	Not Victimized	Victimized	Total
One-off Offender	92 (93)	7 (7)	99 (100)
Persistent Offender	78 (78)	23 (23)	101 (100)
Total	170 (85)	30 (15)	200 (100)

All figures are No. (row %). Chi Sq = .002.

Table 6.2   Mean victimization rates persistent and one-off offenders.

Offence Type	Group	No.	Mean	Std Dev	Sig.
Public Order	Persistents:	101	.08	.337	***
	One-Offs:	99	.00	.000	
Court Order	Persistents:	101	.02	.199	NS
	One-Offs:	99	.01	.101	
Violent and Sex	Persistents:	101	.40	1.379	***
	One-Offs:	99	.05	.262	
Property	Persistents:	101	.14	.491	***
	One-Offs:	99	.02	.141	
Total victimization	Persistents:	101	.46	1.044	***
	One-Offs:	99	07	.258	

NS = not significant, ***p = <.000.

Clearly, then, our persistent offenders were more likely than our sample of one-off offenders to have experienced victimization. In terms of the number of times they were victimized, the persistent offenders appeared to be more frequently victimized than the one-off offenders (see Table 6.2). Our persistent offenders had, in total, experienced forty-five victimizations, whilst the one-off offenders had experienced far fewer—only seven between all ninety-nine of them. We coded the victimizations experienced by offenders into four groups: public order offences (drunkenness, obscene language, vagrancy and the like); court orders (maintenance and other awards of court); violent and sexual offences (assaults, threats, rape, indecent assault and attempted murder); and property offences (mainly theft) and explored the extent to which one-off and persistent offenders were similarly victimized.

Thus it would appear that persistent offenders were much more likely to have been victimized than one-off offenders, and that they also experienced a greater number of victimization events.

However, with a mean number of convictions of 9.5 and a mean number of victimizations of 0.5, persistent offenders were still, by this measure, more likely to have appeared in court as offenders rather than as victims.

What was the Causal Ordering of Victimization and Offending?

As noted above at Table 6.1, there were twenty-three persistent offenders who had been victimized and turned to the courts for redress, and only seven one-off offenders who had experienced victimization. An analysis of their involvement with the courts provided further insight into their involvement in crime. Because we had the entire sixty-one-year span of court actions, it was possible for each case to be classified as to whether victimization preceded or followed offending. With such a small number of cases (thirty in all), firm statements ought to be avoided, but, nevertheless, some patterns emerged.

For four of the seven one-off offenders, offending (ie an appearance in court as the accused) preceded victimization. For the remaining three cases, the dates of appearance as both the accused and the victim were identical and were almost certainly the result of cross-summonses (ie both parties involved in a dispute take one another to court). When we turn to consider the persistent offenders, we see a slightly different picture. Nineteen of the twenty-three persistent offenders had appearances in court as the accused prior to taking others to court. One of the remaining four cases had a victimization prior to an appearance as the accused. Two made their first appearances in court in cross-summonses, and there was one further case where it was impossible to ascertain which event took place first as the court records were recorded by quarters and there was no way to date-order appearances. Overall, therefore, it would appear that offending preceded victimization (when both occurred in an individual's history of involvement with the courts).

However, to merely summarize the relationship with the words 'offending precedes victimization' is to hide an extremely complex set of relationships and contingencies. In order to investigate these relationships, we explored each of the twenty-three persistent offenders' life histories, looking for an explanation of why they had experienced both victimization and been offenders themselves. Five explanations emerged, summarized in Table 6.3 below.

Table 6.3 Explanations for victim/
offender overlap.

	No.
Lifestyle	5
Aggressive nature	6
Work-related	8
Family dispute	2
Randomly victimized	2
Total	23

Two of our persistent offenders appeared to have experienced victimization randomly, well after their main period of offending was over and at the hands of individuals who it did not appear were previously known to them. Those cases classified as having experienced both victimization and offending that was related to their lifestyle included cases where the individual concerned had life-circumstances that left them open to victimization. For example, Wilbur Boswell (whose full and extensive offending history is recorded in Chapter Three) took Terrence Olwins to court for attempting to burgle his home. In fact, possibly because Wilbur Boswell took out a private prosecution on summons, rather than the police prosecuting, the charge was reduced to breaking a window—presumably to try and gain entry to the property—and 'settled out of court' (in some way). At this time, Wilbur's wife (Sally) was in prison for the neglect of three of their children, and Wilbur was living with his mother, presumably because he could not look after their six children on his own. Terrence Olwins, it would appear, took advantage of Boswell's temporarily unoccupied premises.

People who were repeatedly in court for fighting form a group where victim/offender overlap was caused by the cross-summonsing of neighbours in street fracas. This can be seen in the history of Walter Green (Table 6.4).

In all, during a fifteen year period, Walter Green was charged with seven assaults and charged seven others with eight counts of assaulting him.

The line of work that some people pursued meant that they were before the courts as both victims and as offenders. For instance, Alison Peavey and her husband (Timothy) ran a lodging house on Oak Street, one of Crewe's less salubrious streets at that time. In

Table 6.4   Offending and victimization career of Walter Green.

1880	Assaulted Anna Shipway Assaulted by Anna Shipway
1882	Assaulted by Richard Young twice Assaulted Richard Young
1886	Assaulted neighbour Mabel Johnson, eight-year-old girl Assaulted by Paul Johnson (Mabel's brother and a persistent offender himself) Assaulted by neighbour Willy Dickens, aged thirteen Assaulted by neighbour Michael Dolittle
1887	Indecent assault on widow Emily Johnson (Mabel and Paul's mother)
1890	Assaulted by Tony Halls and John Timmis
1892	Assaulted Gerry Himpson Assaulted by Jeremiah Stephens
1894	Assaulted Sally-Ann Allan Assaulted by Wallace Ringlow

1870 Timothy was charged with lodging twenty-one people in four rooms (a breach of lodging house regulations). He was found guilty of a further lodging house offence in 1874, and in 1875 moved to new lodgings himself. He died at the age of sixty-five and Alison kept the lodging house business on. She was convicted for a string of lodging house offences (ten in all) between 1875 and 1892.[6]

In 1874 Alison had been assaulted by a Frenchman who had been lodging with her and her husband. Arnold Toulouse and his family of nine had lodged with the Peaveys, but he made off without making payment. Alison tracked him down to the Express Vaults on Mill Street, where her irritation must have been only further increased, as he was enjoying a glass of ale. Alison confronted him, and asked him for the money owed to her, he declined to pay her again, they tussled, resulting in Toulouse striking Alison three times and pulling a knife on her. For this Toulouse was imprisoned for three weeks. In 1881 Alison was assaulted by Timothy Bellows (striker at the Works and frequent lodger in the Crewe area) and in 1882 a man called James James stole a blanket from her lodging house. Her victimization, like her offending, appeared to be the result of her trade, the culture that permeated it at that time, and the people it brought her into contact with.

---

[6] She died in 1895.

In two cases we found evidence to suggest that it was family disputes that led to the victimization of our persistent offenders. Take, for example, the case of Adam Toshack. He was born in Crewe in 1866 and married Aurelia Paisley in 1885. Their marriage was not a happy one, and in 1886 she took him to court for aggravated assault, of which he was found guilty and fined 30s. (at that time he was earning 26s. a week at the railway works as a painter). In 1889, Adam took his wife and a local bricklayer (Graeme Rowley, another of our persistent offenders) to court for theft following Aurelia's elopement with Graeme Rowley. Aurelia accused Graeme Rowley of compelling her to pawn the things, saying that he had threatened to act 'Jack the Ripper' on her, but the case was dismissed due to lack of evidence. In the same year Aurelia in turn took Adam to court for assault (also dismissed). An already rocky relationship went from bad to worse in 1890, when Adam took his father-in-law, James Paisley, and brother-in-law Casper Low to court for attempted murder. Casper Low (born 1866) was married to Adam's wife's sister (Molly). Casper Low was committed to trial and found guilty and sentenced to imprisonment, part of which he served in Knutsford Prison. Adam and Aurelia's marriage stumbled on despite these setbacks until 1896 when Aurelia died. Adam followed her in 1914.

The strong relationship between victimization and offending at an individual level suggests that as one desists from crime, one may also experience a reduction in victimization. This hypothesis was explored by Farrall and Calverley (2006), who found that in their contemporary sample, desisters were just as likely to experience victimization as persisting offenders. The explanations offered by Farrall and Calverley (2006) were that desisters often remained living in housing estates that experienced high levels of crime and that they often persisted with lifestyles which, whilst not criminal, made their victimization more likely. It would appear, therefore, that as an individual's offending career slowed, their changes of victimization did not follow this. Was this also the case for our persistent offenders from the late nineteenth century and early twentieth century? Table 6.5 reports on our classification of the criminal histories of our twenty-three persistent offenders who experienced victimization.

In the case of those whose offending and victimization ceased suddenly, this was mainly due to them becoming incapacitated in

Table 6.5 The end of offending and victimization careers.

	No.
Yes—both burn out	7
Yes—both stop suddenly	4
No—victimization persists	8
No—offending persists	2
No—both persist	1
Impossible to code	1
Total	23

some way (imprisonment or extreme old age for example). The main two groups are those whose offending and victimization burn out together, and those whose victimization persists. Those for whom victimization persisted beyond their own apparent desistance often appeared to become victims as they entered their older years, having left offending behind during their middle-age. Anthony Ellison, for example, was found guilty of failing to send his children to school (five times in all), using unjust weights and being drunk (twice) between 1878 and 1888 when he was aged thirty to forty. He remained in Crewe until his death in 1909 (at the age of seventy-two), but it is only when he is in his mid-sixties that he appears in court as a plaintiff (for the theft of a hen). Similarly, Wally Newman, a greengrocer, was convicted for using unstamped weights in 1870 (when he was twenty-five years old) and then for seven counts of failing to send his children to school between 1879 and 1889. Then, when he was fifty-seven (three years before his death in 1905) Newman became a victim of assault.

For one of our persistents (John Jasker) his victimization appeared to play a part in his desistance. Jasker (born in 1876 in Crewe) was a petty thief. He was twice convicted of larceny in 1887 (when he was eleven), once in 1888 (from his father, and for which he was sent to the Training Ship Clio, once in 1890 and finally once in 1910 (resulting in a month's stay in Stafford prison).[7] In 1892 he

---

[7] The Clio was a former Royal Navy corvette anchored off the Anglesey coast. She became an industrial training ship in 1877, housing 250 boys aged between eleven and fifteen. Destitute, difficult, and 'criminal' children were sent there for moral and physical education. Some children suffered fatal accidents there, and life

took Hilary Smith (another of our persistent offenders) and her daughter Nancy to court for the theft of some Ulster cloth he owned (Nancy) and the receiving of it (Hilary). After this, although Jasker remained in Crewe until he died at age forty-five, he was not charged with any other offences. It would appear that Jasker put his offending behind him after being victimized—possibly by one of the people to whom he regularly fenced goods. Following this, marriage and employment came rapidly. Perhaps Jasker simply got fed up with leading the life of a petty crook?[8]

Other persistent offenders had criminal histories that suggested that victimization and offending slowly became less and less a feature of their lives. Bill Coldwell was the publican of the Lion and Swan Inn on West Street. He was in and out of court between 1887 and 1910 for offences including permitting drunkenness on his premises, allowing cattle to stray, having a chimney fire, and having no name on his cart, with these offences slowly becoming less and less frequent. In 1930 (when he was aged seventy-four) he was convicted for the last time for not paying his rates. His victimization also diminishes over this time too. Between 1888 and 1903 he took various people to court for failing to quit his public house when asked to do so, and for stealing from his till. His last appearances in court as a complainant were in 1912 and 1913 when he took two groups of boys to court for damaging grass in his field (presumably by playing football). Slowly, as he aged, Coldwell became involved in crimes as defendant or complainant less and less frequently and which were less and less serious.

A not too dissimilar trajectory was followed by Graeme Rowley. He was, at least for a while, both a private bailiff and a bricklayer.

was very hard for them (with many public allegations of bullying and cruelty). For example, it was reported in April 1906 that 'A disagreeable incident had occurred on the ship and [. . .] a poor boy died, probably killed, by reason of some violence on the part of other boys on the ship. It was a mild case of ragging [. . .] it appeared that the boy, who was probably little more than half-witted, was set upon by some of the others and his head was knocked against the piece of wood.' Interestingly, visitors were ferried over to the Clio by L&NWR steamship service. The involvement of L&NWR may be the reason why so many of Crewe's juvenile delinquents ended up on the Clio.

[8] A not uncommon occurrence, it would appear. Farrall and Calverley (2006) report one of their modern-day desisters saying 'I got pissed off walking round early morning in the rain looking for places to burgle and coming home empty-handed.' (George, case 108, TPP4).

Born in 1860, Rowley was first in court in 1882 when he was charged with being drunk in Mill Street and assaulting his father. In 1886 he had another charge of assault against him dismissed. Rowley and his father were then accused of an assault on a seventy-one year-old woman who they 'slapped and pushed' according to the *Crewe Chronicle*. They were acquitted as they had a warrant to enter her home as bailiffs. The same year he was found guilty of a breach of the peace after fighting, and was again taken to court in 1888 by Ellen Smith for bastardy (a case which went against him) and in 1889 by Adam Toshack (see above) for larceny after Rowley eloped with Adam's wife. The next year he was in court on a charge of being drunk. Eventually, between the ages of twenty-two and thirty, Rowley racked up seven appearances in court as the accused. Then, about a decade later, he appeared in court as a complainant (in 1898 when he unsuccessfully took Chris Bateman to court for assault and wounding). 1900 saw him charge Amelia Dullace (the friend of another of our persistent offenders, Ellie Oldfield) with unlawful wounding, although this case was later withdrawn. In 1903 he was convicted of making threats against Fran Lumper, in 1915 he was convicted of obscene language, and in 1918 took Jason Simpkins to court for assault. He died in Crewe in 1932. Over time his involvement in crime appears to have become less and less intense—the frequency of his appearances petered out, and the charges against him reduced in seriousness—dropping from assault, to breach of the peace, to threats, to obscene language. His victimization follows a similar trend, becoming less common over time.

In What Ways did the Relationship between Victimization and Offending Change Over an Individual's Life-course?

Of course, as individuals age, so their position in the family, the workplace, and the neighbourhood changes. Errant sons become responsible fathers, 'hard' men 'soften', drunken girls become mothers, troublesome youths become offending adults and parents become grandparents. Some of these processes have been outlined above. What we seek to do in this section is to explore in greater detail how these changes were experienced by one of our persistent offenders and the impact that this had upon her engagement in crime as both victim and offender.

Eunice Round (née Espinal) was born in Whitchurch, Shropshire in 1846 and began her working life there as a domestic servant. By 1870 she had moved to Crewe, where she was employed by Thomas Bolshaw (an Assistant Overseer of the Poor) as a general servant. In 1871 she married Harold Round, a twenty-three year-old blacksmith, and two years later she gave birth to her first child, Martha, whilst they lived with his parents at the back of Oak Street. By 1874 they had moved into their own rented property in Duke Street. Eunice and one of her new neighbours (Margaret Griston) cross-summonsed one another that year. Eunice said that she had been cleaning snow from her doorstep when Margaret threw water over her—Margaret said that Eunice was 'in the habit of taking drink and insulting her daily' (*Crewe Chronicle*). The magistrates bound them both over to keep the peace. Three further children were born (all boys), and from the early 1880s the family started to take in lodgers to supplement their incomes.

Eunice does not appear in the court records again until 1886 when she was brought before the magistrates for being drunk in Lockitt Street and Mill Street, two of the streets, like Oak and Duke Street, where lodging houses were to be found in some number (she was fined 2s.). By this time she has three children, aged seven, ten and thirteen respectively. Three years later her husband appears before the court on two charges of drunkenness, whilst Eunice appears on a charge of drunkenness, being fined 2s. 6d. and costs or seven days. Over the next three years, Eunice is before the court ten times for drunkenness, and in 1892 she appeared with her daughter Martha on charges of drunkenness and assault upon Howard Birkin, the child of Alice Birkin (who was the girlfriend of Eunice's son Jerry). The *Crewe Chronicle* of 3 December 1892 reported that 'it was one of those family rows which sometime happened in Crewe streets, and especially Lockitt Street, which seemed to be a famous resort for pugilists' and reported a witness as stating that she 'thought the best place for the two defendants was the middle of a forest'.

After this fracas, for which she was fined 5s. and costs, Eunice's offending career appears to slow down; she appears only twice more on drunkenness charges before the turn of the century, despite her family life seemingly being an unhappy one. Her sons Jerry and Wilbur were repeatedly prosecuted for obscene language and drunkenness. Eunice also became the victim in an assault case and two larceny cases (in 1896, 1901 and 1902 respectively). In 1896 Eunice, by now a woman of forty, was assaulted by Betty Elbows. Although her family continued to offend quite regularly between 1896 and 1901 (two of her sons, her daughter and husband are variously convicted of using bad language, obscene language, profane language and of being drunk) Eunice kept out of trouble. In 1901, however, she was back in court, this time as a victim of a theft by Ellie Oldfield (another persistent offender) and a friend of Ellen's, Amelia Dullace (who Graeme Rowley took to court for unlawful wounding, see above). 1902 sees Eunice victimized again, when one of her lodgers (Rebecca Broadfields) stole a bed quilt from her. Rebecca had been lodging at Eunice's for two years, and during that time had born a child by one of Eunice's sons (Wilbur). During this time, Rebecca appeared not to get on well with either her common-law husband or his mother, as a report from the *Crewe Chronicle* in 1903 records: 'Broadfields had lodged there for two years, and had quarrelled with Wilbur many times, and did not get on with Eunice.' The case was in the *Crewe Chronicle* as Rebecca had now died, and Wilbur had been charged with her murder. Rebecca had been on bail for neglecting her child and the *Crewe Chronicle* reported that 'the prisoner [Wilbur] threw a poker at her and said she wanted hanging'. The poker hit Rebecca's leg, and, being drunk, Wilbur then left the house. Rebecca died of pyaemia (blood poisoning) a week later. The wound to her leg had been dressed by Eunice, 'without which she would not have died' asserted the *Crewe Chronicle*. Wilbur is reported as saying that he 'did not know what had happened. My mother always told me to keep my mouth shut, and to say I don't know, and then I should get out of it.' The charge against Wilbur was dropped to manslaughter and then dismissed at Assizes.

Eunice appeared very infrequently in court thereafter. In 1903 she was charged with obscene language a number of times and with being drunk, but her offending stopped dramatically after her forty-third birthday. She remained in Crewe until 1930, when she died. It appears that her drinking days were well behind her. Maybe the impact of the victimization against her had curbed her enthusiasm for the bottle. Despite the fact that she clearly did not get on with Rebecca Broadfield, she still attempted to dress her wounds, suggesting some level of care for her erstwhile daughter-in-law. Like several of the other cases, Eunice became a victim towards the end of her life. However, unlike Walter Green who became vulnerable through age, Eunice Round does not appear to be a particularly vulnerable individual. Her victimization appears to have been the result of her trade (lodging-house keeper) and the characters it would have brought her into contact with (in this respect she is similar to Alison Peavey). However, in Peavey's case, her victimization appears to be incidental to her running of a lodging house and to have had little impact on her offending. In Round's case, we think, the victimizations she experienced and saw (particularly Broadfield's death) may have profoundly altered her behaviour: she ceased to be as heavily involved in offending as she once was. Eunice 'moved' from being a drunken, rowdy neighbour in a relatively powerless position, into a more powerful position (in that she ran a lodging house). Perhaps the care (albeit fatal) that she showed towards Rebecca Broadfield reflected the adoption of a more matriarchal role?

Conclusion

It is clear that, in line with other studies reviewed above, persistent offenders were also more likely to have experienced victimization (measured herein as taking another individual to court) and also to have experienced more victimization episodes when compared to one-off offenders in the courts. However, it remained the case that only a rather small proportion of our persistent offenders had experienced any victimization. It also appeared that offending preceded victimization, which, we ought to stress, does not imply that somehow the offender was 'asking for it' or in any way 'deserved' the victimization that they experienced. We identified a number of reasons why our persistent offenders who had experienced victimization had done so. Having a lifestyle that exposed them to various risks was one such explanation. Another was appearing to have an aggressive nature (identified as repeated involvement in violent crimes). A third explanation, surrounding employment, also emerged. Some areas of the economy were more easily regulated by agents of the courts (such as weights and measures inspectors, or lodging house inspectors). These arenas of the economy were more likely to result in opportunities to offend (since the parties involved may meet only briefly and have few strong bonds to one another), risks of being victimized (since services were often provided ahead of payment) and detection (since legislation existed to support such inspections and the individuals being inspected were not often structurally located to be able to resist or avoid inspections). Hence those running small businesses (lodging houses, shops and market stalls) were likely to appear in court as victims and offenders. A further, and all too common, explanation for the victim/offender overlap emerged from within families: disputes between spouses and their respective families of origin resulted in abuse and victimization on both 'sides'.

In keeping with contemporary analyses, we found that often when a persistent offender ceased to offend they continued or started to be victimized. Some of this appeared to be the result of the ageing process making offenders more likely to cease offending and simultaneously more vulnerable to assault. However, there also appeared to be a sizeable group of offenders who ceased offending and at roughly the same period also ceased to appear as victims in the magistrates court. The explanations for this are not easy to uncover. It could be that, like Eunice Round, they experienced a set of events that made them look at their behaviour in a new light (similar factors have been observed to occur in contemporary studies, eg Cusson and Pinsonneault, 1986; Farrall, 2005), or it could be that these individuals desisted from victimization and offending at the same time. What is interesting is that contemporary studies suggest that once one has become heavily involved in offending, one is likely to remain at risk of victimization for some considerable time (Farrall and Calverley, 2005). This suggests that contemporary society is organized in such a way as to make escape from aversive situations and locales in which crime is common (and hence victimization all the more likely) a rarity.

7
Conclusions

'Go away and let me earn an honest shilling. Go and catch burglars . . . I would rather give £1–00 to the poor box than come here [*Crewe magistrates' court*], it is breaking my wife's heart'.

(Defendant appearing for the thirty-eighth time, *Crewe Chronicle* 21 May 1938)

The defendant quoted above, and some others perhaps, might have questioned why we also were taking such an interest in persistent offenders in this period, and what we have learned for our troubles. We therefore commence this chapter with a short overview of the key findings reported in Chapters Three to Six, before going on to outline our own thinking on how best to combine historical, structural and 'agentic' factors in explanations of those processes associated with criminal careers and victimization. In so doing we return to some of the debates surrounding agencies and structure which have emerged time and again in the writings of criminologists.

Looking Back

Looking back over what we have discovered from our investigation of crime in Crewe at the end of the nineteenth century, there are a number of findings which appear to stand out. Whilst there was undoubtedly a perception of the existence of a 'criminal class' at this time, the likely reality is that there were few hardened, persistent offenders around at that time. As we noted in an earlier chapter, Hay and Snyder (1989) stated that in the 1850s, there were 'under 10,000 serious offenders in England and Wales', and this low level of persistence is reflected in our research for the period 1880–1940 in Crewe.

True, we have concerned ourselves with 'resident' offenders, and there were, of course, those peripatetic offenders who plied their trade around the North West or Midlands. However, these cases were also relatively few. We found that for the period 1880–1890 some 152 individuals were committed to the Chester Quarter Sessions from Crewe at the rate of approximately one per month. The vast majority of these serious offenders were not Crewe residents and the number of Cohort A offenders who appeared at the higher courts could be counted on one hand.[1] We could not, as we noted above, find much evidence to support the notion that persistent criminality was 'passed on' from father to son or mother to daughter in a way which supports biological or genetic theories of criminality. Instead, it is more likely that the 'criminal' class, which in the middle- and upper-class imagination consisted almost exclusively of idle, violent, immoral and drunken males, was in fact a continually varying cohort of individuals with individual failings or desires, rather than an easily categorized group of like-minded people capable of undermining the cohesion of society. Our research has shown that even amongst the relatively small percentage of persistent offenders in Crewe there were often more differences than similarities (supporting therefore the suggestion that heterogeneity not homogeneity predominates, Laub and Sampson, 2003; Ezell and Cohen, 2005; Shapland and Bottoms, 2005). With the exception of habitual drunkards, it has not proved easy to identify a particular 'type' of persistent offender. In one respect however, the empirical evidence for a 'criminal class' was unimportant to contemporary commentators—it was a popular belief in its existence that fuelled so much of both the debate and the resultant actions in the field of crime and punishment during the latter decades surrounding the turn of the twentieth century (and the early twenty-first century, as Tony Blair's comments referred to at the outset of this book illustrate). A strong aspect of historical debates on the criminal class was their incorrigibility. Despite the possibilities of the reform and rehabilitation of juveniles—an idea which grew in respectability from the eighteenth century onwards and which led to the introduction of separate juvenile courts, prisons, and probation in the nineteenth and twentieth centuries—once juveniles became adults, it was assumed they could not change their ways (see Emsley, 2004; Godfrey, 2005; Taylor, 1998; see also Farrall, 2005). Nevertheless,

---

[1] It would be interesting to trace the offending and life histories of these serious offenders (Cox, Godfrey and Farrall, forthcoming).

as stated in Chapter Three, 40% of Cohort A offenders did desist from crime before they died, and three-quarters of those desisted well before they died (see Table 3.7).

In Chapter Four we turned to consider those factors associated with their desistance. Naturally, we were constrained to considering only those factors that we had access to data about, and these, of course, were 'social' (rather than psychological or psychosocial) in nature. Marriage and having children, as modern commentators have found, appear to act as mechanisms for reforming men who wish to please or win approval from their spouses or who generally accept the responsibility that parenthood brings. We suggested that in times when gender inequalities are less pronounced than they were in the late-nineteenth and early-twentieth centuries, females are able to exert (willingly or otherwise) a greater degree of control over their boyfriends and husbands (and for that matter, maybe over their fathers and brothers too). However, our data led us to conclude that because the nature of marriage in the late-nineteenth and early-twentieth centuries was different from its modern character, the impact it had on male behaviour was not so strong, nor so persuasive.

When we turned to consider employment we were reasonably confident that employment at the railway Works for persistent offenders stabilized their offending. The number of convictions recorded against them after they commenced at the Works steadied, and the rate at which they were convicted went down slightly too. When persistent offenders left the employ of the Works, their offending increased, especially so if they had been dismissed.

On the other hand, for the occasional offenders, employment at the Works appeared to be associated with the onset of their (brief) contact with the criminal justice system. Offending receded after they left the Works. Why was this? Our explanation rested on an understanding not of employment as simply an economic activity, but also as a social activity. The work environment today is where people form friendships; in mixed workplaces it is one of the routes employed to finding a partner; it is an organization which operates as an arena for the planning and organizing of social activities; it is also where people find some sort of 'communion', even if this means for some expressions of dissatisfaction with one's job. Employment formed a similar function for the employees of the Works (apart from as a direct route to a marriage partner, as the

Works employees were overwhelmingly male), and, as today, many of these activities involved alcohol. When we looked at the persistent offenders we saw that the nature of their offending was closely related to their life-stage as it related to their employment. Before they commenced employment at the Works, a mere 7% of them had been convicted for drunkenness. This rose during the time that they were employed, to 27%, and after they had left the Works over half of them (56%) were convicted at least once for an act of drunkenness in Crewe. When we turned to the occasional offenders we saw a different pattern. None of them had been convicted for drunkenness before they started at the Works, but whilst they were working for the L&NWR at Crewe, almost a fifth of them were convicted of drunkenness. After they left the Works however, only 4% were convicted of drunkenness. Thus a significant proportion of the occasional offenders appeared in front of the magistrates at Crewe for acts of drunkenness during their working lives. However, these acts were limited in frequency—the bulk being whilst they were employed at the Works. The engagement at the Works for the 'essentially law-abiding' was associated with an increase in offending behaviours, probably, we feel, the result of the group of offenders' immersion in a culture in which heavy drinking was common, if only limited to the weekends. For the persistent offenders, on the other hand, it was promotion at work that reduced their offending quite dramatically (by more than half). This suggests a number of points to us. First, that the same process can produce different outcomes for different groups of people—encouraging one type of offending for one group and suppressing offending for another—and it is therefore the quality of the process which must be factored, eg the speed and nature of career advancement; workers' enjoyment of or attachment to their jobs and employers. Second, that an understanding of the local culture of an organization is required before one can think through the ways in which this may affect the individuals who find themselves—via their own choices or through other means—operating within it. Of course, this understanding needs to be located in time and space.

In Chapter Five we explored the transmission of persistent offending between generations of the same family. Our data suggested to us that the transmission of intergenerational patterns of persistent criminality may have existed only in the short term and may not persist over longer periods of time. Therefore, it would appear that in the late-nineteenth and early-twentieth centuries short-term transmission was reasonably common, longer-term transmission was a rarity—the commonly held belief that there are generations of people within 'criminal families' is erroneous. Instead, our data suggest that whilst patterns of persistent offending may have existed over the short term within families, after the third generation this diminished considerably.

It is clear that, in line with other studies, persistent offenders were also more likely to have experienced victimization and also to have experienced more victimization episodes when compared to one-off offenders in the courts. However, it remained the case that only a rather small proportion of our persistent offenders had experienced any victimization. We identified a number of reasons why some of the persistent offenders had experienced victimization. Having a lifestyle that exposed them to various risks was one such explanation. Another was appearing to have an aggressive nature. A third explanation, surrounding employment, also emerged. Some areas of the economy were more frequently regulated by agents of the courts; these arenas of the economy were also more likely to present opportunities to offend; risks of being victimized were therefore also accentuated; detection was also more common. Hence those running small businesses were likely to appear in court as victims and offenders. But of course, had we located our study some years prior to this, when the regulatory arm of the Victorian state was still embryonic and less capable of detecting and acting against such trades, we may not have found this group of victim/offenders. A further, and all too common, explanation for the victim/offender overlap emerged from with families: disputes between spouses and their respective families of origin resulted in abuse and victimization on both 'sides'.

Making Sense of Offending, Victimization and Desistance: Historical, Structural and Agentic Factors in Processes of 'Transmission' and 'Reform'

In this section of our closing thoughts, we wish to focus on two areas which our studies have shed light upon: processes associated with the transmission of engagement in persistent offending between one generation and the next, and those processes associated with desistance from crime and reform. A number of key principles dominate our thinking in terms of how best to 'make sense' of the processes that we have uncovered during our exploration of offending, transmission and desistance. In this section of our closing chapter, we seek to draw lessons from our studies of the late-nineteenth and early-twentieth centuries which may be of use to those studying these issues today. But why, first of all, ought criminologists studying desistance using contemporary data be concerned with what was happening around 100 years earlier? We think that there are a number of reasons why they might wish to take an interest in studies such as our own.

Crewe in 2004, just as we commenced our fieldwork, was in some respects little different from Crewe in 1904. The railway was still an important part of 'what' Crewe was (even if it had been severely cutback in the 1990s). The Works are, along with Rolls-Royce/Bentley, a major employer (although with a much reduced number of employees), and Crewe is still a major hub for train travel in the North West and along the west coast main line from London to Glasgow. There is still a sizeable locomotive depot to the south of Crewe station and a large set of sidings further south still. Much of the housing stock is still Victorian terraces, although this too is changing as new houses are built to meet local housing needs. Many people in Crewe live and work there or in the immediately surrounding area and there are still parts of Crewe where crime appears more likely to occur, and still places were it is less likely to occur—and these regularities appear to have changed little over 100 years or so. Many of the buildings built by or at the time of the Works' ascendancy are still standing (the market, Lyceum theatre, and Town Hall, for example). On the other hand, it is a very different place. There are fewer jobs related to the locomotive-building industry, fewer public houses, less rented accommodation, more police officers, a university campus and a host of other social changes.

These changes help us to make sense of crime and offending as part of a social process as well as simply the outcome of a series of individual choices. Societies change, and 'change' at that level is often about change in structural factors foremost and individual-level change which follows it. As societies change they reveal continuities and discontinuities which can help us to make sense of the processes at play when individuals desist from criminality. This is not to suggest that we ought to exclude from our consideration all individual-level processes, but rather that when we are able to explore processes of desistance over 100 years ago, it is inevitably the structural factors which will draw our focus.

Structural Influences in Transmission

As discussed in Chapter Five, we could not find a statistical relationship which suggested that there was a family effect in processes of transmission. Instead, and like others before us (eg Sampson and Laub, 1994; Hagan, 1988), we developed a model which accounted for the transmission of persistent offending between two generations of the same family which drew upon individual-level factors, structural level processes and those processes which took place within families, such as spousal abuse. What this suggested was that transmission was affected by not simply individual-level characteristics, but also by changes at the societal-level (ie those brought about and caused by the move from the countryside to growing urban areas, such as Crewe). Our final model (reproduced below as Table 7.1) suggested that four variables were important in this process: if the offending parent had migrated to Crewe from a rural area; the number of house moves as measured by changes in addresses we found the family at in the censuses from 1861–1901; the child's gender, and whether or not the child joined a gang. This drives us back towards historically-informed sociological models of transmission, and away from the 'pure-individual' models seemingly favoured by psychologists and psychiatrists.

Gender is a correlate with offending, and it enters our model too. Similarly, gang membership, which is strongly associated with gender, is strongly related to offending. Thus, at this level we find

Table 7.1 Transmission of offending G1 to G2.

Variable	B	S.E.	Wald	DF	Significance
G1 from rural area	.693	.344	4.049	1	*
N of family moves	.845	.434	3.791	1	*
Gender of G2	1.897	.369	26.471	1	***
G2 gang member	3.996	1.117	12.792	1	***
Constant	1.477	2.344	.397	1	NS

No. of cases = 304. Corrected predicted cases: 82.2%, No. = 250. *p <= .05, **p <= .01, ***p <= .001, NS = not significant.

that some individual characteristics at the G2 level are associated with transmission, but they are the ones that are commonly associated with offending. If we move 'back up' the individual-superstructure chain, we find that the number of home moves experienced by the family while a child was a member of it (some children in the same family experienced fewer moves, of course, due to being born after a substantial period of upheaval for that family) was associated with their offending. This variable speaks to the disruptive and unsettled nature of some families. Persistent offenders who had migrated from a rural area were more likely to have children who would become offenders. As the wider economy changed, and communities became increasingly urbanized, so the effects of this were felt amongst the children of persistent offenders. Criminal careers, and the transmission of persistent criminality amongst the children of persistent offenders, appear to be as much the result of macro-level social change as they are of individual level processes.

From the children ($n = 318$) of all 101 G1 persistent offenders, of those whom we could definitely identify, only sixteen were G2 persistent offenders. This represents a transmission rate of around 16%. These sixteen G2 persistent offenders had, in turn, three G3 persistent offenders, a transmission rate of about 19%. These figures suggest that the rate of transmission did not change greatly between G1/G2 and G2/G3, and as such, over time will slowly 'fade out'.

Thinking about Desistance

The findings which we have reported above, especially those which relate to the processes of desistance, offer a new perspective on established theories. Previously, many researchers had reported that individuals desisted when they embarked on 'decent' careers, became emotionally engaged with a life partner or underwent a host of other social and personal changes (moving home, reflecting on past events, or some dramatic incident whilst offending, see Chapter Four above). However, we have found a slightly different set of findings with regard to two of these. Employment actually increased offending amongst previously non-offending employees (although these were often one-off offences and related to drinking) whilst it appeared to stabilize the offending of our persistent group for the time that they worked at the Works. This suggests to us evidence of a change in the meaning of employment to people (and in particular, men) since that period. Many of the men employed in locomotive construction and associated trades used to drink heavily during their working days.

As such, and unlike many jobs in the contemporary period where alcohol consumption was frowned upon whilst at work, drinking at work and afterwards with one's workmates was condoned by the employers.[2] This, allied with the men's own desire to socialize with their work colleagues, rather than stay at the centrally provided canteen (Drummond, 1995), itself sustained the already strong culture of drinking after work, which resulted in some previously unconvicted employees appearing in court. That this did not result in them losing their jobs, as we suggested at the end of Chapter Four, was likely to be the result of cultural norms surrounding the labouring man's right to a drink after a hard day's work. Alongside this there was the tacit acceptance on the part of the Works that, given that they would find it hard to challenge this norm, they would need to accommodate themselves to it or run the risk of depleting the number of men whom they were prepared to employ. This was suggested by Stevenson's quote that it was hard to find good men who could read and write, and the tolerance of drinking to which this gave rise. Thus agency (choosing to drink, choosing to drink too much or perhaps choosing to allow oneself to be pressured into drinking by one's work colleagues) is situated both within the local context which the Works was trying to establish (a good, hard working workforce who turned up on time and in a fit state to work) and the wider working class culture of 'hard drinking' and nights out in town. Thus we see in historical context Sampson and Laub's contention that 'human agency cannot be divorced from the situation or context, once again making choice situated or relational rather than a property of the person or even the environment; agency is constitutive of both' (2005: 27).

These observations—that wider social and cultural values and norms are important in attempts to account for changes in commonly observed regularities which relate to crime—bring us to the consideration of a remark made by our colleagues Tony Bottoms and Joanna Shapland. In their paper given to the European Society

---

[2] There are, of course, some trades in which heavy drinking is still an accepted or favoured aspect of employment—building work being one of these. However, even here, the consumption of exaggerated amounts of alcohol is reserved for the period after work, especially at the end of the working week. By and large, however, alcohol consumption during working hours is unacceptable in contemporary British society.

of Criminology in Krakow (2005) they note that 'criminologists get obsessed with crime' (2005: 5), a point with which we broadly concur. Our intention with this study was to add to those like Bottoms and Shapland who situate crime within wider social and cultural processes. This aim sent us further along a path towards and understanding of the role of institutions in the social production of crime and trajectories of offending over the life course. We wish to refer to this, building upon a body of work referred to as 'New Institutional Economics', as 'institutional criminology'.

Institutional Criminology

There have been a number of attempts to understand the role of institutions in the production of crime already (see, for example, Messner and Rosenfeld, *Crime and The American Dream* and the work of Sampson and Laub). What we wish to do, however, is to formalize these approaches into a relatively coherent set of statements in order to develop our own thinking with regards to change in societies over time. New Institutional Economics (NIE) was an attempt to answer some fundamental puzzles haunting neo-classical economics. In short, NIE attempted to provide a solution to the gulf between the perfectly rational actors of classical economic theorizing and the well-documented irrational decisions of actual economic actors (Harris, Hunter and Lewis, 1995: 2). Borrowing from NIE, we use the word 'institutions' to refer to those regulatory systems of formal laws, informal conventions and norms of behaviour which govern or regulate most forms of behaviour in a particular domain of activity. Douglass North, one of the pioneers of NIE writes that 'Institutions are the rules of the game of a society, or, more formally, are the humanly devised constraints that structure human interactions. They are composed of formal rules (statute law, common law, regulations), informal constraints (conventions, norms of behaviour and self-imposed codes of conduct), and the enforcement characteristics of both.' (North, 1995: 23).

'Organizations', on the other hand, are more concrete bodies, such as individual actors, groups of individuals, political parties, governments and 'middle-range' collectivities such as regional governments, police forces, and such like. Of course, there is no 'clear blue water' between the two, and it is possible for organizations to shape and be shaped by institutions, which in turn are open to influence by organizations. In this respect the NIE is structurationist at heart. Given this, we drawn upon some elements of the work surrounding structuration theory (Giddens, 1984; Stones, 1991) in our summary of NIE. NIE addressed its chief concerns from a standpoint which made the following assumptions: first, that information is rarely complete and that individuals and groups of individuals have different ideas about how the world around them works ('mental models' in NIE, 'agents context analysis' in structuration theory; Stones, 1991). Second, that these mental models are employed by actors to make choices and are culturally derived, differ widely and are not easily altered in the short term. Third, that institutions are formed in order that the costs and uncertainties associated with human exchange are minimized. Fourth, that institutions create the circumstances under which private concerns and the public interest can be reconciled, thus transcending social dilemmas (Harris, Hunter and Lewis, 1995: 3).

By 'social dilemmas' economists associated with this school are referring to the sorts of outcomes which are produced when rational actors, *en masse*, produce socially undesirable outcomes. In other words, individuals when faced with the limitations of individual level rationality create institutions which, by creating new incentives or by imposing new constraints, enable them to transcend such limitations. That change, when it occurs, is usually an incremental process, and whilst the formal rules of any organization can be changed speedily, informal norms change only slowly, and this change may be unevenly realized. In other words, position practices (in structuration theory) do not change greatly, even if the formal structures of an organization change around individuals. Whilst two organizations may have similar (or identical) formal rules, these may have very different performance characteristics because both the informal norms and the ways in which enforcement is delivered may be very different. Institutions will only be stable if they are supported by organizations which have an interest in the perpetuation of the institutions. As such, a prerequisite of successful reform is the creation of such organizations. Because it is the mental models of actors which shape choices and decision-making, it is essential to change both the institutions and the belief systems for lasting changes to take place. Not all of these considerations need delay us here with further discussion, however, what these do suggest to us is that in order to account for why it is that some of our findings, especially those relating to the processes surrounding desistance, differ from those findings made by criminologists studying the lives of contemporary offenders, we need to consider which institutions and organizations have changed between the late 1800s and the early 2000s.

Age- and Historically-graded Institutional Influences on Criminal Careers

In Victorian times, many sons followed their fathers into their line of work (Harris, 1993: 68, Drummond, 1995: 75). Not only did this happen, but boys would start work at a far earlier age than they do now. We found, amongst our data set of Works employees, boys starting as apprentices as early as twelve years old, and a quarter of our sample of 139 Works employees started before they were fifteen years old. Many of these apprenticeships lasted seven years, with the men taking up a trade from the age of nineteen to twenty-one. Thus the 'transition' from child to adult was one which was structured almost exclusively around employment. Today, of course, things are rather different. The transition to adulthood is normally taken to be completed with completion of full-time education (which can now last to twenty-two or twenty-three with the increases in those attending university), the commencement of full-time employment and independent living. The completion of full-time education is of particular interest to criminologists, since the peak age of offending was, for a while at least, closely tied to it.

As Barclay (1990) notes, the peak age of offending used to be the age at which compulsory schooling ended plus one year. When the final year of compulsory schooling was fourteen, the peak age was fifteen, when it was raised to fifteen, the peak age of offending rose to sixteen. In the late 1980s and early 1990s as more and more young people elected to study to further and higher education levels, so the peak age of offending increased. Of course, we are not saying that it was these students who were to blame for the rise, but rather that their collective decisions to stay on in education altered for many in the generation the nature and the timing of the transition to adulthood. Naturally, the late 1980s and the reintroduction to the UK of long-term unemployment for many young people would also have altered transitions and their timing, as was argued at the time (Willis, 1984). What this suggests to us is that changes at the macro level influence timings at the individual level, and in some instances these changes find expression in those behaviours which we call crime. There has been a long debate about the meaning of the peak age of offending (eg Hirschi and Gottfredson) which does not need to be rehearsed here. However, what is clear is that, in many respects as the peak age of offending for males has been rising, achieving important markers of adulthood (engagement in the labour force, independent living, partnership formation and childrearing) has become more difficult for many in our society.

Marriage was an important part of the social markers which indicated 'adulthood'. It is our contention that whilst marriages were not loveless vehicles designed purely for economic necessity, marriages in the late 1800s were of a different character to those in the late 1900s. It is clear from several authors that marriages, especially those of the working classes, were as much economic affairs as they were expressions of love and affection. Harris has this to say on the topic:

Even more important [than children of school-age working] for most working class households was the economic contribution made by mothers: as wage-earners, as unpaid domestic servants, and, almost invariably, as managers of the domestic budget. [. . .] the life of most working class mothers was an incessant round of cooking, laundering, childcare, ironing, cleaning grates, laying fires, emptying slop pails and keeping dirt at bay, much of this labour was not merely of domestic significance but an essential (if invisible) part of the wider process of industrial production. (1995: 72).

In this respect, whilst not on the surface different from many women's assumed domestic roles today, the wife was an important economic resource, as well as an emotional one. With no welfare state to provide assisted pre-school places, schooling or income in times of hardship, and with employers who cared little for compassionate leave if a family member was ill and children needed looking after, 'a wife', as well as being a sign of the accomplishment of masculine identity, was an unpaid domestic servant and child-carer. This perhaps explains why we found so many men who remarried so quickly after their first wife had died (especially if they had had children by that time) and why it appeared that marriage did so little to curb many men's offending. Few women had access for very long periods of their lives to independent sources of income, few had a livelihood outside of marriage, those who refrained from marriage were often viewed with suspicion and none had the vote (until 1918). Again, this suggests to us that an understanding of the role played by social institutions in the production and termination of criminal careers requires an understanding of those institutions in their historical and cultural contexts.

Changes in Working-class Aspirations

Grayson has argued that the type of industrial or urban environment must have had a considerable effect on working-class aspirations (Grayson, 1998: 42–57). Her study suggested that many industrial towns such as Sheffield or Birmingham were characterized by many hundreds of small workshops run by 'little masters', and she argues that is was much more difficult for workers in such operations to improve their lot. In Crewe, where the majority of employment was provided by a single employer, there was a highly stratified employment structure, and whilst it remained difficult, it was possible to rise through the ranks of such employment. Many of the individuals that we researched during the course of this project can be traced as rising from engine cleaners to apprentice locomotive firemen to locomotive engine drivers. The post of locomotive engine driver was much sought after and highly regarded; they earned considerably more than unskilled or semi-skilled labourers and often sought residential segregation from less-skilled workers (Chaloner 1950: 48). Working-class attitudes to crime and respectability are also glimpsed in the Cross Street brothel case of 1875, in which the *Crewe Chronicle* of 11 September 1875 reported that 'respectable inhabitants of the neighbourhood' complained about the presence of an illegal brothel.

A certain set of aspirations of Victorian working-class men and women can be discerned from portions of the relevant literature. For many, decent housing was a priority. Such accommodation would usually be thought of as self-contained (ie not shared with another family)—although in reality many families, especially those amongst the very poor, would share accommodation. Drummond (1995: 19) notes that the Works provided the housing which they built for their employees with water and gas, thereby raising the living standards of their workforce, in order to attract them to Crewe from their previous residences. As time progressed, and as some areas of Crewe started to become associated with the 'lower' social groups and/or with inferior housing stock, those of higher employment status started to demand and seek out accommodation which marked their higher status via residential segregation. Of course, key to many people's dreams of what the future holds for them is the notion of a family of some sort, and this was true also for Victorian men and women. As we noted in Chapter Four, the family was an economic unit as well as being a source of emotional support born out of romantic attachment. Nevertheless, the family was a social institution which existed both in reality and as an element of the hopes and aspirations of many Victorians of all social ranks. For those who were working, either for the railways or for other sectors of the economy within Crewe and further afield, the desire to rise through the ranks of their firm or industry was another important aspect of their aspirations. Some loftier sociopolitical aspirations, such as the right to vote, also formed part of their desires (and it must be remembered that the Works at Crewe was embroiled in various disputes over union and Liberal Party membership in the late 1880–90s). Often associated with such hopes were desires for better pay and working conditions for not just themselves, but for their fellow employees.

And what of today's working-class dreams? Bottoms *et al* (2004), in a paper devoted to theoretical issues relating to desistance, refer to what they call an 'English Dream'. Drawing directly from the notion of an 'American Dream', Bottoms *et al* propose a similar English Dream for working-class children and adolescents living in contemporary Sheffield. This dream consists of a secure job, 'enough' money, consumption of certain desired products and services (clothes, meals out, cars and so on), a steady romantic attachment and the likelihood of parenthood (2004: 384).[3] This, of course, is only one form of one dream—doubtless there are other dreams which draw their precise configuration from cultural, ethnic, class and other considerations, as Bottoms *et al* acknowledge. Whilst it would be easy (and fruitless, we think) to compare and contrast these sets of aspirations, what is clear from them is the following. First, that these aspirations are strikingly similar to the processes associated with desistance from crime (employment, marriage, family formation and personal progression resonate); and second, that these processes are not automatically achievable for all, and

---

[3] Politicians as well as academics have articulated the 'English Dream'—notably Michael Howard MP, former leader of the Conservative Party.

that, by implication, for an individual to retain their desires for these objects, they must feel that they are in a set of circumstances which allow them to *hope* that they will one day achieve these goals.

Hope—that the future will enable the individual to achieve various goals and aspirations—it is being increasingly recognized, is an important emotion not just in the recovery from various life-threatening ailments (see Simpson, 2004), but also in those processes associated with desistance from crime (Burnett and Maruna, 2004; Farrall and Calverley, 2006). And yet, there are concerns (eg as expressed by Bottoms *et al*, 2004) that amongst all the changes experienced by UK society, these dreams may no longer be achievable for many young working-class men and women, and especially for those people with criminal convictions. Willis (1984) highlighted the role that the wage plays in assisting many young men and women commencing the journey towards full adulthood, and the ways in which this can be damaged by large-scale economic restructuring. Alongside these considerations, we must remember that when opportunities for achieving success via legitimate means are removed or made harder to achieve, so people re-orient their aspirations towards new goals, some of which may either be illegitimate or require illegitimate activities to be achievable. MacLeod (1987/1995), especially in the second edition of his book which includes an eight-year follow-up of the lives of the respondents living in a poor neighbourhood in the US, charts the connections between individual criminal careers and community structures and forms. As MacLeod notes:

Aspirations reflect an individual's view of his or her own chances for getting ahead and are an internalization of objective probabilities. But aspirations are not the product of rational analysis; rather, they are acquired in the habits of the individual. A lower-class child growing up in an environment where success is rare is much less likely to develop strong ambitions than is a middle-class boy or girl growing up in a social world peopled by those who have 'made it' and where the connection between effort and reward is taken for granted. (1995:15)

Macleod's work suggests that as some opportunities are eroded (in this case, employment and opportunities to 'make it') so behaviours are altered, and that this in turn frequently has implications for individuals' involvement in crime. Poor employment prospects encourage engagement in offending which may ultimately serve to block subsequent opportunities for legitimate employment and desistance. Hagan (1997) has argued that western industrialized nations have, during the last quarter of the twentieth century, witnessed an overall slow-down in economic growth. He suggests that this has been 'characterized by increased unemployment and income inequality, led by the loss and only partial replacement of core sector manufacturing jobs with less stable and poorer paying service sector jobs' (Hagan, 1997: 289).

Many of the poorest men and women were amongst those who lost most during this period of economic upheaval. These economic changes have resulted in huge social changes. For example, a significant proportion of young people leaving school (depending on the period during which they enter the labour market) will either expect *not* to work, will experience economic instability or may become accustomed to periodic unemployment. As well as helping to maintain the concentration of poverty, such changes will create 'a social context that includes poor schools, inadequate job information networks, and a lack of legitimate employment opportunities [*that*] not only gives rise to weak labour force attachment, but increases the probability that individuals will be constrained to seek income derived from illegal and deviant activities' (Wilson, 1991: 10, cited in Hagan, 1997: 292).

Evidence of similar processes can also be found in the UK. Downes (1997: 3) reports the evidence given to the House of Commons Select Committee on Employment by John Wells in 1994, in which Wells argues that unemployment and crime (especially property crime) are strongly related to one another. Wells adds that:

prolonged unemployment, particularly where it is spatially concentrated, is likely to prove a fertile breeding-ground for crime. [. . .] The absence of future employment prospects de-legitimizes school and results in many pupils becoming cynical, bored and rebellious. The future no longer holds out the prospect of material and social success, and so young people see no point in making a 'stake in conformity' (1994: 43–4).

As Downes himself (1997: 4) notes, school exclusions have soared since schools were given the right to select which pupils they take. We posit here that it is the hope and expectation that their aspirations will one day be met which encourages many people towards developing a 'stake in conformity' and which prevents them from becoming so disillusioned with their lot that they resort to offending as a common solution to the difficulties they face. In short, when goals are achievable and seen to be achievable via legitimate means, many people will choose these means; when such routes are blocked, and especially blocked by structural impediments which are organized in such a way as to discriminate against people on the basis of their social, ethnic or geographical grouping, they will not. Providing people with legitimate routes towards realizing their hopes then matters, since this motivates people towards socially acceptable behaviour. Or, to cite Emirbayer and Mische (1998: 971), 'the imaginative generation by actors of possible future actions, in which received structures of thought and action may be creatively reconfigured in relation to actors' hopes, fears and desires for the future'. These 'desires for the future' at an individual level (Giordano et al, 2002; Farrall, 2005) have been found to be related to patterns of desistance. However, such dreams and desires must also exist at a societal level in order to create and sustain the particular set of circumstances and position practices associated with them. One cannot realistically dream of finding good work, a partner and starting a family if those roles do not exist as cultural scripts in one's society and if they are not at some level achievable.

The majority of persistent offenders in the nineteenth and twentieth century came, in many ways, from a section of society which was much poorer and disadvantaged than the lowest strata of today's society. Welfare provision was uneven and designed merely to prevent and mitigate the very worst features of endemic poverty. Today the welfare system, though as a whole inadequate, provides a low but adequate level of income for all but the very excluded and marginalized in our society. However, when it comes to ex-offenders, the situation is reversed. In the 1880 to 1940 period, ex-offenders (who were mostly unschooled, or had low levels of education) could still find gainful employment, virtually at will. Even the 1930s depression which ravaged the country did not heavily affect Crewe. The vast range of available labouring jobs (inside and outside the Works) allowed ex-offenders to both change their 'identities' (and assume respectability) and also gain the structural features that helped inhibit recidivism—fairly good housing, regular wages, community, and so on. However, it is our contention that various socio-economic changes and shifts in public policy over the last thirty years or so (Farrall, 2006) have made the realization of the 'English Dream', the securing of gainful employment, and a 'new start' all the harder for some in our society.

Appendix A
Our Data Sets: Origins and Architecture

During the course of the analyses undertaken for this project, we naturally enough relied upon a number of data sets. These frequently, in one way or another, were related to each other. In this section, we outline the data sets we produced and the key aspects of their structure.

'Main' Data Set: Petty Sessions Cases 1880–1940

Our main data set—main in that it is by far the largest of those that we developed and that all other data sets stem from it in some way—is a record of all cases resulting in court action in the Crewe Petty Sessions from 1 January 1880 until the end of December 1940. Not all cases were included in this data set, however. In some cases, the parties settled out of court (in which case the register was marked 'settled'), the defendant failed to appear and the case was adjourned to a further date, with or without the issue of an arrest warrant, or where the court felt that an alternative charge should be put, or that there was no case to answer (in which case the file was marked 'withdrawn'). For one short period (1892–1895) the Petty Sessions records books have been lost and so data for this 'lost' period was not collected directly from the Petty Sessions, but from newspaper trial reports as reported in the *Crewe Chronicle*. By collecting a small segment of data either side of the lost period (ie 1892 and 1895) we were able to estimate the extent to which the *Chronicle* reported Petty Sessions proceedings. It appeared that they reported around one in four appearances. Although there were juvenile sessions running alongside adult courts in Crewe from 1909, in 1933 Crewe started a separate Juvenile Court, and these cases have been included in the Petty Session/Main data set (though they are marked as juvenile court cases).

This data set was recorded at the level of the individual defendant, and (through the combined use of court, newspaper, and census records) now contains the following information: date of appearance; name of the agency bringing the case; full name of the defendant; the name(s) of any children who were involved in the case; the gender of the defendant; and their age (if recorded); the full name of the complainant; the gender of the complainant; the age of the complainant (if recorded); the offence the defendant was charged with; the place where the offence took place; the occupations of both the defendant and the complainant; the residences of both parties; the plea entered at court; and the sentence passed by the court. We also recorded extraneous notes relating to the case, any aliases used, if the case was linked to other appearances (for example, when a number of people were charged with offences arising out of one collective incident, an affray, or poaching, for example) and previous convictions when they were revealed. For the sake of completeness, we note that in many cases the name of the magistrate was also recorded in the Petty Sessions records, however, we decided not to include this information since there were at least three magistrates involved in each case, and sentencer volatility would make this information impossible to reliably account for. This data base contains the records of some 49,202 court actions.

Quarter Sessions Records

In order to assist the identification of persistent offenders, provide further information on previous convictions outside the Crewe area and to ascertain the eventual outcomes of those cases referred to Quarter Sessions, we also collected data relating to these courts for all cases so committed. We found that we could trace about 75–80% of such cases.

This data set included, for all those committed to Quarter Sessions, all of the information recorded from the Petty Sessions and all of the data relating to previous convictions (some of which took place outside of the jurisdiction of the Crewe courts, and some which took place in Crewe but before 1880, when our data set starts (in fact the court registers do not exist for the period before 1880). In some cases too, extra details were given (such as familial relationships or further aliases). This data set contained the details of some 152 individuals.

Newspaper Records of Crewe Petty Sessions, 1880–1940

In order to supplement the information gleaned from petty sessions' registers about persistent offenders, we turned to newspaper trial reports. The Petty Session reports provided by the *Crewe Chronicle* gave a much greater flavour of the lives of our persistent offenders. No two entries were totally alike, but the data which we recorded often related to home addresses, the nature of the offences (ie if this had been just one in a long string of feuds between neighbours), demeanour and physical appearance in court, employment of the parties involved, where the offence had taken place and, sometimes, quite long descriptions of the people involved. In some cases, what appeared to be verbatim quotes of magistrates, advocates, and witnesses were also reported.

Crewe Railway Works Employees Data Set

The data set contained the records of all persistent offenders (ie those with five or more convictions) identified in the main data set who were known to be Works' employees and whose records could be located. This small sample of cases was supplemented by two further groups of employees: one group who had between one and four convictions, and a group with no convictions.

Identifying and Matching Cases

The task of identifying individuals from the main data set and then matching them to materials from the other records which we were interested in took over a year to complete. The process was an iterative one and the 'stages' undertaken as part of this process have no clear demarcation from one another. Because of the nature of our interest, we started by identifying all those individuals in the main data set who appeared to be the same person. This included searching for the individuals recorded in the main data set in the available censuses (1841–1901) to make an assessment of the 'uniqueness' of any one individual. In some cases, where more than one person with the same name was found in the census, it was possible to eliminate some potential people in the census by examining dates of birth or the nature of their employment.

This process was aided by an examination of those cases which were committed to the Quarter Sessions, since the Quarter Sessions listed all known aliases and all known previous convictions (giving dates and offence type). The *Crewe Chronicle* provided another source of information that allowed for the matching of cases. Often, it was observed, for even the most petty of crimes, other information about the defendant or the complainant was provided. This included, age, occupation, the names of family members, home addresses or the address of an individual's employment. Other sources of local information, such as directories of publicans and shopkeepers, and electoral registers assisted with the identification of cases. Through a triangulation of data sources, which in practice meant moving between several data sets to securely identify cases, we were able to draw up a list of persistent offenders who started their offending careers between 1880 and 1890 and who were persistently offending some time between 1880 and 1940.

Appendix B
The Mechanics and Validity of the Censuses, 1841–1901

For the identification of individuals, we relied upon seven censuses, those from 1841 to 1901. There are several important caveats which need to be mentioned when using census data from the UK at this time, and this *Appendix* introduces readers who might not be familiar with such data to these considerations. We draw heavily upon Edward Higgs' excellent *A Clearer Sense of the Census*, HMSO, London, 1996.

The UK's first modern census was undertaken in 1801. Ever since, with the exception of 1941 (when the census was postponed due to the Second World War), the census has been carried out every ten years. The first four of these censuses (ie the 1801–1831 censuses) were little more than head-counts, with limited information on named individuals (Higgs, 1996: 7), and in any case were destroyed in 1913. (There is no evidence that we know of to suggest that any of the returns for the Crewe censuses of 1841–1901 have been systematically damaged or lost). The 1841 census represents something of a transition from the earlier 'headcount' variety towards something much more like the census as we know it today. In this respect the 1841 census is a rather strange beast—special provisions for night-workers and merchant vessels, for example, were not introduced until the 1851 census. For these reasons, and the difficulties of comparing data from 1841 and subsequent censuses, the earliest census that we rely upon is that conducted in 1851, although the 1841 census was occasionally consulted in order to provide extra confirmation of an individual's details.

From 1851, the census followed a similar administrative cycle (Higgs, 1996: 11–12). An Act of Parliament was sought (it was only later that censuses became a permanent institution). Following this, negotiations took place between the General Register Office and various bodies to recruit enumerators, to house the enumerators during the fieldwork and to provide security by the police. All of this work took place in a matter of months, as the Act of Parliament was often only passed seven to eight months before census day. Higgs (1996) provides further details such as rates of pay ('insufficient'), age of enumerators (eighteen to sixty-five) and general demeanour ('respectable'). The records that we have relied upon normally contained the following information for each individual:

Address

Name

Age

Relation to head of household

Gender

Employment

Place of birth

Marital status

Mental or physical handicaps

For our purposes this was often enough to trace an individual (eg one of our persistent offenders or, say, their offspring) in the census. From 1841 the census collected information from people residing in institutions (such as prisons, workhouses, hospitals and almshouses). However, it would appear that for 1841 it is rather unclear how exactly and even if this took place (Higgs, 1996: 35–6). From 1851, those institutions with 200 or more inmates were returned in special institutional books, and this remained the practice from 1861 to 1881. In 1891 the threshold was dropped to 100 inmates. Identifying individuals is not always easy for those in institutions, since in some censuses (eg 1861) enumerators were only required to list initials rather than full first names. Relationships between inmates are also impossible to identify as this information was not recorded. Nevertheless, for the period which we are interested in, most institutions were recording details about their inmates—and indeed we succeeded in finding several of them in prisons, gaols, army barracks and training ships.

Another group that we were interested in were those who were of no fixed abode or who were tramping. From 1851 censuses were held in March-April so as to avoid an undercount of residents because of the travel associated with migration to sites of agricultural work, although in 1841 the census was held in June (Higgs, 1996: 46, 171). Many of the serious offenders who were sent from Crewe petty sessions for trial at the quarter sessions or assizes were people who were not resident in Crewe for very long. However, there were some amongst our sample who were physically in Crewe but without a home of their own (eg the prostitute Minnie Valler). From 1861 those sleeping in outhouses, barns and so on were returned in the main records. Starting with the 1851 census, night-workers, those working in pits, mines, and in factories were recorded at their home address if they were to return to that address in the morning.

Data relating to place of birth was clearly crucial to our efforts to identify specific individuals. Before 1851 residents were simply recorded as 'born in the same county or not' and 'born in Scotland, Ireland or Foreign Parts or not', and this is unsatisfactory for many reasons. From 1851 people had to state their birthplace. Whilst there are still problems with this (some people appear to have 'changed' their birthplaces between censuses), most of these are fairly easily accounted for and are not of major concern. For example, misspellings were common as a) the spelling had not been settled upon ('Crewe' or 'Crew'), b) some enumerators were not local and they often guessed at the spellings of place names, and c) geographical knowledge was not especially good (hence some towns or cities are given as being in incorrect counties). In some cases, recent immigrants to a locale changed their birthplace to the place where they were living at the time of the census. Employment appeared to be fairly accurately recorded, at least for males (Higgs, 1996: 95), although, as was the case in Crewe, this was sometimes simply too vague to tell us much (eg 'general labourer'). Female employment is a different matter, with many married women simply listed as 'wife' or for example 'farmer's wife'. Some, of course, are listed by details of their employment. Those who had retired or ceased for other reasons to work, were instructed to be entered as 'former . . .' or 'retired . . .', but they were often just listed by their former employment. This is understandable when one takes into account the fact that many people were employed either on a day basis, or were periodically laid off or had no precise end of working life and start of retirement, there being virtually no pension provision.[1]

Regardless of these caveats, most of which are easily allowed for when collecting and analysing data, we feel that the censuses between 1841 and 1901 provide a record of the resident population of Crewe which is 'fit for purpose'. True, there are some aspects of the censuses which we wish were different (eg the use of initials rather than full names of inmates in the 1861 census), but this is the nature of historical documents recorded for purposes other than crime history research in the twenty-first century.

---

[1] Examples of the difficulties faced by census enumerators can be found in the following report of the taking of the 1911 census in Crewe, reprinted from the *Crewe Chronicle*, 8 April 1911:

Most of the town enumerators found their work of collecting the papers very difficult. In many cases the papers had not been filled in when they called, and they had to instruct how they should be filled in. In others they had been only partially filled in, and in others again the enumerators had to make liberal corrections. In one street only one of the papers had been filled in rightly. Some of the people were out when the collectors called, and they had to make several journeys over the ground in order to get the papers.

Appendix C
Nested Data and Appropriate Statistical Techniques
by Jonathan Jackson and Stephen Farrall

Children in the same family share certain characteristics. They are alike by dint of genetics, a mutual environment and complex *nature-nurture* interactions. Our interest here is in the offspring of persistent offenders in late-nineteenth-century Crewe: which factors are related to these children having a criminal record and are siblings more likely to commit crime than unrelated individuals?

In statistical parlance, observations such as these are known as nested—with children nested in families, or pupils nested in classrooms nested in schools. A dataset based on such observations is said to have a clear hierarchical or clustered structure. But many statistical methods such as ordinary least squares regression or standard logistic regression cannot take into account the clustered nature of such data, requiring instead independence of observations. Such methods are inappropriate tools for analysing hierarchical data since the structure of the data violates the assumption of standard methods that observations of the response variable are independent given the explanatory variables. Standard methods effectively overstate the amount of information in the data. They produce deflated standard errors, leading to a higher probability of rejection of a null hypothesis.

Moreover if one is aware of the statistical challenges of analysing hierarchically structured data, and consequently of the problems of aggregating, then one is likely to avoid analysing data at one level but drawing conclusions at another level (Hox, 1995). Consider the ecological fallacy: one can draw inferences at the ecological level from aggregating analyses at the individual level and produce grossly misleading results (Robinson, 1950). Consider also the atomistic fallacy: one can draw inferences at a higher level from analyses performed at the individual level and also produce invalid conclusions (Alker, 1969).

Consequently, when one wishes to analyse such data one needs to take into account their hierarchical nature. Multilevel analysis is a methodology for the analysis of data with complex patterns of variability, with a focus on nested sources of variability (Bryk & Raudenbush, 1992; Goldstein, 1995). Multilevel modelling assumes hierarchical data, with one response variable at the lowest level and explanatory variables at all levels. It produces statistically efficient estimates of regression coefficients, correct standard errors, confidence intervals and significance effects, and can identify covariates at any level of the hierarchy.

Analysis of the Crewe Data

The technique of multilevel modelling was used to analyse the data on the children of persistent offenders. Observations exist within other observational units. The base-level here is the individual, with measured characteristics of the individual known as level-1 variables and the response variable being criminal conviction (n = 318). Higher-level observations are at the family level, or level-2 units (n = 64).

Multilevel models estimate, test and explain the nature of the level-1 relationship across different higher-level units. Fixed effects are the identified associations with the explanatory variables and the response variable. Multilevel modeling also estimates random effects. This is the group-level or intra-correlation effect that is unexplained by level-2 variables. In the case of the Crewe data it is the effect of being in a given family on conviction.

Before one undertakes such an analysis, one might be concerned about the average size of the number of cases in each family. In many families there were less than five children in a given family. One might conclude that there is not enough information going around to estimate the family effect. This is true if one treats the family effect as a fixed parameter. In practical terms this means having a dummy variable for each family. However we avoid this problem in the current analysis by treating the family effect as a sample of a population of families (Snijders & Bosker, 1999: 44). We only estimate the variance of the random effect. The analysis pools information from all observations and avoids the issue of low group sizes.

Of course, just because they were siblings does not mean they shared a particular propensity to commit a crime. It is actually an empirical question whether these siblings were more likely to be convicted compared to unrelated individuals. If the random effect is found to be statistically significant then the next step is to include all explanatory variables in the model. If there is no family-level effect, the data are not clustered on the issue of criminal conviction, over and above the explanatory variables in the model. The practical implication of this is that the analysis can proceed with the use of standard logistic regression models.

Because the response variable was binary, a logistic regression multilevel model was estimated. Since the first goal was to assess whether there were random group-level effects of family on individual-level criminal conviction, the initial step was to assess within-family dependence on the probability of being convicted.

Results

Stata 8.0 was used to run the model. The first model specified our response variable, one explanatory variable (whether the parent had been found guilty of a violent offence) and a random effect representing the family effect. The p-value attached to the likelihood ratio test of the random effect was 0.160. We therefore fail to reject the hypothesis that the variance of the random effect is zero. The practical implication of this is that we can proceed with standard logistic regression modelling: there is no within-family dependence on the probability of conviction.

```
xtlogit gen2_off g1_violent, re i(level)
```

Fitting comparison model:

Iteration 0:	log likelihood =	-157.76646
Iteration 1:	log likelihood =	-156.00330
Iteration 2:	log likelihood =	-155.99321
Iteration 3:	log likelihood =	-155.99321

Fitting full model:

tau = 0.0	log likelihood =	-155.99321
tau = 0.1	log likelihood =	-155.69137
tau = 0.2	log likelihood =	-155.61325
tau = 0.3	log likelihood =	-155.79244
Iteration 0:	log likelihood =	-155.61325
Iteration 1:	log likelihood =	-155.49993
Iteration 2:	log likelihood =	-155.49878
Iteration 3:	log likelihood =	-155.49878

Random-effects logistic regression	Number of obs	=	304
Group variable (i): level1	Number of groups	=	63
Random effects u_i ~ Gaussian	Obs per group: min =		1
	avg	=	4.8
	max	=	11

Wald chi2(1) = 3.18
Log likelihood = -155.49878 Prob >chi2   =   0.0745

gen2_off	Coef.	Std. Err.	z	P>|z|	[95% Conf. Interval]	
g1_violent	−.6136539	.3440373	−1.78	0.074	−1.287955	.0606469
_cons	−.4811568	.5079429	−0.95	0.344	−1.476707	.514393
/lnsig2u	−1.198111	1.226385			−3.60178	1.205559
sigma_u	.5493304	.3368452			.1651518	1.827191
rho	.0840186	.0943819			.0082225	.5036779

Likelihood-ratio test of rho = 0: chibar2(01) = 0.99 Prob > = chibar2 = 0.160.

Bibliography

Adams, K. (1997) 'Developmental Aspects of Adult Crime', in Thornberry, T. (ed.) *Developmental Theories of Crime and Delinquency*, London, Transaction Press.

Alcock, P. (1995) 'Back to the Future: Victorian values for the 21st century', in Lister, R. (ed.) *Charles Murray and the Underclass: the developing debate*, London, Institute of Economic Affairs.

Alker, H. R. (1969) 'A typology of fallacies', in M. Dogan and S. Rokkan (eds.) *Quantitative Ecological Analysis in the Social Sciences*, Cambridge, MIT Press.

Anon. (1938) *Report on Road Accidents in Great Britain Involving Personal Injury (Fatal and Non-fatal) Year Ending 31/03/1937*, London, HMSO.

Ballintyne, S. (1999) *Unsafe Streets*, London, IPPR.

Barclay, G. (1990) 'The Peak Age of Known Offending by Males', in *Home Office Research Bulletin 28*, pp. 20–23.

Bell, I. A. (1991) *Literature & Crime in Augustan England*, London, Routledge.

Benson, J. (1989) *The Working Class in Britain*, London, Longman.

Blumstein, A. and Cohen, J. (1987) 'Characterising Criminal Careers', in *Science*, 237, pp. 985–91.

Bottoms, A., Shapland, J., Costello, A., Holmes, D. and Muir G. (2004) 'Towards Desistance: Theoretical Underpinnings for an Empirical Study', in *Howard Journal of Criminal Justice*, 43(4), pp. 368–89.

Bourgois, P. (1996a) *In Search of Respect: Selling Crack in El Barrio, New York*, Cambridge, CUP.

—— (1996b) 'In Search of Masculinity: Violence, Respect and Sexuality among Puerto Rican Crack Dealers in East Harlem', in *British Journal of Criminology*, 36 (3), pp. 412–27.

Brogdan, M. and Harkin, S. (2000) 'Community Rules Preventing Re-offending by Child Sex Abusers—A Life History Approach', in *International Journal of the Sociology of Law*, 28, pp. 45–68.

Bryk, A. S. and Raudenbush, S. W. (1992) *Hierarchical Linear Models, Applications and Data Analysis Methods*, London, Sage.

Budd, T., Sharp, C. and Mayhew, P. (2005) *Offending in England and Wales: first results from the 2003 Crime and Justice Survey*, Home Office Research Study 275, London, Home Office.

Burnett, R. (1992) *The Dynamics of Recidivism*, Oxford, Centre for Criminological Research.

Burnett, R. (1994) 'The Odds of Going Straight: Offenders' Own Predictions', in University of Loughborough (ed.), *Sentencing, Quality and Risk: Proceedings of the 10th Annual Conference on Research and Information in the Probation Service*, Birmingham, Midlands Probation Training Consortium.

—— and Maruna, S. (2004) 'So "Prison Works", Does it? The Criminal Careers of 130 Men Released from Prison under Home Secretary, Michael Howard', in *Howard Journal of Criminal Justice*, 43 (4), pp. 390–404.

Caddle, D. (1991) 'Parenthood Training for Young Offenders: An Evaluation of Courses', in *Young Offender Institutions, Research and Planning Unit Home Office Paper 63*, London, HMSO.

Carpenter, M. (1853) *Juvenile Delinquents, their Conviction and Treatment*, London, W. & F. G. Cook.

Chaloner, W. H. (1950) *The Social and Economic Development of Crewe 1780–1920*, Manchester, Manchester University Press.

Chassaigne, P. (2003) 'A new look at the Victorian Criminal Classes: a view from the archives', paper given at *Social Deviance in England and France c. 1830–1900* Conference, Maison Française d'Oxford, Oxford Brookes 4–5 July.

Colquhoun, P. (1815) *Treatise on the Wealth of the British Empire*, London, Joseph Mawman.

Cook, D. (1997) *Poverty, Crime and Punishment*, London, Child Poverty Action Group.

Cox, D. J. (2006) 'A certain share of low cunning: an analysis of the work of Bow Street Principal Officers 1792–1839', unpublished PhD thesis, Lancaster University.

—— and Godfrey, B. (2005) *Cinderellas & Packhorses: A History of the Shropshire Magistracy*, Almeley, Logaston Press.

Cox, P. and Shore, H. (2002) *Becoming Delinquent: British and European Youth 1650–1950*, Aldershot, Ashgate.

Critchley, T. (1970) *The Conquest of Violence: Order and Liberty in Britain*, London, Constable.

Cromwell, P. F., Olson, J. N. and Avary, D. W. (1989) *Breaking and Entering*, London, Sage.

Cusson, M. and Pinsonneault, P. (1986) 'The Decision to Give up Crime', in Cornish, D. B. and Clarke, R. V. (eds.) *The Reasoning Criminal*, New York, Springer-Verlag.

Darwin, C. (1859) *On the Origin of Species*, London, John Murray.

David, M. (1995) 'Fundamentally Flawed', in Lister, R. (ed.) *Charles Murray and the Underclass: The Developing Debate*, London, Institute of Economic Affairs.

Davidoff, L., Doolittle, M., Fink, J. and Holden, K. (1999) *The Family Story Blood, Contract and Intimacy, 1830–1960*, London, Longman.

—— and Hall, C. (1987) *Family Fortunes: Men and Women of the English Middle Class, 1780–1850*, London, Hutchinson.

Davies, A. (1999) 'These viragoes are no less cruel than the lads: young women, gangs and violence in late Victorian Manchester and Salford', in *British Journal of Criminology*, 39 (1), pp. 72–89.

—— (2000) 'Youth gangs, gender and violence, 1870–1900', in D'Cruze, S. (ed.) *Everyday Violence in Britain, 1850–1950*, Harlow, Longman Pearson.

Davis, J. (1980) 'The London Garrotting Panic of 1862: A Moral Panic and the Creation of a Criminal Class in mid-Victorian England', in Gatrell, V. A. C., *et al* (eds.) *Crime and the Law: A Social History of Crime in Western Europe since 1500*, London, Europa.

—— (1999) *A History of Britain, 1885–1939*, Basingstoke, Macmillan.

D'Cruze, S. (1998) *Crimes of Outrage: Sex, Violence and Victorian Working Women*, London, London University College Press.

De Groot, G. (1996) *Blighty: British Society in the Era of the Great War*, Harlow, Longman.

Dennis, N. and Erdos, G. (2005) *Cultures, Crime and Policing in Four Nations*, London, Civitas.

Ditton, J. (1977) *Part-time Crime: An Ethnography Of Fiddling And Pilferage*, London, Macmillan.

——, Bannister, J., Gilchrist, E. and Farrall, S. (1999) 'Afraid or Angry? Recalibrating the "Fear" of Crime', in *International Review of Victimology*, 6 (2), pp. 83–99.

Downes, D. (1997) 'What the next government should do about crime', in *The Howard Journal of Criminal Justice*, 36 (1), pp. 1–13.

Drummond, D. (1995) *Crewe: Railway Town, Company and People, 1890–1914*, Aldershot, Scolar Press.

Elder, G. and Pellerin, L. (1998) 'Linking History and Human Lives', in Giele, J. and Elder, G. (eds.) *Methods of Life Course Research*, London, Sage.

Emirbayer, M. and Mische, A. (1998) 'What is Agency?', in *American Journal of Sociology*, 103 (4), pp. 962–1023.

Emsley, C. (1993) ' "Mother, what did policemen do before there weren't any motorists?". The law, the police and the regulation of motor traffic in England, 1900–1939', in *Historical Journal*, 37, pp. 357–81.

—— (1996) *The English Police: A Political and Social History*, Harlow, Longman.

—— (2005) *Crime and Society in England, 1750–1900*, 3rd edition, Harlow, Longman.

Ezell, M. E. and Cohen, L. E. (2005) *Desisting from Crime*, Oxford, OUP.

Fagan, J. (1989) 'Cessation of Family Violence: Deterrence and Dissuasion', in Ohlin, L. and Tonry, M. (eds.) *Crime and Justice: An Annual Review of Research*, Vol. 11, Chicago, University of Chicago Press.

Fagan, J., Piper, E. and Cheng, Y-T. (1987) 'Contributions of Victimisation to Delinquency in Inner Cities', in *Journal of Criminal Law and Criminology*, 78 (3), pp. 586–613.

Farrall, S. (2000) 'Introduction', in Farrall, S. (ed.) *The Termination of Criminal Careers*, Aldershot, Ashgate.

—— (2002) *Rethinking What Works With Offenders*, Willan Publishing, Cullompton.

—— (2005) 'On The Existential Aspects of Desistance From Crime', in *Symbolic Interaction*, 28 (3), pp. 367–86.

—— (2006) 'Rolling Back the State: Mrs Thatcher's Criminological Legacy', in *International Journal of the Sociology of Law*, 34 (4), pp. 256–77.

—— and Calverley, A. (2006) *Understanding Desistance From Crime*, Milton Keynes, Open University Press, Crime and Justice Series.

—— and Maltby, S. (2003) 'The Victimisation of Probationers', in *Howard Journal of Criminal Justice*, 42 (1), pp. 32–54.

Farrington, D. P. (1992) 'Juvenile Delinquency', in Coleman, J. (ed.) *The School Years*, London, Routledge.

—— (2002) 'Developmental Criminology & Risk-focused Prevention', in Maguire, M., Morgan, R. and Reiner, R. (eds.) *The Oxford Handbook of Criminology*, Oxford, OUP.

——, Gallagher, B., Morley, L., St. Ledger, R. J. and West, D. J. (1986) 'Unemployment, School Leaving and Crime', in *British Journal of Criminology*, 26 (4), pp. 335–56.

——, Barnes, G. C. and Lambert, S. (1996) 'The Concentration of Offending in Families', in *Legal & Criminological Psychology*, 1, pp. 47–63.

——, Lambert, S. and West, D. J. (1998) 'Criminal Careers of Two Generations of Family Members in the Cambridge Study of Delinquent Development', in *Studies on Crime and Crime Prevention*, 7, pp. 85–106.

——, Jolliffe, D., Loeber, R., Stouthamer-Loeber, M. and Kalb, L. M. (2001) 'The concentration of offenders in families, and family criminality in the prediction of boys' delinquency', in *Journal of Adolescence*, 24, pp. 579–96.

Fattah, E. (1993) 'The rational choice/opportunity perspectives as a vehicle for integrating criminological and victimological theories', in Clarke, R. V. and Felson, M. (eds.) *Routine Activity & Rational Choice*, New Brunswick, Transaction Publishers.

Feld, S. L. and Straus, M. A. (1989) 'Escalation and Desistance of Wife Assault', in *Criminology*, 27, pp. 141–61.

—— and —— (1990) 'Escalation and Desistance of Wife Assault', in M. A. Straus, and R. J. Gelles (eds.) *Physical Violence in American Families: Risk Factors and Adaptations to Violence in 8,145 Families*, New Brunswick, Transaction Publishers.

Ferguson, T. (1952) *The Young Delinquent in his Social Setting*, Oxford, OUP.

Fleming, Rebecca B. (2000) 'Scanty Goatees and Palmar Tattoos: Cesare Lombroso's Influence on Science and Popular Opinion', in *The Concord Review*, pp. 195–217.

Flood-Page, C., Campbell, S., Harrington, V. and Miller, J. (2000) *Youth Crime: Findings From the 1998/99 Youth Lifestyles Survey*, London, Home Office Research Study, No. 209.

Gadd, D. (2006) 'The role of recognition in the desistance process: A case analysis of a former far-right activist', in *Theoretical Criminology*, 10 (2), pp. 179–202.

Galton, F. (1864 and 1865) 'Hereditary Character and Talent' (published in two parts, in *MacMillan's Magazine*, 11, November 1864 and April 1865, pp. 157–66 and pp. 318–27).

Garland, D. (2001) *The Culture of Control*, Oxford, OUP.

Garside, R. (2004) *Crime, Persistent Offenders and the Justice Gap*, London, Crime and Society Foundation Discussion Paper Number 1.

Geeson, A. W. (1969) 'The Development of Elementary Education in Crewe 1840–1918', unpublished M.Ed thesis, University of Dumfries.

Giddens, A. (1984) *The Constitution of Society*, Cambridge, Polity Press.

Giordano, P. C., Cernkovich, S. A. and Rudolph, J. L. (2002) 'Gender, Crime and Desistance: Toward a Theory of Cognitive Transformation', in *American Journal of Sociology*, 107, pp. 990–1064.

Glueck, S. and Glueck, E. (1950) *Unravelling Juvenile Delinquency*, New York, Commonwealth Fund.

Godfrey, B. (2003) 'Counting and accounting for violence', in *British Journal of Criminology*, 43 (2), pp. 340–53.

—— (2004) 'Rough Girls: A "recent" history of violent young women, 1900–1930', in Alder, C. and Worrall, A. (eds.), *Criminal Girls*, New York, University of New York Press.

—— and Dunstall, G. (eds.), (2005) *Crime and Empire 1840–1940: Criminal justice in local and global context*, Cullompton, Willan.

——, Farrall, S. and Locker, J. (2006) 'Persistence in Crime and the Impact of Significant Life-Changes: A Pilot Study of Crewe, 1881', in Briegel, F. and Porret, M. (eds.) *Le Criminel Enduci*, Geneva, Droz.

——, —— and Karstedt, S. (2005) 'Explaining Gendered Sentencing Patterns for Violent Men and Women in the Late Victorian Period', in *British Journal of Criminology*, 45 (5), pp. 696–720.

—— and Lawrence, P. (2005) *Crime and Justice 1750–1950*, Cullompton, Willan.

Goffman, E. (1963) *Stigma*, Harmondsworth, Penguin.

Goldstein, H. (1995) *Multilevel Statistical Models*, London, Arnold.

Gottfredson, M. (1984) *Victims of Crime: Dimensions of Risk*, Home Office Research Study, No. 81, London, HMSO.

Gottfredson, M. and Hirschi, T. (1990) *A General Theory of Crime*, Stanford, Stanford University Press.

Graham, J. and Bowling, B. (1995) *Young People And Crime*, Home Office Research Study 145, London, HMSO.

Grayson, R. (1998) 'Class relationships in nineteenth-century Sheffield', in Kidd, A. and Nicholls, D. (eds.) *The Making of the British Middle Class? Studies of Regional and Cultural Diversity since the Eighteenth Century*, Thrupp, Sutton Publishing.

Gregory, R. L. (ed.) (1987) *The Oxford Companion to the Mind*, Oxford, OUP.

Grove, W. M., Eckert, E. D., Heston, L., Bouchard, T. J. Jr., Segal, N. and Lykken, D. T. (1990) 'Heritability of substance abuse and antisocial behavior: a study of monozygotic twins reared apart', in *Biological Psychiatry*, 27, pp. 1293–304.

Gurr, E. (1981) 'Historical trends in violent crime: a critical review of the evidence', in *Crime and Justice: An Annual Review of Research*, 3, pp. 295–353.

Gurr, T. R., Grabosky, P. and Hula, R. (1977) *The Politics of Crime and Conflict: A Comparative History of Four Cities*, Beverly Hills, Sage.

Hagan, J. (1988) *Structural Criminology*, Cambridge, Polity Press.

—— (1997) 'Crime and Capitalization: Toward a Developmental Theory of Street Crime in America', in Thornberry, T. (ed.) *Developmental Theories of Crime And Delinquency*, New Brunswick, Transaction Press.

Hall, S. (1992) 'The West and the Rest: Discourse and Power', in Hall, S. and Giebden, B. (eds.) *Formations of Modernity*, Oxford, Polity Press.

Harman, T. (1567) *A Caveat for Common Cursitors*, reprinted (1990) in Kinney, A. F. (ed.) *Rogues, Vagabonds and Sturdy Beggars: A New Gallery of Tudor and Early Stuart Rogue Literature*, Amherst: University of Massachusetts Press.

Harris, J. (1993) *Private lives, public spirit: a social history of Britain 1870–1914*, Oxford, OUP.

——, Hunter, J. and Lewis, C. (eds.) (1997) *The New Institutional Economics and Third World Development*, London, Routledge.

Hartless, J., Ditton, J., Nair, G. and Phillips, S. (1995) 'More Sinned Against than Sinning', in *British Journal of Criminology*, 35 (1), pp. 114–33.

Head, F. B. (1849) *Stokers and pokers, or the London & North Western Railway, the electric telegraph and the railway clearing house*, reprinted (1968), Newton Abbot, David & Charles.

Hennessy *et al* (1978), 'Broken Homes and Middle Class Delinquency: A Re-evaluation', in *Criminology*, 15, pp. 505–27.

Henry, S. (1978) *The Hidden Economy: the Context and Control of Borderline Crime*, Oxford, Martin Robertson.

Hetherington, E. M. and Elmore, A. M. (2004) 'The intergenerational transmission of couple instability', in Chase-Lansdale, P. L., Kiernan, K.

and Friedman, R. J., *Human development across lives and generations*, Cambridge, CUP.

Higgs, E. (1996) *A Clearer Sense of the Census*, London, HMSO.

Hindelang, M. J., Gottfredson, M. R. and Garofalo, J. (1978) *Victims of Personal Crimes*, Cambridge, MA, Ballinger.

Hirschi, T. and Goffredson, M. (1983) 'Age and the Explanation of Crime', in *American Journal of Sociology*, 89, 552–84.

Hobbs, D. (1988) *Doing the Business*, Oxford, OUP.

Hodkinson (née Roberts), W. W. (1969) 'Crewe—as I once knew it', unpublished manuscript, Crewe Library.

Holden, C. (1986) 'Growing Focus on Criminal Careers', in *Science*, 233, pp. 1377–8.

Holstein, J. A. and Miller, G. (1990) 'Rethinking victimization: an international approach to victimology', in *Symbolic Interaction*, 13, pp. 103–22.

Horn D. (2003) *The Criminal Body*, London, Routledge.

Horney, J., Osgood, D. W. and Haen Marshall, I. (1995) 'Criminal Careers in The Short Term: Intra-Individual Variability in Crime and Its Relation to Local Life Circumstances', in *American Sociological Review*, 60, pp. 655–73.

Hox, J. J. (1995) *Applied Multilevel Analysis*, Amsterdam, TT-Publikaties.

Hughes, M. (1997) 'An Exploratory Study of Young Adult Black and Latino Males and the Factors Facilitating their Decisions to Make Positive Behavioural Changes', in *Smith College Studies in Social Work*, 67 (3), pp. 401–14.

—— (1998) 'Turning Points in the Lives of Young Inner-city Men Forgoing Destructive Criminal Behaviours: A Qualitative Study', in *Social Work Research*, 22, pp. 143–51.

Indermaur, D. (2000) 'Violent Crime in Australia: Patterns and Politics', in *Australian and New Zealand Journal of Criminology*, 33 (3), pp. 287–99.

Irwin, J. (1970) *The Felon*, New Jersey, Prentice Hall.

Jamieson, J., McIvor, G. and Murray, C. (1999) *Understanding Offending Among Young People*, Edinburgh, The Stationery Office.

Johnson, D. R. and Booth, A. (1998) 'Marital Quality: A Product of the Dyadic Environment or Individual Factors?', in *Social Forces*, 76, pp. 883–904.

Juvenile Organisations Committee (1920) *Children: Juvenile Delinquency*, TNA HO45/16515.

Karstedt, S. and Farrall, S. (forthcoming), *Respectable Citizens—Shady Practices: Crime, Social Change and the Moral Economy*.

Kearon, T. and Godfrey, B. (forthcoming) 'Setting the Scene: The History of Victims', in Walklate, S. *The Handbook of Victims and Victimology*, Cullompton, Willan.

Kelves, D. J. (1985) *In the Name of Eugenics: genetics and the uses of human heredity*, Berkeley, University of California Press.

Kerr, A. and Shakespeare, T. (2002) *Genetic Politics: From Genetics to Genome*, Cheltenham, New Clarion Press.

Kidd, A. and Nicholls, D. (eds.) (1998) *The Making of the British Middle Class? Studies of Regional and Cultural Diversity since the Eighteenth Century*, Thrupp, Sutton Publishing.

King, P. (1984) 'Decision-Makers and Decision-Making in the English Criminal Law, 1750–1800', in *Historical Journal*, 27, pp. 25–58.

—— (1996) 'Punishing assault: the transformation of attitudes in the English courts', in *Journal of Interdisciplinary History*, 27 (1), pp. 43–74.

—— (2000) *Crime, Justice and Discretion in England, 1740–1820*, Oxford, OUP.

Knight, B. J. and West, D. J. (1975) 'Temporary and Continuing Delinquency', in *British Journal of Criminology*, 15 (1), pp. 43–50.

Laslett, P. (1983) *The world we have lost*, London, Methuen.

Laub, J., Nagin, D. and Sampson, R. (1998) 'Trajectories of Change in Criminal Offending: Good Marriages and the Desistance Process', in *American Sociological Review*, 63, pp. 225–38.

—— and Sampson, R. J. (1993) 'Turning Points in the Life Course: Why Change Matters to the Study of Crime', in *Criminology*, 31 (3) pp. 301–25.

—— and —— (2001) 'Understanding Desistance From Crime', in Tonry, M. (ed.) *Crime and Justice: An Annual Review of Research*, Vol. 26, Chicago, University of Chicago Press.

Lauritsen, J., Sampson, R. and Laub, J. (1991) 'The Link Between Offending and Victimisation Among Adolescents', in *Criminology* 29 (2), pp. 265–92.

Leibrich, J. (1993) *Straight to the Point: Angles on Giving up Crime*, Otago, New Zealand, University of Otago Press.

—— (1996) 'The Role of Shame in Going Straight: A Study of Former Offenders', in Galaway, B. and Hudson, J. (eds.) *Restorative Justice*, Monsey, NJ, Criminal Justice Press.

Loeber, R., Stouthamer-Loeber, M., Van Kammen, W. and Farrington, D. P. (1991) 'Initiation, Escalation and Desistance in Juvenile Offending and their Correlates', in *Journal of Criminal Law and Criminology*, 82 (1), pp. 36–82.

Lombroso, C. (1876) *L'Uomo Delinquente*, Milan.

Lown, J. (1990) *Women and Industrialization: Gender and Work in Nineteenth-Century England*, Cambridge, Polity Press.

MacLeod, J. (1987/1995) *Ain't No Makin' It*, Oxford, Westview Press.

Maruna, S. (1997) 'Going Straight: Desistance from Crime and Life Narratives of Reform', in Lieblich, A. and Josselson, R. (eds.) *The Narrative Study of Lives*, 5, London, Sage.

—— (2000) 'Desistance from Crime and Offender Rehabilitation: A Tale of Two Research Literatures', *Offender Programs Report*, 4 (1).

—— (2001) *Making Good: How Ex-Convicts Reform and Rebuild their Lives*, Washington DC, American Psychological Association Books.

—— and Farrall, S. (2004) *Desistance from Crime: A Theoretical Reformulation*, Kölner Zeitschrift für Soziologie und Sozialpsychologie, No. 43.

Maudsley, H. (1873) *Body and Mind*, London, Macmillan.

—— (1874) *Responsibility in Mental Disease*, London, Henry King.

Mawby, R. I. and Walklate, S. (1994) *Critical Victimology*, London, Sage.

May, C. (1999) *Explaining Reconviction Following A Community Sentence: The Role of Social Factors*, Home Office Research Study No. 192, London, HMSO.

Mayhew, P. and Elliott, D. (1990) 'Self-reported Offending, Victimisation and the British Crime Survey', in *Violence and Victims*, 5 (2), pp. 83–96.

McCord, J. (1977) 'A comparative view of two generations of native Americans', in Meier, R. (ed.) *Theory in Criminology*, Beverly Hills, Sage.

—— (1982) 'A longitudinal view of the relationship between paternal absence and crime', in Gunn, J. and Farrington, D. (eds.) *Abnormal Offenders, Delinquency and the Criminal Justice System*, Chichester, Wiley.

—— (1991) 'The cycle of crime and socialisation practices', in *Journal of Criminal Law & Criminology*, 82, pp. 211–28.

McGowan, R. (1990) 'Getting to know the criminal class in nineteenth-century England', in *Nineteenth Century Contexts*, 14, (1), pp. 33–54.

Meisenhelder, T. (1977) 'An Exploratory Study of Exiting from Criminal Careers', in *Criminology*, 15 (3), pp. 319–34.

Messner, S. F. and Rosenfeld, R. (1994) *Crime & The American Dream*, Belmont, CA, Wadworth.

Miers, D. (1990) 'Positivistic Criminology: a Critique. Part Two: Critical Victimology', in *International Review of Victimology*, 1 (3), pp. 219–30.

Mischkowitz, R. (1994) 'Desistance from a Delinquent Way of Life?', in Weitekamp, E. G. M. and Kerner, H. J. (eds.) *Cross-National Longitudinal Research on Human Development and Criminal Behaviour*, Boston, Kluwer-Nijhoff.

Moffitt, T. E. (1993) ' "Life-Course Persistent" and "Adolescent-Limited" Antisocial Behaviour: A Developmental Taxonomy', in *Psychological Review*, 100, pp. 674–701.

—— (1997) 'Adolescence-Limited and Life-Course Persistent Offending: a Complementary Pair of Developmental Theories', in Thornberry, T. (ed.) *Developmental Theories of Crime and Delinquency*, London, Transaction Press.

Monkkonen, E. H. (2001) *Murder in New York City*, Berkeley, UCLA Press.

Morrison, B. (2005) 'Ordering disorderly women: female drunkenness in England c. 1870–1920', unpublished Ph.D thesis, Keele University.

Mulvey, E. P. and Aber, M. (1988) 'Growing out of Delinquency: Development and Desistance', in Jenkins, R. L. and Brown, W. K. (eds.) *The Abandonment of Delinquent Behaviour: Promoting The Turnaround*, New York, Praeger.

Murray, C. (1995) 'The emerging British underclass', in Lister, R. (ed) *Charles Murray and the Underclass: The Developing Debate*, London, Institute of Economic Affairs.

Nagin, D., Pogarsky, G. and Farrington, D. P. (1997) 'Adolescent Mothers and the Criminal Behaviour of their Children', in *Law & Society Review*, 31 (1), pp. 137–62.

Newburn, T. and Stanko, E. (1994) 'When men are victims', in Newburn, T. and Stanko, E. (eds.) *Just Boys Doing Business?*, London, Routledge.

Norris, J. (1988) *Serial Killers: the growing menace*, New York, Doubleday.

North, D. (1995) 'New Institutional Economics and Third World Development', in Harris, J., Hunter, J. and Lewis, C. (eds.) (1997) *The New Institutional Economics and Third World Development*, London, Routledge.

O'Donnell, I. and Edgar, K. (1996a) *The Extent and Dynamics of Victimisation in Prisons*, Oxford, Centre for Criminological Research.

—— and —— (1996b) *Victimisation in Prisons*, Home Office Research Findings 37, London, Home Office.

Osborn, S. G. (1980) 'Moving Home, Leaving London and Delinquent Trends', in *British Journal of Criminology*, 20 (1), pp. 54–61.

Ouimet, M. and Le Blanc, M. (1996) 'The Role of Life Experiences in the Continuation of the Adult Criminal Career', in *Criminal Behaviour and Mental Health*, 6, pp. 73–97.

Parker, H. (1976) 'Boys Will be Men: Brief Adolescence in a Down-Town Neighbourhood', in Mungham, G. and Pearson, G. (eds.) *Working Class Youth Culture*, London, Routledge.

Pearson, G. (1983) *Hooligan: A History of Respectable Fears*, Basingstoke, Macmillan.

Peelo, M., Stewart, J., Stewart, G. and Prior, A. (1992) *A Sense of Justice: Offenders as Victims of Crime*, London, Association of Chief Officers of Probation.

Pezzin, L. E. (1995) 'Earning Prospects, Matching Effects and the Decision to Terminate a Criminal Career', in *Journal of Quantitative Criminology*, 11 (1), pp. 29–50.

Pick, D. (1989) *Faces of Degeneration: A European Disorder, c.1848–1918*, Cambridge, CUP.

Philips, D. (1977) *Crime and Authority in Victorian England: the Black Country, 1835–60*, London, Croom Helm.

Quigley, B. M. and Leonard, K. E. (1996) 'Desistance of Husband Aggression in the Early Years of Marriage', in *Violence and Victims*, 11, pp. 355–70.

Rafter, N. H. (1997) *Creating Born Criminals*, Urbana, University of Illinois Press.

Rand, A. (1987) 'Transitional Life Events and Desistance From Delinquency and Crime' in Wolfgang, M. E., Thornberry, T. P. and Figlio, R. M. (eds.) *From Boy To Man, From Delinquency to Crime*, Chicago, University of Chicago Press.

Reed, B. (1982) *Crewe Locomotiove Works and its Men*, Newton Abbot, David & Charles.

Robins, L. (1979) 'Sturdy childhood predictors of adult outcomes', in Barrett, J. E., Rose, R. M. and Klerman, G. L. (eds.) *Stress and mental disorder*, New York, Raven Press.

Robinson, W. S. (1950) 'Ecological correlations and the behaviour of individuals', in *American Sociological Review*, 15, pp. 351–7.

Rosenheim, M. K. (2003) *A Century of Juvenile Justice*, Chicago, Chicago University Press.

Rowe, D. C. and Farrington, D. P. (1997) 'The Familial Transmission of Criminal Convictions', in *Criminology*, 35 (1), pp. 177–201.

Rudé, G. (1985) *Criminal and Victim Crime and Society in Early Nineteenth-century England*, Clarendon Press, Oxford.

Rutter, M. and Giller, H. (1983) *Juvenile Delinquency*, New York, Guilford.

Rylands, L. G. (1889) *Crime: its causes and remedy*, London, T. F. Unwin.

Sampson, R. J. and Laub, J. H. (1993) *Crime in the Making: Pathways and Turning Points through Life*, London, Harvard University Press.

——and—— (1994) 'Urban Poverty and the Family Context of Delinquency: A New Look at Structure and Process in a Classic Study', in *Child Development*, 65, pp. 523–40.

Savage, M. (2005) 'Revisting Classic Qualitative Studies', in *Forum Qualitative Social Research*, 6 (1), published online at www.qualitative-research.net/fqs/fqs-eng.

Shapland, J. and Bottoms, A. (2005) 'Between Conformity and Criminality: Theoretical Reflections on Desistance', paper presented to European Society of Criminology Conference, Krakow, August 2005.

Shore, H. (1999) *Artful Dodgers: Youth and Crime in Early Nineteenth-Century London*, Woodbridge, Boydell.

Shover, N. (1983) 'The Later Stages of Ordinary Property Offender Careers', in *Social Problems*, 31 (2), pp. 208–18.

—— and Thompson, C. (1992) 'Age, Differential Expectations and Crime Desistance', in *Criminology*, 30 (1), pp. 89–104.

Simmons, J. (1978) *The Railway in England and Wales 1830–1914: The System and Its Working*, Leicester, Leicester University Press.

Simpson, C. (2004) 'When hope makes us vulnerable: a discussion of Patient-Healthcare Provider interactions in the context of Hope', in *Bioethics* 18 (5), pp. 428–7.

Singer, S. (1981) 'Homogeneous Victim-Offender Populations: A Review and Some Research Implications', in *Journal of Criminal Law and Criminology*, 72 (2), pp. 779–88.

Slipman, S. (1995) 'Would you take one home with you?', in *Charles Murray and the Underclass. The developing debate*, London, Institute of Economic Affairs booklet 33.

Smith, C. and Farrington, D. P. (2004) 'Continuities in antisocial behaviour and parenting across three generations', in *Journal of Child Psychology and Psychiatry*, 45 (2), pp. 230–47.

Snijders, T. and Bosker, R. (1999) *Multilevel Analysis*, London, Sage.

Sommers, I., Baskin, D. R. and Fagan, J. (1994) 'Getting out of the Life: Crime Desistance by Female Street Offenders', in *Deviant Behaviour*, 15 (2), pp. 125–49.

Soothill, K. (2003) 'The persistent offenders debate: a focus on temporal changes', in *Criminal Justice*, 3 (4), pp. 389–412.

—— (2005) 'Sex crime in a small English city', in Briegel, F. and Porret, M. (eds.) *Le Criminel Edurci. Recidive et recidivists du moyen age au XX siecle*, Droz, Geneva.

Stanko, E. (1985) *Intimate Intrusions*, London, Virago.

—— (1988) 'Hidden Violence against Women', in Pointing, J. and Maguire, M. (eds.) *Victims of Crime: A New Deal?*, Milton Keynes, Open University Press.

Stedman Jones, G. (2002) *Outcast London. A Study in the Relationship between Classes in Victorian Society*, Milton Keynes, Open University Press.

Stones, R. (1991) 'Strategic Context Analysis: A New Research Strategy for Structuration Theory', in *Sociology*, 25 (3), pp. 673–95.

Storch, R. (1975) 'The plague of blue locusts: police reform and popular resistance in northern England 1840–57', in *International Review of Social History*, 20, pp. 61–90.

—— (1976) 'The policeman as domestic missionary: urban discipline and popular culture in northern England, 1850–1880', in *Journal of Social History*, 9, pp. 481–511.

Sugden, P. (2002) *The Complete History of Jack the Ripper*, London, Constable and Robinson.

Taylor, D. (1998) *Crime, Policing and Punishment in England, 1750–1914*, Basingstoke, Macmillan.

Taylor, I. (1996) *A tale of two cities global change, local feeling and everyday life in the North of England. A study in Manchester and Sheffield*, London, Routledge.

Tolman, R. M., Edleson, J. L. and Fendrich, M. (1996) 'The Applicability of the Theory of Planned Behavior to Abusive Men's Cessation of Violent Behavior', in *Violence and Victims*, 119 (4), pp. 341–54.

Trasler, G. (1979) 'Delinquency, Recidivism and Desistance', in *British Journal of Criminology*, 19 (4), pp. 314–22.

Turner, L. (ed.) (1891) *Fifty Years on the LNWR, and Other Memoranda of the Life of David Stevenson*, Crewe, Turner.

Uggen, C. (2000) 'Work as a Turning Point in the Life Course of Criminals: A Duration Model of Age, Employment and Recidivism', in *American Sociological Review*, 67, pp. 529–46.

—— and Kruttschnitt, K. (1998) 'Crime in the Breaking: Gender Differences in Desistance', in *Law and Society Review*, 32 (2), pp. 339–66.

Van Dijk, J. and Steinmetz, C. (1983) 'Victimisation Surveys: Beyond Measuring the Volume of Crime', in *Victimology: An International Journal*, 8 (1–2), pp. 291–309.

Vincent, D. (1980) 'Love and death and the nineteenth-century working class', in *Social History*, 5, pp. 23–47.

Von Hentig, H. (1948) *The Criminal and his Victim: Studies in the Sociobiology of Crime*, New Haven, Yale University Press.

Walklate, S. (1992) 'Appreciating the Victim: Conventional, Realist or Critical Victimology?', in Matthews, R. and Young, J. (eds.) *Issues in Realist Criminology*, London, Sage.

—— (1996) 'Can There be a Feminist Victimology?', in Davies, P., Francis, P. and Jupp, V. (eds.) *Understanding Victimisation*, Newcastle, Northumbria Social Science Press.

—— (1998) 'Crime and community: fear or trust?', in *British Journal of Sociology*, 49 (4), pp. 550–69.

Wallace, C. (1986) 'From Girls and Boys to Women and Men: The Social Reproduction of Gender Roles in the Transition from School to (Un)employment', in Walker, S. and Barton, L. (eds.) *Youth, Unemployment and Schooling*, Milton Keynes, Open University Press.

—— (1987) *For Richer, For Poorer: Growing up in and out of Work*, London, Tavistock.

Warr, M. (1998) 'Life-Course Transitions and Desistance from Crime', in *Criminology*, 36 (2), pp. 183–215.

Weitekamp, E., Kerner, H. J., Stelly, W. and Thomas, J. (2000) 'Desistance from Crime: Life History, Turning Points and Implications for Theory Construction in Criminology', in Karstedt, S. and Bussmann, K. D. (eds.) *Social Dynamics of Crime and Control: New Theories for a World in Transition*, Oxford, Hart.

West, D. J. (1982) *Delinquency: Its Roots, Careers and Prospects*, London, Heinemann.

—— Farrington, D. (1973) *Who Becomes Delinquent?*, London, Heinemann.

West, G. W. (1978) 'The Short Term Careers of Serious Thieves', in *Canadian Journal of Criminology*, 20, pp. 169–90.

White, J. (1986) *The Worst Street in North London: Camden Bunk, Islington between the Wars*, London, Routledge and Kegan Paul.

Wiener, M. (1990) *Reconstructing the Criminal. Culture, Law and Policy in England, 1830–1914*, Cambridge, CUP.

Wiener, M. (2004) *English Culture and the Decline of the Industrial Spirit*, Cambridge, CUP.

Willis, P. (1984) 'Youth Unemploment' (as three articles), in *New Society*, Mar–Apr.

Wilson, W. J. (1987) *The truly disadvantaged*, Chicago, Chicago University Press.

—— (1991) 'Studying Inner-City Social Dislocations: The Challenge of Public Agenda Research', in *American Sociological Review*, 56, pp. 1–14.

Wittebrood, K. and Nieuwbeerta, P. (1999) 'Wages of Sin? The Link between Offending, Lifestyle and Violent Victimisation', in *European Journal on Criminal Policy and Research*, 7, pp. 63–80.

Wolfgang, M. E., Figlio, R. M. and Sellin, T. (1972) *Delinquency in a Birth Cohort*, London, University of Chicago Press.

Young, J. (1986) 'The failure of criminology: the need for a radical realism', in Matthews, R. and Young, J. (eds.) *Confronting Crime*, London, Sage.

Index

Specific case studies